Currents in Transatlantic History

NUMBER FORTY-SEVEN
Walter Prescott Webb Memorial Lectures,
published for the University of Texas at Arlington
by Texas A&M University Press

Currents in Transatlantic History

Encounters, Commodities, Identities

Edited by Steven G. Reinhardt

Contributors
Marcus Rediker
Benjamin Mark Allen
Emmanuel M. Mbah
Julie L. Holcomb
Tom Aiello
Gregory Kosc
Pawel Goral

Published for the University of Texas at Arlington
by Texas A&M University Press
COLLEGE STATION

First edition

This paper meets the requirements of
ANSI/NISO Z39.48–1992 (Permanence of Paper).
Binding materials have been chosen for durability.
Manufactured in the United States of America

Library of Congress Cataloging-in-Publication Data
Names: Reinhardt, Steven G., 1949– editor. | Rediker, Marcus, author. | Rediker, Marcus. Slave revolt at sea. | University of Texas at Arlington, issuing body.
Title: Currents in transatlantic history : encounters, commodities, identities / edited by Steven G. Reinhardt ; contributors, Marcus Rediker, Benjamin Mark Allen, Emmanuel M. Mbah, Julie L. Holcomb, Tom Aiello, Gregory Kosc, Pawel Goral.
Other titles: Walter Prescott Webb memorial lectures ; 47.
Description: First edition. | College Station : Published for the University of Texas at Arlington by Texas A&M University Press, [2017] | Series: Walter Prescott Webb memorial lectures ; number forty-seven | Includes bibliographical references and index.
Identifiers: LCCN 2016052464| ISBN 9781623495428 (hardcover (printed case) : alk. paper) | ISBN 9781623495435 (ebook)
Subjects: LCSH: History, Modern. | Civilization, Modern. | International relations. | Commerce.
Classification: LCC D210 .C84 2017 | DDC 909/.09821—dc23 LC record available at https://lccn.loc.gov/2016052464

A list of other titles in this series appears at the back of the book.

To Stanley H. Palmer, Transatlantic Historian

Contents

Contents

Preface

The forty-ninth annual Walter Prescott Webb Memorial Lectures, "Currents in Transatlantic History: Encounters, Commodities, Identities," were organized to commemorate the fifteenth anniversary of the creation of UTA's doctoral program in Transatlantic History and to honor the contribution of Stanley H. Palmer, who was instrumental in its formation. Accordingly, we invited six of our graduates to return to Arlington on March 6, 2014, to present papers that dealt with various aspects of Transatlantic History, the field of study that focuses on the complex process of interchange and adaptation that began when Africans, Amerindians, and Europeans first came into contact, a process that continues today. The expanded versions of their presentations found herein are based on the authors' current scholarly interests and focus on topics representative of the diverse research conducted under our Transatlantic History program during the past fifteen years.

Acknowledgments

UTA's Department of History wishes to acknowledge several benefactors and friends of the Walter Prescott Webb Memorial Lecture Series. The lectures were inaugurated in 1965 by Will Holmes, Harold Hollingsworth, and the department chair, E. C. Barksdale. In recent decades—under the successive leadership of Richard G. Miller, Stanley H. Palmer, Ken Philp, Don Kyle, Robert Fairbanks, W. Marvin Dulaney, and Scott Palmer—the lecture series and publications have grown in stature and gained a national reputation. The lectures are published by means of a generous endowment from C. B. Smith of Austin, a graduate of UTA and a former student of Walter Prescott Webb. Additional funding is now provided by a generous grant from the Rudolf Hermanns Endowment for the Liberal Arts. Thanks also go to the late Jenkins and Virginia Garrett of Fort Worth, who long demonstrated both loyalty and generosity to UTA's Special Collections and the Department of History. Additionally, we would like to acknowledge the support of UTA's president, Vistasp M. Karbhari. And finally, the invaluable contribution of Dr. Jennifer Lawrence, coordinator of the actual Webb Lecture Series, deserves special mention.

Introduction

Although the chapters assembled here focus on diverse subjects and take different approaches to the complex field of Transatlantic History, the contributions can nonetheless be grouped according to certain unifying themes or general issues: encounters, commodities, and identity.

Marcus Rediker reminds us that a subject of central concern to Transatlantic History is the forced movement of Africans, mainly from West Africa, during the slave trade that spanned the fifteenth through the nineteenth centuries. Perhaps no single incident other than the *Amistad* slave rebellion of 1839 better brings into focus the various issues that make up Transatlantic History: the commodification of human labor and its violent confinement and forcible transportation across the Atlantic; the sense of *déracinement* and longing for a fictive or real "home" felt by all immigrants, whether they be voluntary or involuntary; the creolization process that transformed people who came into contact with one another, altering not just their language but other facets of their cultures; the intersection of efforts at self-liberation with campaigns to emancipate enslaved people globally. Ironically, Rediker observes, the *Amistad* incident has been transformed into a courtroom drama and a self-congratulatory event that celebrates the same American legal system that in 1839 held two and a half million in bondage; as a result, the emancipatory actions of the African rebels have been eclipsed. Rediker's goal is to view "history from below" and thereby restore them—not the abolitionists, attorneys, judges, and politicians—to the center of their own story. He explores how captives from ten different ethnicities were melded into a "strange, new, accidental collective" both by the common experience of captivity and slavery and by their transatlantic voyage below deck. As a result, they were transformed into a "motley crew" of rebels with a shared solidarity and common purpose: the attainment of freedom and return to their homeland, which they finally achieved in 1842.

The themes of "home" and "family"—themes related to a sense of belonging—pervade Benjamin Mark Allen's and Emmanuel M. Mbah's chapters. Although their topics are separated by centuries, both chapters deal with similar issues. Allen imaginatively pieces together the family saga of the Talon children who survived the disastrous second expedition of René-Robert Cavelier, sieur de La Salle, and were adopted by the Caddo and the Karankawa Indians in Texas. When they were finally "recovered" by the Spanish and turned over to the French, they saw the world with new eyes and could barely recognize their original world as being "home." Having lived among and identified with the Indians, they were no longer Europeans. Indeed, Allen tells us, the Talon children—although glad to reunite with their other family members—"greeted the Spanish with trepidation and ambivalence" and hesitated to join them. He argues that members of the Talon family "entered the Texas Gulf Coast as Frenchmen but left it with altered identities." Allen further contends that their tale can best be seen as "heroic" in a literary-mythic sense, that is, a saga that recounts how the heroes are thrust into a liminal space and then, in their quest to regain an ill-conceived and only partially remembered "home," they subsequently emerge into a post-liminal space effectively transformed. In short, they have been "creolized."

Three centuries later, Cameroon immigrants to the United States also experienced a significant transition that was generally less traumatic but nonetheless equally transformative. Depending on their age, personal resilience, and receptivity to change, immigrants (especially the young) emerged from their extended "ordeal" with identities that were more or less altered. They also found that their arrival in the New World was only the beginning of their transformation. Emmanuel M. Mbah explores the tensions felt by Cameroonians who continue to leave their homeland voluntarily but nonetheless struggle to retain a degree of connectedness. In other words, although they, too, have attempted to create a "home away from home," the older generation often finds itself perpetually "at sea" or lost between two worlds. Migrants from the Cameroons become, figuratively speaking, people without a country: neither accepted in the United States where they are fated to remain perpetual "strangers" nor able to return to their former homeland where they are no longer welcome. The result is that they are never fully comfortable in either their former home or their new.

The second group of essays approaches Transatlantic History by focusing on the commodity of cotton and the problems related to the mobilization of a labor force (enslaved or free) for its production as well as the organization of the trade networks that linked sources of raw materials to manufacturing sites. Julie L. Holcomb examines the career of William Adam, a nineteenth-century Scottish-born, English-educated missionary to British India who eventually broke from his fellow Baptists to become a Unitarian and then the editor of a radical newspaper. There he began to campaign for more enlightened policies that respected India's indigenous people and their culture. But his educational proposals and general denunciation of missionaries proved too radical for the British government, prompting him to leave for the United States, where he accepted a teaching appointment at Harvard and later associated with prominent US abolitionists. Taken altogether, his life experiences illuminate the global origins and dimensions of the transatlantic anti-slavery movement. Holcomb shows how Adam became convinced that slavery in the British East Indies was as severe as African slavery in the West Indies and antebellum United States, leading him to dedicate himself to a lifelong campaign for the abolition of slavery throughout the empire and its former colonies. Holcomb recounts how Adam fought passionately (yet largely unsuccessfully) for the major social issues of the century and became an advocate for women's rights everywhere—even while his own marriage and family life collapsed in ruin. His various life experiences shaped the development of his complex understanding of indigenous cultures and conditions of servile labor throughout the world. They also attest to the challenge he confronted of "creating a global economy based on justice and humanity rather than profit and loss."

The demand for commodities that supplied the expanding global economy contributed to the rise to prominence of Dallas (Texas), which supplied raw cotton via transatlantic trade networks to textile mills in Lancashire (Great Britain), the home of the Industrial Revolution. Since 1803, the United States had become Britain's primary source of raw cotton. But even before the close of the US Civil War, the center of cotton production in the United Sates had shifted westward. Lancashire merchants were eager to establish connections with growers in the productive blackland cotton fields of East Texas and with the ginning facilities newly established in Dallas in 1851. As a result, Tom Aiello explains, the Dallas regional economy shifted its focus away from general agriculture and toward monoculture and became an important staging area for marketing and distributing the region's cotton crop. As a result, even in the postwar era, Dallas was well on its way to becoming a key player in the Atlantic world and a veritable outpost on the frontiers of the British Empire.

But this Anglo-American partnership between the two regions cannot be explained only by facts of economic geography. Dallas's ties with Lancashire transcended economic relations, and those who were involved in the trade formed a single community. British migrants to the city not only molded and shaped the economy but also constituted an "English Colony" that influenced the city's cultural and intellectual life well into the 1930s.

Rather than investigate the impact of the Old World on the New, in the final section Gregory Kosc and Pawel Goral examine how the reality and myth of the American West influenced the self-perception of Europeans. Ever since the very first transatlantic encounters, Europeans have continuously sought to expand their horizons, both literally and intellectually. Both authors explore European reactions to and reflections on the American West—whether actual or only imaginary—and the role they played in the construction of European identities. The fourth Earl of Dunraven (1841–1926) was a hunter-writer who identified as an Irishman but, like many men and some women of his era, was drawn to the challenging environment of the American West. Therein he sought out an adventurous life of violence and hardship that would prove his mettle by experiencing "therapeutic pain." Simultaneously, Dunraven hoped his voyages would be ones of self-discovery. Europeans perceived the West as an egalitarian society of rugged, self-made Americans disdainful of traditional elites and as a natural habitat populated by wild animals and hardy indigenous natives. Both were well-suited opponents against whom elite Englishmen could match their cunning and intellect. In other words, the West seemed to be the perfect testing ground to prove one's "true grit." Because the West radiated "Americanness" and epitomized the qualities that many refined Brits rejected, it attracted Dunraven and other adventurers-travelers-hunters who sought to reaffirm and validate their own self-worth on a level playing field. By emerging victorious, Kosc contends, they could dispel their own insecurity and prove to themselves and others that their worthiness was genuine, not artificial, and that they truly merited inclusion among the "natural" elite.

Dunraven may also have sensed that a contest pitting him against the American West and its denizens would reveal his true identity, that is, unveil an essential, masculine self that lay hidden within him—an identity that could only emerge in the proper circumstances. It is more probable, however, that by successfully surmounting challenges and working hard to overcome ordeals, he actually became the man he wished to be. By performing the tasks he regarded as characteristic of such a person, he became that person. In effect, he was effectively constructing his own identity as a hunter-writer and becoming the protagonist of his own narratives. Why was Dunraven impelled to embark on transatlantic adventures? Kosc describes the ways in which modern forces were challenging his traditional, hierarchical, masculine way of life: both the "New Woman" and the working class were demanding equality and extension of the suffrage, and non-whites were calling for greater recognition. In response, Dunraven did not so much seek to preserve or even reconstruct his traditional world, but instead sought self-regeneration via the crafting of a new identity. In this task, the American West served essentially as a playing field on which he was confident he could excel.

In Cold War Poland, Goral tells us, socialists opposed to Western capitalism as well as those workers who joined the Solidarity movement against the Socialist government turned to mythic tales and cinematic versions of the American West for inspiration. In many ways, the West—because it was idealized—was a perfect setting for morality plays inhabited by stock characters locked in struggles between good and evil, a place where the outnumbered hero could overcome adversity and triumph in the name of truth and justice against overwhelming odds. In tales of the West, they found a story they could tell themselves, about themselves. Here was a mirror for their own struggle between generic "Good Guys" and prototypical "Bad Guys"—whether they were fascists (e.g., Ukrainian nationalists or Nazis) or unspecified "gangsters" seeking to rob the community of its buried treasure. Even before the Cold War, translations of the enormously popular German-language novels of Karl May, whose works first appeared in 1899, had familiarized Poles with the conventional plot lines and tropes of the Western novel. Unsurprisingly, both sides drew upon May's work for inspiration. May's plot lines and characters were malleable and lent themselves to adaptation. Poland's southeastern borderlands could be substituted for the frontier of the American West, the Bieszczady Mountains for the Black Hills, and the Polish People's Republic's Army for the US Cavalry that came to the rescue. What remained the same, regardless of the setting and characters, was the final victory of good versus evil.

Why the American West? On the one hand, it provided a safe, familiar option in popular culture for filmmakers eager to align their films with the Socialist government's official propaganda. Working with the typical formulaic story line of the American Western, they avoided commenting (at least overtly) on the more contentious issues of contemporary politics and social issues. On the other hand, filmmakers were always eager to communicate with their audiences in an idiom they recognized. Therefore, they perhaps subversively embraced the Western because the United States had always represented for them hope for the future and the promise of stability and prosperity in a land of opportunity. After all, Polish heroes had been instrumental in helping the Americans win their freedom during the American Revolution. Poles had even settled on the Texas frontier. In effect, however, Polish Western films probably had even less to do with the reality of the American West than did American Westerns. In a scene that Lord Dunraven would have applauded, we find an armed Polish hero who sets aside his weapon and chooses to fight with a knife to prove to his Native American opponent that the Polish fight fair and are noble human beings! As Goral concludes, Polish filmmakers of all persuasions did their best to creatively combine Polish history and culture with the appealing myth of the American West. In this respect, Goral suggests that these two cultures were continuing their transnational, transatlantic dialogue.

Currents in Transatlantic History

1

Slave Revolt at Sea

The Rebels of the Amistad, *1839*

Marcus Rediker

During the moonless early hours of July 1, 1839, several captive Africans quietly slipped out of their chains in the hold of the slave schooner *La Amistad.* One of them had managed to break a padlock, which made it possible to remove the chain that reeved them together and held them down in the hold below the main deck of the vessel. Forty-nine men and four children made up the human cargo of the *Amistad.* They had sailed from Havana, bound for the new plantations of Puerto Príncipe (Camaguey), Cuba. A few hours earlier, in cramped, airless quarters below deck, they had made a collective decision to seek a different fate.[1]

A group of four men—Cinqué, Faquorna, Moru, and Kimbo—led the way as they climbed up and out of the hatchway onto the main deck, although they were not the sole leaders of the revolt. They moved with the grace and precision of warriors accustomed to daring midnight attacks. They picked up belaying pins and barrel staves and moved toward the ship's boat, where the cook lay sleeping. They bludgeoned him to death. As more men escaped their irons and swarmed up on deck, they opened a box of "cane knives"; tools that were meant for cutting sugar cane would now serve the purpose of self-emancipation. The sight of flashing blades caused the two sailors who were meant to guard against such uprisings to leap over the side of the vessel into the water. Captain Ramón Ferrer armed himself and fought back against the insurgents, killing one and mortally wounding another. Four of their comrades counterattacked, surrounding the captain and slashing him to death.

In a matter of minutes, the *Amistad* rebels had turned their wooden world upside down. They captured the two men who had considered themselves their owners, José Ruiz and Pedro Montes, clapped them in manacles, and sent them below deck as prisoners. They took control of the ship and organized themselves to do the hard work of sailing it. But in their newly won freedom lay a dilemma: they wanted to return to their homes in Sierra Leone, but none of them knew how to navigate the schooner. After some debate they decided to keep the surviving Spaniards alive in order to help them sail the vessel eastward, toward the rising sun, which had been at their backs as they made the Middle Passage on a slave ship two weeks earlier.

Montes had been a merchant ship captain; he was experienced in the ways of the sea and shrewd in the ways of men. He used his specialized knowledge of the deep-sea sailing ship to deceive his new masters. During the day, he followed orders, sailing east, but he kept the sails loose and flapping in the wind to slow the *Amistad*'s progress. By night he steered the vessel back to the west and the north, hoping to stay near the islands of the Caribbean and the coast of North America in order to be intercepted and saved. After eight weeks, he got his wish: a US Navy survey ship captured the *Amistad* off Culloden Point, Long Island, and carried the Africans, the Spaniards, the cargo, and the schooner to New London, Connecticut.

What would happen to these African rebels now anchored in one of the world's leading slave societies? Would they be returned to Cuba to be tried—and certainly executed—for their crimes of mutiny, murder, and piracy as the diplomats of Spain, and many American slave owners, demanded? Or would they, as Lewis Tappan and other abolitionists on both sides of the Atlantic insisted, in the aftermath of the abolition of the slave trade, be allowed to go free? Had they not defended their own natu-

Death of Capt. Ferrer. *Engraving by John Warner Barber, 1840.*

ral rights by killing the tyrant who enslaved them? These questions would occupy people of all stations and several nations in fierce debate, projecting the *Amistad* rebels to the center of a massive controversy about slavery and the rights of people who were not free to shape their own destiny. The *Amistad* rebellion became one of the most important events of its time.

An epic struggle ensued. Assisted in their legal battles by distinguished attorneys Roger S. Baldwin and former president John Quincy Adams, who made dramatic speeches before the US Supreme Court in March 1841, the *Amistad* rebels won their freedom, to the joy of half the nation and the consternation of the other half. After a successful fund-raising tour organized by abolitionists, they returned to their African homelands in November of that year. The abolitionist movement claimed a great, historic, and altogether unlikely victory.

• • •

The popular memory of the *Amistad* rebellion has ebbed and flowed with the political tides. In its own day, the event captured the popular imagination. A mere six days after the vessel had been towed ashore, a drama troupe at New York's Bowery Theater performed a play about its story of mutiny and piracy. Commercial artists converged on the jail where the *Amistad* Africans were incarcerated, drew images of Cinqué, the leader of the rebellion, reproduced them quickly and cheaply, and sent them off to be hawked by boys on the streets of eastern cities. Artist Amasa Hewins would paint a 135-foot panorama depicting the *Amistad* Africans as they surrounded and killed Captain Ferrer and seized their freedom by force of arms. Another artist, Sidney Moulthrop, would create twenty-nine life-size wax figures of the Africans and the *Amistad* crew, which he cast and arranged to dramatize the shipboard insurrection. Both artists would tour with their creations, charging admission to those eager to see a visual reenactment of the uprising. Meantime, thousands of people lined up daily to pay admission and walk through the jails of New Haven and Hartford to get a glimpse of the *Amistad* rebels, who were "political prisoners" before the phrase had been invented. When the case moved to the legal system, citizens jammed the courtrooms to capacity and beyond, refusing to leave their seats during breaks for fear of losing them. Meantime, ministers delivered thundering sermons; correspondents wrote hundreds of highly opinionated newspaper articles; poets penned romantic verses; and those for and against slavery debated furiously about the *Amistad* rebels, what they had done, the morality and meaning of their acts, and what their fate should be. Discussed in public as never before, slave resistance became not only a main political issue of the day, but also commercial entertainment, a commodity that circulated in the ever-growing American marketplace, influencing the public opinion that would itself shape the fate of the *Amistad* rebels.

The fascination would not last. After the Civil War, the memory of the *Amistad* waned, barely kept alive by two related groups: abolitionists and African American writers and artists, who wanted to bask in the glory of victory and remember the long, arduous struggle against slavery. In the dark times of Social Darwinism and scientific racism, the *Amistad* uprising faded from public view. It disappeared from histories of the United States written in the late nineteenth and early twentieth centuries, and indeed it saw no major revival until new social movements exploded in the 1960s and 1970s. Especially important in this regard were the Civil Rights and Black Power movements and their demands for a new history of the United States that took seriously the long, bloody battle against slavery and racism. The Mississippi Freedom Summer Schools taught about the *Amistad* rebellion, and some activists named their sons Cinqué after its heroic leader. "History from below" raised the consciousness of struggles past and present, and post-'60s historians made the *Amistad* story part of a new, more democratic, and inclusive vision of the American past. Yet knowledge of the shipboard insurrection among the general public remained limited.

A new phase in popular memory and culture began in 1997 with the release of Steven Spielberg's movie *Amistad*, which carried the history to millions of viewers, many of whom had never before known of it. Although not a commercial success, the film had a broad impact, creating a veritable cottage industry around the history of the event: school curricula incorporated the rebellion; children's coloring books depicted it; museum galleries and art projects celebrated it; novels fictionalized aspects of it; plays and operas dramatized it; and the state of Connecticut financed a multimillion-dollar recreation of the vessel, a floating embodiment of the event that would have its home at Mystic Seaport.[2]

The history and especially the movie gave the *Amistad* insurrection a renewed presence in American popular culture. The rebellion rapidly became one of the best-known events involving slavery in all of American history, and Cinqué joined Underground Railroad conductor Harriet

Tubman and runaway slave-turned-eloquent-abolitionist Frederick Douglass as the most recognizable individuals of African descent associated with the histories of slavery and resistance in America.[3]

Yet the history and the movie have told only part of the story, because the drama of the courtroom has eclipsed the original drama that transpired on the deck of the slave schooner. The American actors—abolitionists, attorneys, judges, and politicians—have elbowed aside the Africans whose daring actions set the train of events in motion. Curiously, the American legal system has emerged as the story's hero—the very same system that, in 1839, held two and a half million African Americans in bondage. This triumphalism may be comforting to an American audience still haunted by the legacy of slavery, but it is deeply misleading.

I have chosen to tell the story of the *Amistad* in a different way. It begins in southern Sierra Leone, West Africa, and leads to an understanding of how the *Amistad* Africans were originally captured and enslaved, initiating an odyssey of epic proportions. These multiethnic people—mostly Mende, but also Temne, Gbandi, Kono, Gola, Sando, and Loma—came from humble backgrounds. They were commoners and workers; a few had been slaves. Born of societies that shared commonalities of belief and culture, these West Africans began a long, slow process of social bonding and self-organization, first at the Lomboko slave-trading factory on the Gallinas Coast, where they were held for several weeks awaiting Atlantic transport on a slave ship called the *Teçora*. Under the extreme, terrifying conditions of the Middle Passage they bonded as "shipmates," cooperating for the sake of survival. The process continued in the barracoons of Havana, where they were held and, after two weeks, sold under humiliating circumstances as if they were cattle. Guided by the practices of a powerful all-male secret society in their homelands called the Poro Society, they organized themselves to carry out the rebellion aboard the *Amistad*. Under the pressure of necessity, they worked together to sail the vessel 1,300 miles from the north coast of Cuba to the northern tip of Long Island; several of their comrades died of dysentery and dehydration along the way. Captured by the US Navy and charged with piracy and murder, they were incarcerated in New Haven, Connecticut. The first maritime leg of the odyssey featured violence, suffering, and self-emancipation.

The rebels now took their drama of slavery and freedom on to an American stage. Once they reached the shores of Connecticut, they inspired profound popular interest in what they had done among artists, playwrights, actors, theatergoers, artists, correspondents, writers, readers, lawyers, judges, politicians, and citizens, but most especially among abolitionists, who flocked to the jail in large numbers. The *Amistad* Africans slowly built an alliance with other antislavery activists as they studied reading, writing, and religion, all the while organizing themselves, developing their own independent African identity as "the Mende People." They worked with abolitionists such as Tappan and political figures such as Adams to keep their case before the public and to mount a strong legal defense of the freedom that they had won by arms aboard the *Amistad.* This small group of African captives who took desperate action on the high seas caused some of the most powerful people in the world to debate the meaning of what they had done, including monarchs (Queen Charlotte of Britain and Queen Isabella II of Spain), presidents and former presidents (Adams, Martin Van Buren, and John Tyler), statesmen, high-ranking government officials, and Supreme Court justices, among many others.

The meeting of African insurrectionists and American reformers in the New Haven jail was an unprecedented and historic moment. The rebels had made a revolution in miniature aboard the ship, which inspired sympathetic coverage in the press, especially the *New York Sun*, and in turn intense fascination among the public. Tappan and other abolitionists responded, struggling to control and direct the enormous popular interest toward their own purposes, building in the process a determined, energetic, interracial defense campaign. Many who supported the *Amistad* struggle were not, strictly speaking, abolitionists; moreover, they celebrated the heroic insurrection in ways that made moderate abolitionists uneasy. The Africans themselves, through their actions on the vessel and their noble bearing in jail, continued to inspire an unprecedented interest in the fearsome subject of slave revolt. To many, especially African Americans enslaved and free, the *Amistad* rebels rekindled the radical egalitarian hope of the American Revolution.[4]

The insurrectionists and reformers who met in Connecticut jails represented the two main wings of a global movement against slavery. Black rebels had long played an important role in America's antislavery movement, especially by their audacious escapes from slavery, which inspired and mobilized abolitionists throughout the northern states. The *Amistad* case publicized a more controversial form of resistance, outright rebellion, and gave enslaved rebels and their resistance a more important place in an expanded, radicalized movement against slavery. It would help to establish the right of people who were not free to seize freedom through armed self-defense and to claim their place in society as equals.[5]

Even though slave resistance was ubiquitous throughout the turbulent 1830s, revolts were infrequent, even rare, occurrences, especially in the United States. Slaveholders always made clear the consequences of a failed revolt with hangings, maimings, and many other forms of violent repression. Most slaves, like most people, did not want to risk everything in a gamble few before them had won. But an example of success changed everything. This was part of the importance of the Haitian Revolution, 1791–1804. During that revolution the black men and women of Saint-Domingue had demonstrated that the bottom rail could be placed on top. Until the *Amistad* rebellion of 1839, slaves in mainland North America could find no similar example of success. Slave rebels had failed in New York in 1712 and 1741; in Richmond, Virginia, in 1800; in Louisiana in 1811; and in Charleston, South Carolina, in 1822. That record of failures changed in 1839, and with it changed the worlds of American slavery and abolition.

A history of the *Amistad* rebellion "from below" is supported by a collection of sources unique in the annals of New World slavery. Because the makers of the maritime insurrection spent twenty-seven months in Connecticut, nineteen of them in jail, and because their cause was both controversial and well publicized, they met thousands of people from all walks of life, on both sides of the jail's walls. Journalists and ordinary citizens visited them, conversed with them through translators such as the Mende sailor James Covey, and transcribed their life stories, noting their work and nationality (hunter, Temne), where they lived in Africa ("two moons march to the coast"), and how they were enslaved (captured in war, kidnaped). Other visitors drew their portraits and silhouettes. Phrenologists measured the size of their skulls. Yale professor Josiah Gibbs compiled vocabularies of their languages. Many of these visitors published their findings in business newspapers such as the *New York Journal of Commerce*; in penny press papers such as the *New York Sun* and *New York Morning Herald*; and in abolitionist periodicals such as the *Emancipator* and the *Pennsylvania Freeman*. As many as 2,500 articles were published, many of them written by correspondents who had visited the African rebels in jail. No other makers of a modern slave revolt generated such a vast and deep body of evidence, which in turn makes it possible to know more about the *Amistad* Africans than perhaps any other group of once-enslaved rebels on record—to get to know them, individually and collectively, in intimate, multidimensional ways, from their personalities and senses of humor to their specifically West African ways of thinking and acting during their ordeal.

Throughout their odyssey, the *Amistad* rebels struggled—sometimes alongside the American abolitionists, sometimes against them—for a voice of their own. As abolitionist Joshua Leavitt noted soon after they came ashore, "These unfortunate persons, who have been committed to prison and bound over to be tried for their lives" could not "say a word for themselves."[6] Of course, the rebels could and did say many words for themselves, but for weeks no one could understand them. At this point, a group of African sailors entered the picture, most notably James Ferry, Charles Pratt, and James Covey, whose cosmopolitan knowledge of multiple languages finally allowed the rebels to tell their stories of origin, enslavement, and insurrection. Ferry had been liberated from slavery in Colombia at age twelve by Simón Bolivar; Pratt and Covey, by the British naval anti–slave trade patrols. They were experienced in the struggle against slavery and they would be denounced by proslavery critics as "half-civilized, totally ignorant" sailors, who, like the other men of color and low standing, were not to be trusted or believed. The motley crews of ship and waterfront played a critical role in the *Amistad* case.[7]

Leavitt's observation lingers. The *Amistad* rebels' struggle for voice led them to learn English, to study American political culture and to use it for their own ends, to tell both individual and collective stories about what had happened to them and why. Even so, it was no easy matter for them to be heard, in their own times, above or even alongside the voices of evangelical Christians; lawyers, politicians, and diplomats; middle-class antislavery reformers; and proslavery ideologues. And it has proved to be no easy matter to hear them today. This is a history of the *Amistad* rebellion "from below." That, literally, is how and where the *Amistad* case began, with the eruption of armed rebels from the hold onto the main deck of the vessel. By viewing the courtroom drama in relation to the shipboard revolt, or put another way, the actions taken from above in relation to those taken from below, the entire event, from causes to consequences, appears in a new light. This history puts the *Amistad* rebels back at the center of their own story and the larger history they helped to make. Theirs was an epic quest for freedom.

• • •

A new interpretation of the *Amistad* rebellion begins in Sierra Leone and emphasizes the people who made the uprising. Who were the rebels? How did they carry out a successful revolt? Uprisings were commonplace on slave ships during the three and a half centuries of the gruesome trade in human bodies, but *successful* revolts were extremely rare, because slaving captains possessed and used a body of knowledge and practice designed to prevent revolt; moreover, the vessels themselves were designed to make uprisings difficult if not impossible.[8]

The success of the revolt lay in a set of common experiences that served as bases for the rebels' collective action. Most of these commonalities were based in the West African cultures from which they came. Others had emerged during their various captivities, in Lomboko (the slave-trade factory in southern Sierra Leone where they were held); on the transatlantic Brazilian/Portuguese slave ship, the *Teçora*; in the barracoons of Havana; and on board the *Amistad*. From these experiences grew the cooperation and solidarity manifested in the uprising.[9]

The rebels consisted of at least ten different ethnicities or nationalities. Yet they shared an unusually large capacity for communication among themselves: almost two-thirds were Mende, several others could speak Mende, and almost all were multilingual, as was common in their region of origin. All came from societies in which they were accustomed to working together for the good of the whole. Almost all were commoners: many practiced communal rice farming; others knew the common occupation of urban weaver. All came from communities governed by the Poro Society—the powerful all-male secret society that trained warriors, declared war, organized rites of passage, settled disputes, and maintained social discipline. It was observed that leader Cinqué had been accustomed to command. The meaning of that phrase was twofold: he had military experience and discipline and he had wielded authority in the Poro Society, which was by far the most culturally significant means of self-organization known by, and practiced among, the *Amistad* Africans.[10]

The rebels also shared a set of profound experiences based on their common misfortune of enslavement. All had been expropriated from the land and enslaved, although by various means, whether judicial ruling, kidnaping, or military action. All had endured a long, debilitating march, by land and water, to the coast. All except the four children were young, strong, able-bodied men, who had been separated from the families and kinship systems that had previously governed their lives. The very characteristics that made them desirable as slaves, whose youthful labor power could be exploited, made them dangerous as potential rebels. All had been imprisoned at Lomboko on the Gallinas Coast. It was here that Cinqué and Grabeau, Cinqué's second in command, began a conversation about freedom that would last for years. Grabeau testified that he "met the others for the first time" at Lomboko, where they began to take shape as a strange, new, accidental collective.[11]

All had experienced the Portuguese slave ship *Teçora* and its Middle Passage, jammed together with five to six hundred others in miserable circumstances for "two moons," many dying along the way, the survivors developing a "fictive kinship" that grew among the "brothers" and "sisters" of a common ordeal. Those bound for the *Amistad* cried when they were separated from other shipmates upon sale in Havana, and those who remained together repeatedly explained that "they were all brought from Africa in the same vessel," a powerful source of solidarity. Shared sufferings in the Havana barracoons and aboard the *Amistad* strengthened these ties.[12]

The *Amistad* Africans, in sum, boasted commonalities of work, culture, government, enslavement, youth, geographic origins, sites of cooperation (factory, ship), and fictive kinship as "shipmates." In the broader context of the history of the slave trade, they exhibited an unusual degree of common experience, number of social characteristics, and depth of cultural connection, all of which combined to create a broad basis for collective rebellion, in a small place at a specific moment in time. They did not choose their way into the dilemma that confronted them aboard the *Amistad*, but they did, collectively, choose their way out.

These commonalities made the rebellion aboard the *Amistad* possible, but they did not guarantee its success. The overwhelming majority of slave ship revolts, including many that shared the characteristics of the *Amistad* revolt, were abject failures that resulted in massive violence against the rebels—flogging, torture, and murder, all meant to create the most extreme terror, which was intended to break the solidarity expressed in resistance.

Uprisings aboard slave ships proceeded through stages, which is to say, a rebellion was a *process*. They could—and did—break down, allowing the conspiracy to be discovered, and thereby to fail, at any point along the way. The phases of the process of a rebellion were the formation of an original core of rebels, the vanguard that would lead the rebellion; the formation of a collective that would carry it out; then the processes of getting out of the chains, finding weapons, and eventually sailing the ship to freedom. Movement through the stages aboard the *Amistad* was made easier by the fact that it was not a proper slave ship, lacking as it did a lower deck, a defensive barricado, and an isolated gun room, all designed to prevent revolts from below.[13]

Cinqué and Grabeau, both Mende, constituted the original core of the rebels. Cinqué was, in the idiom of the society from which he came, a "head war man," experienced and selected as such by his comrades in the hold of the *Amistad* in the run-up to the rebellion, which he in turn led, with bravery and success. Grabeau was apparently a high-ranking member of the Poro Society, evidenced by his extensive scarification and a fact offered later by someone who knew him in Mende country before his enslavement. He was connected with a high family, though poor himself. These two men thus represented a perfect combination of military, spiritual, and political authority as it existed on the Gallinas Coast and in its hinterlands—and, finally, in the displaced, mobile circumstances of the African diaspora aboard a slave ship in the northern Caribbean. Everyone on board would have recognized them immediately as leaders.[14]

Around these two leaders formed a secondary group: Burna, the third leading figure, and Moru, both Gbandi; Shule (fourth in command on board the schooner) and Kimbo, both Mende; and Fa and Faquorna, culture unknown. All had been warriors in their native societies. They now stepped forward because of their knowledge and combat experience. They studied the ship and whispered their findings to one another in the hold. They wanted to know how the vessel worked (some may have worked on the *Teçora*), how many were in the crew, what were their habits, what were their arms. (The crew was small; they kept no regular watch; they had muskets, pistols, and whips.) These warriors would have seen that the prospects for rebellion aboard the *Amistad* were much greater than they had been on the *Teçora*.[15]

The collective was formed (phase two) through the organizing efforts of the vanguard and the working principles of the Poro Society. The collective, created by the host of experiences above, came into purposeful existence during the meeting, described by Kinna as the time when "we consider." During the "palaver" held in the hold, someone, probably

Cinqué, asked, "Who is for War?" By the end of the meeting, the group had achieved what the Mende called *ndehun*, which meant "one word" or unity. The oral history of the rebellion kept by the rebels themselves recalled their decision: all had "one word WAR!! and war immediately."[16] They decided as a group to rise up, seize the ship, and sail home, or to die trying. Even though a clear leadership had been established immediately before and during the uprising, the collective continued to meet and act together as the situation unfolded. As Ruiz noted, a few days after the rebellion, the group met and officially chose Cinqué as their leader; he had earned the position through action, in the customary Mende way. Other positions were also allocated among themselves: Sesse, who apparently had some seafaring knowledge (probably aboard the *Teçora*), would steer and "make sail." Foone would be delegated as the group's cook. The process of self-organization would continue during the voyage to freedom, the time in American jails, in court, and even at sea again during the repatriation to Sierra Leone.

Two aspects of previous experience were critical to the success of the revolt. First, warfare—much of it connected to the slave trade—had been extensive in the homelands of the *Amistad* Africans from the mid-1820s up to the moment of their shipment out of Lomboko in April 1839. All of the men aboard the *Amistad* had been trained as warriors and many had experience in combat. Gnakwoi had been a "war boy" who fought with the notorious mercenary warlord Goterah. Cinqué and Bau explained that "they had been in battles, in their own country, using muskets." They had been soldiers in the army of King Amara Lalu, who fought the aggressive expansion of King Siaka, the paramount king allied with the Spanish slave traders. Indeed, it was Siaka's soldiers who captured, enslaved, and sold them both to Pedro Blanco. Grabeau also had military experience of a distinctly ironic, not to say contradictory, sort: he had, at one point in his life, fought in a war against "insurgent slaves," not far from the American colony of Liberia. He would now use his martial skills to fight as an insurgent slave himself.[17]

The fundamental practices of Mende warfare were apparent in how the uprising took place. The weapon of choice was a knife. Mende warriors always preferred knives—the cutlass at home, the very similar cane knife aboard the *Amistad*, the discovery of which must have seemed a gift from the ancestral spirits. Moreover, they used typical Mende tactics: they waited for a moonless night and launched a surprise guerilla attack, using war shouts and swinging their blades wildly in a successful effort to make their opponents abandon position so that victory might be more easily achieved. The goal of warfare was not slaughter but capture, of people and place, both of which were quickly achieved on board the vessel. Once they had captured the schooner, the warriors engaged in a ritual called *kootoo*—martial singing, dancing, and the beheading of a vanquished enemy, in this case, Captain Ferrer.[18]

Perhaps even more important, the subversive experience of slave ship revolt was already present aboard the *Amistad* as noted by the two sailors who jumped overboard during the mutiny and managed to get back to Havana: "the Captain, owner of the schr., [Ferrer] was warned, previous to sailing, to keep a look out for the negroes, as they had attempted to rise and take the vessel in which they were brought from Africa." Nothing more is known about the rebellion, as it was never mentioned in any other documentation surrounding the *Amistad* case. Yet it is of first significance that the veterans of a failed rebellion aboard the *Teçora* would have another chance to get it right, and get it right they would.[19]

How did the Africans get out of the irons—the manacles, shackles, neck rings, chains, and padlocks—that rendered them immobile and unable to move about the ship? This question too had an answer in West African practice. The ability of the rebels to pick or break the padlock must have owed something to the fact that two of insurgents were blacksmiths who knew the properties of iron intimately from their work. Sesse

Temne warrior with poisoned arrows, 1820s.

was described as "a blacksmith, having learnt that trade of his brother; he made axes, hoes, and knives from iron obtained in the Mendi country." When speed was crucial to avoiding detection, getting so many people out of irons was necessarily a communal undertaking.[20]

The next phase of the rebellion concerned the acquisition of weapons. At the beginning of the uprising the rebels used tools, handspikes, sticks (probably barrel staves), whatever they could find lying around on the deck. Then came a decisive discovery in the hold of the *Amistad*: a box of cane knives meant to be used by workers in Puerto Príncipe. At the first trial of the *Amistad* Africans, for piracy and murder, a cane knife was presented as evidence to the grand jury and described by a newspaper correspondent: "It is a most formidable weapon in the hands of a resolute man, [c]ould be wielded with deadly effect; it is about 3 feet long, 3 or 4 inches wide at the end, and narrowing until it enters the handle, where it is about one inch and half wide; the handle is of horn with a knob at the end." The rebels quickly transformed a tool of exploitation into its opposite—a tool of emancipation. It also helped that some of the *Amistad* captives knew how to use pistols and muskets.[21]

How the captives found their weapons of self-emancipation has long been one of the mysteries of *Amistad* rebellion. It so happened that British diplomat Richard Robert Madden, who was stationed in Havana, knew how it happened and explained the process in a letter of October 1839. Writing of the *Amistad*, he noted:

> There was much merchandize also on board, and amongst the rest a package of swords or machetes as they are called, which are used for cutting down canes. The female negroes of the party, true to their sex, indulged their curiosity in examining the contents of various packages around them whenever there was an opportunity, and faithful also to the communicative character of the fair part of humanity, they imparted the information they had acquired to their male friends, and the latter true to themselves, and faithful to one bold man among them who became their chief, they acted on it.[22]

The so-called female negroes were the three little girls—Margru, Kagne, and Teme—each about nine years old.

They were not, as Madden seems to suggest, on a shopping expedition. They were, rather, trapped on a slave ship, but they had freedom of movement that others did not have. They used their intelligence, their ability to range freely, and their ability to communicate to find the cane knives and inform their male shipmates of the location, thereby making the successful rebellion possible.

The final phase of the rebellion was the biggest challenge of all. Could they sail the schooner to freedom? The decision was taken to keep Montes alive because he knew how to navigate the vessel. Even though Ruiz and Montes "made fools of us, and did not go to Sierra Leone," as Cinqué explained, he and his comrades did learn to handle the ship well enough to make it to a place that was not "slavery country." They set sail, operated the windlass, hauled anchor, used the boat, and managed to go ashore at least thirty times during the voyage after the rebellion, all of which bespeaks considerable maritime skill. Most of the places they anchored and went ashore remain unknown: Did they go ashore in South Carolina or Virginia, only to discover that these places *were* "slavery country"? Their ability to sail the ship may have owed something to the sickness of white crew members aboard the *Teçora*, a common problem on Atlantic slave ships, which was solved by bringing African men out of the lower deck and teaching them the rudiments of sailoring—how to hand, reef, and steer on a sailing ship.[23]

Why were they able to make a successful revolution in miniature? Was it, as the escaped sailors of the *Amistad* claimed, because of the carelessness of Captain Ferrer, who took too small a crew and too rebellious a gang of enslaved people, whom he then failed to keep properly in chains, below decks with the hatchway locked, without arms, and without opportunities to rise up and kill him? Or was it the shrewdness of the *Amistad*

Margru. Pencil drawing by William H. Townsend.

Africans that made them able to draw on a rich fund of culture and experience and thereby to recognize the weaknesses and seize the opportunities before them?

The planning and execution of the rebellion—and no less the long, dangerous, even torturous voyage afterward—were great and historic achievements. Acting on shared common experiences and West African precepts of self-organization, the *Amistad* Africans had done what few of the millions before them had done: waged a successful uprising aboard a slave ship, then sailed the vessel to a place where they might secure the freedom they had fought for and won. Their armed self-defense forced abolitionists, in America and around the world, to make revolutionary arguments in defense of their resistance and against the institution of slavery itself. As attorney Roger Baldwin explained to the justices of the Supreme Court, the *Amistad* "had been taken by force out of the hands of Spanish subjects, was not sailing under Spanish colors, had lost its national character, and was in the full possession of the Africans."[24] John Quincy Adams made the same point before the same court: "The Africans were in possession, and had the presumptive right of ownership" of the *Amistad*; "they were on a voyage to their own native homes. . . . the ship was theirs."[25] And of course the *Amistad* Africans themselves knew what they had achieved, even as posterity was beginning to paint them as hapless victims. Indeed, young Kale wrote to Adams, telling the great man exactly what he should say to the Supreme Court: "If court ask you who brought Mende people to America? We bring ourselves. Ceci hold rudder."[26]

The shock waves of the *Amistad* rebellion reverberated in many different directions—throughout the Caribbean and Brazil, where a successful revolt put a regional master class on the defensive; back to Europe, where monarchs, middle-class reformers, and workers took great interest in the case; to Africa, where the *Amistad* rebels returned in January 1842, bringing missionary abolitionists and an international track of the Underground Railroad with them; and throughout the United States, where the movement against slavery took a radical turn, especially among African American abolitionists, leading in a direct line to John Brown's raid on Harper's Ferry in 1859 and the Civil War in 1861. Word of the mutiny—and agency—of fifty-three enslaved Africans on a small vessel in the northern Caribbean in 1839 spread far and wide around the Atlantic. Neither the rebellion nor its broad influence can be understood without a "history from below," in which the African rebels created their own freedom and, in so doing, helped to create a path for millions of other enslaved people to follow in the years ahead.

NOTES

1. This chapter was first presented as a lecture at "Les Rendez-vous de l'histoire" in Blois, France, and published as "Révolte d'esclaves en mer, les rebelles de l'*Amistad* en 1839," *l'Histoire* 410 (May 2015). It is republished here with permission. The article draws on Marcus Rediker, *The* Amistad *Rebellion: An Atlantic Odyssey of Slavery and Freedom* (New York: Penguin, 2012).

2. Julie Roy Jeffrey, "*Amistad* (1997): Steven Spielberg's 'True Story,'" *Historical Journal of Film, Radio and Television* 21 (2001): 77–96; Marouf Hasian Jr. and A. Cheree Carlson, "Revisionism and Collective Memory: The Struggle for Meaning in the *Amistad* Affair," *Communications Monographs* 67 (2000): 42–62. Novels include Barbara Chase-Riboud, *Echo of Lions* (New York: William Morrow, 1989); Alexs D. Pate, *Amistad* (New York: Signet, 1997); and David Pesci, *Amistad* (Marlowe, 1997). A poetic reflection on the history and meaning of the case is Kevin Young, *Ardency: A Chronicle of the* Amistad *Rebels* (New York: Knopf, 2011).

3. The historiography of the *Amistad* rebellion is rich: William A. Owens, *Black Mutiny: The Revolt on the Schooner* Amistad (New York: John Day, 1953); Mary Cable, *Black Odyssey: The Case of the Slave Ship* "Amistad" (New York: Viking Press, 1971); Maggie Montesinos Sale, *The Slumbering Volcano: American Slave Ship Revolts and the Production of Rebellious Masculinity* (Durham: Duke University Press, 1997); and Iyunolu Folayan Osagie, *The* Amistad *Revolt: Memory, Slavery, and the Politics of Identity in the United States and Sierra Leone* (Athens: University of Georgia Press, 2000). Important recent contributions include Michael Zeuske, Amistad*: A Hidden Network of Slavers and Merchants* (Princeton: Markus Wiener, 2014); and Benjamin Lawrance, Amistad*'s Orphans: An Atlantic Story of Children, Slavery, and Smuggling* (New Haven: Yale University Press, 2015). Valuable new work is forthcoming by Robert S. Wolff and Joseph Yannielli.

4. The best, and most poetic, account of the struggle against slavery and its long aftermath remains Vincent Harding, *There Is a River: The Black Struggle for Freedom in America* (New York: Vintage Books, 1981).

5. Peter Linebaugh and Marcus Rediker, *The Many-Headed Hydra: Sailors, Slaves, Commoners, and the Hidden History of the Revolutionary Atlantic* (Boston: Beacon Press, 2000), chap. 9. Other scholars who have included enslaved rebels in the abolitionist movement include Merton L. Dillon, *Slavery Attacked: Southern Slaves and Their Allies, 1619–1865* (Baton Rouge: Louisiana State University Press, 1990); Stanley Harrold, *American Abolitionists* (Harlow, UK: Longman, 2001); and Douglas R. Egerton, "The Scenes Which Are Enacted in St. Domingo: The Legacy of Revolutionary Violence in Early National Virginia," in *Antislavery Violence: Sectional, Racial, and Cultural Conflict in Antebellum America*, ed. Jack

R. McKivigan and Stanley Harrold (Knoxville: University of Tennessee Press, 1999), 41–64.

6. "Incarcerated Captives," *New York Commercial Advertiser*, September 6, 1839.

7. Howard Jones, *Mutiny on the* Amistad: *The Saga of a Slave Revolt and Its Impact on American Abolition, Law, and Diplomacy* (New York: Oxford University Press, 1987), 210 (quotation about black sailors). On the radicalism of the waterfront, see Linebaugh and Rediker, *Many-Headed Hydra*, chaps. 7 and 8.

8. Marcus Rediker, *The Slave Ship: A Human History* (New York: Penguin, 2007), chap. 8.

9. See Rediker, *The* Amistad *Rebellion*, 122 and chap. 4.

10. "The Long Low Black Schooner," *New York Sun*, August 31, 1839. See also Rediker, *The* Amistad *Rebellion*, chap. 1.

11. "African Testimony," *New York Journal of Commerce*, January 10, 1840.

12. "Deposition of Bahoo [Bau]," *New York Morning Herald*, September 22, 1839; "The *Amistad*," *New York Commercial Advertiser*, October 4, 1839.

13. For more on shipboard rebellion, see Niklas Frykman, Clare Anderson, Lex Heerma von Voss, and Marcus Rediker, eds., *Mutiny and Maritime Radicalism in the Age of Revolution: A Global Survey* (Cambridge: Cambridge University Press, 2014).

14. "Private Examination of Cinquez," *New York Commercial Advertiser*, September 13, 1839; "The Mendians," *Vermont Chronicle*, June 8, 1842.

15. John Warner Barber, *A History of the Amistad Captives: Being a Circumstantial Account of the Capture of the Spanish Schooner Amistad, by the Africans on Board; Their Voyage, and Capture Near Long Island, New York; with Biographical Sketches of Each of the Surviving Africans; Also, an Account of the Trials had on Their case, Before the District and Circuit Courts of the United States, for the District of Connecticut* (New Haven: E. L. and J. W. Barber, 1840), 12.

16. Hannah More to William Harned, Mendi Mission, October 12, 1852, American Missionary Association, Amistad Research Center, New Orleans.

17. "The Mendians," *Vermont Chronicle*, June 8, 1842; "Private Examination of Cinquez," *New York Commercial Advertiser*, September 13, 1839.

18. See Rediker, *The* Amistad *Rebellion*, chap. 2.

19. "Correspondence of the *Journal of Commerce*," *New York Journal of Commerce*, July 25, 1839.

20. Barber, *History of the* Amistad *Captives*, 11.

21. "Case of the Captured Africans," *New York Morning Herald*, September 22, 1839.

22. Richard Robert Madden to A. Blackwood, Esq., October 3, 1839, in Correspondence from Dr. R. R. Madden, Mr. D. R. Clarke, and the Foreign Office relating to the removal of the "Liberated Africans" from Cuba, 1839, Colonial Office (CO) 318/146, National Archives, Kew Gardens, UK.

23. "To the Committee on Behalf of the African Prisoners," *New York Journal of Commerce*, September 10, 1839; "The *Amistad*," *New London Gazette*, October 16, 1839.

24. "The Captives of The *Amistad*," *New York Journal of Commerce*, February 23, 1841.

25. *Argument of John Quincy Adams before the Supreme Court of the United States in the case of the United States, Appellants, vs. Cinque, and others, Africans, captured in the schooner Amistad, by Lieut. Gedney, Delivered on the 24th of February and 1st of March 1841* (New York: S. W. Benedict, 1841).

26. "Ka-le's Letter to Mr. Adams," *New York Journal of Commerce*, March 20, 1841.

I

Encounters

2

The Talons

A Seventeenth-Century Captivity Saga

Benjamin Mark Allen

In July 1714, Louis Juchereau de Saint-Denis, a French envoy accompanied by other compatriots, Native Americans, and two curious-looking scouts, wandered into the Spanish outpost of San Juan Bautista de Rio Grande. Undoubtedly, the fort's commandant, Captain Diego Ramon, greeted the French agents with surprise and suspicion given the intense rivalry between the two colonial powers over this contested area that the Spaniards called *Tejas* (present-day East Texas) in an attempt to pronounce the Caddo word for their alliance with other regional tribes. The competition for control over this area began in the 1680s, when the French first introduced a colony in Spanish territory. Most remarkable was the purpose of Saint-Denis's visit—the establishment of formal trade relations between the French colony of Louisiana and *Nueva España* (New Spain). It was a culmination of three decades or more of French and Spanish rivalry over the coveted region. With the arrival of this small band of French emissaries, Ramon clearly understood and warned the king, Luis I, that if the Spaniards did not settle East Texas then "the French will be masters of this land."[1] It was wishful thinking that any European power could, at that time, dominate and control the expansive region. No one understood this better than Saint-Denis's two scouts, brothers Pierre and Robert Talon, who knew that the Indians remained the true masters, for as former captives, they were living proof that the colonized could at times be the colonizers.

Saint-Denis's adventure is a political narrative of imperial rivalry that spanned the better part of the seventeenth and eighteenth centuries. It is well documented and offers a fascinating tale of international intrigue and calamity, as well as insight into the prominent characters and their motivations. Lesser known are the casualties of this contest, and perhaps none is as significant as that of the Native American societies such as the Caddo and Karankawa of Texas who were wedged between the two imposing powers and, although sovereign for a time, eventually succumbed and perished. Although the interaction between Saint-Denis and Diego Ramon make for an intriguing story that had geopolitical repercussions, the meeting would perhaps never have been possible without the knowledge and labor of common folks often considered expendable by their elite compatriots.[2] Saint-Denis and the French authorities heavily relied on Pierre and Robert Talon to advance French suzerainty into Texas. Once captives of the Caddo and Karankawa, respectively, their linguistic abilities, bodily scarifications that identified them as Indian kin, and knowledge of the territory and its bounty proved vital to gaining safe passage and winning alliances with the dominant native tribes. For most of their lives, the Talons were pawns of the colonial powers that compelled this family to serve the interests of the state without regard to their own welfare. Theirs is a family saga with heroic overtones that exemplifies what some have described as "creolization"—the Talons entered the Texas Gulf Coast as Frenchmen but left it with altered identities. They became acculturated by the collision of diverse societies with very different mentalities who met in the contact zones of North America.[3]

Although the Talons appear in a few official records, none of them describe their lives in the form of narrative prose. I nonetheless describe their ordeal as "heroic" in its literary-mythic ideal in which an unwilling participant is thrust into a terrific journey following an often violent abduction from his or her familiar environment and then forced to negotiate, survive, and finally overcome a very strange world as the person attempts to return home. The experience produces a psychological and sometimes physical metamorphosis of sorts, resulting in intellectual, cultural, and spiritual change. Back home, the "hero" discovers that the once familiar has become strange, and she or he must choose to cross back over the cultural threshold and to teach what was learned in the foreign environment, or she or he must opt to remain behind and embrace the exotic. Scholars have demonstrated that the archetypical hero's journey is in fact a metaphor of life, and the Talons serve as examples of this mythic application to reality.[4] Studies further show that, in general, most European captivity survivors and other secondary narrators either willingly or subconsciously opted to describe the captivity ordeal in terms of heroic prose.[5] Sadly, though, the Talons, like so many others who survived similar experiences, never completed the cycle. Were it not for some buried transcripts, their tale would have been forgotten and their transformative journey from a European to a New World identity never understood. And though almost silenced, their muted voices cry out to be heard.

Narrating this "heroic" epic proves problematic. With so few documents offering the Talons' first-person perspective, historians are reluctant to extrapolate for fear of fabrication and too much reliance on "exact imagining."[6] One scholar has convincingly argued, however, that this fear is not justified because it rests too heavily on the colonizers' historical methodology as taught and practiced by Western academe.[7] Reliance on written documents alone favors the colonizers and remains an institutionalized form of subjugation of the colonized because a majority of the colonized did not possess written records, and the records that did exist were often destroyed by the Europeans, as in the case of the Aztecs. The absence of documentation, however, does not negate the significance of the colonized or their contribution to the evolution of the modern world.[8] If a more complete history is to emerge, consideration must be rendered to the subjugated masses and allow them to speak across time. This secondary voice is described by historian James Axtell as the "second record . . . [that is] entirely personal and individual . . . [and] is everything that (the historian) can bring to bear on the record of the past in order to elicit . . . the best account he can render."[9] The task is especially daunting when attempting to describe captivity ordeals that are intensely traumatic and personal. It requires probing the deepest and darkest chasms of human experience.

In describing this acculturative process, our vocabulary lacks the precision to adequately relay the psychological transformations that resulted in identities unique to the New World.[10] One scholar has described it as a process of "creolization" to relay the idea that "new cultural forms came to life in the New World."[11] To help explain the process, I have found some utility in the hero archetype in mythology as defined in semiotic studies offered by anthropologist Claude Lévi-Strauss. It is a problem of cultural hybridization that often occurred in the contact zones of the Atlantic world. Although clearly of European, African, or Native American origins, a person's cultural homogeneity began to deteriorate because of the mixing that resulted over time, distance, and place, as well as in response to the dynamic sociopolitical realities of colonial America. As English, French, Africans, Spaniards, and a host of other groups began to clash, mingle, and coexist (one result of the Columbian exchange), a syncretic culture emerged.[12] It was unique to the American continent that would ultimately consume the aboriginal cultures, and those Indians who survived would also be tainted, or creolized.[13]

The Talons aptly demonstrated this evolution. The clues indicate that they, like so many other New World captives, lost their original identity as French Europeans. They no longer could relate to their French compatriots or to any other European—because of their heroic ordeals they had morphed into something entirely new as individuals and as a creolized family. The problem, however, is the scarcity of these clues. Considering that historians have dedicated most attention to the more prominent historical figures such as Saint-Denis, a vast majority of New World characters have faded from historical memory. Understandably, historians are most comfortable and more securely grounded in their studies buttressed by heaps of archival manuscripts. Where the Talons are concerned, the records are almost nonexistent. Their names appear only where and when they are of importance to the elite in the larger contest for imperial domination. Considered *roturiers* of the Third Estate in a stratified French society, the two Talon brothers and their heroic tale have remained obscure and nearly forgotten, awaiting a unique methodology to give them a voice at last.[14] A debt is owed to Texas historian Robert Weddle for salvaging the Talons from the dustbin of history. His research into the failed French colony of Fort Saint Louis on the Texas Gulf Coast uncovered a deposition of two teenage brothers whose experience rivaled most epic myths.[15] This study stems from that testimony.

Long before serving as guides for the Saint-Denis party, the Talon family came to Texas in 1684 along with René-Robert Cavelier, sieur de La Salle, the French explorer who two years earlier claimed the lower Mississippi River Valley for his king, Louis XIV. Considering French and Spanish rivalry in the North American Gulf, La Salle hoped to seize the Mississippi's mouth and to guarantee French domination by settling colonists recruited from France and Canada.[16] The Talons were among his first recruits. This family's history is testament to what scholars have described as the "circular transmission of human experience . . . that set the Atlantic currents in motion."[17] Lucien and Isabelle Talon accompanied La Salle to the Gulf Coast along with their six children—Marie-Elizabeth (born 1672), Marie-Madeleine (born 1673), Pierre (born 1676), Jean-Baptiste (born 1679), Lucien (born c. 1681), and Robert (born 1684). Both Lucien and his wife migrated to North America from France and both, most likely, met and married in the French colony of Québec.[18] Their children were born in the Western Hemisphere with the possible exception of Lucien, who may have been born when the couple temporarily returned to France. She then gave birth to their youngest child, Robert, during the ocean voyage from France to the Gulf.

The Talons witnessed and endured one calamity after another as La Salle's attempt to secure a foothold in Texas proved a miserable failure. He sailed from France with four ships and about three hundred colonists, but once in the Gulf of Mexico, a quarrel erupted with the captain of the fleet, Sieur de Beaujeu. One of the four ships carrying the majority of supplies, the *St. François*, fell prey to Spanish privateers in the Gulf of Mexico. After further desertions of crewmembers during ports of call, La Salle and company overshot the Mississippi River and finally landed at Matagorda Bay (near present-day Corpus Christi, Texas) in January 1685. Because of bad blood, Beaujeu abandoned the colonists at first chance, leaving them with only one ship, *La Belle*, which subsequently sank during a storm.[19] If having been stranded in an uncharted land did not prove ominous enough, a skirmish erupted between the French and a local tribe of the Karankawa, resulting in La Salle stripping the natives of various goods and some of their canoes.[20] La Salle's lack of diplomacy would eventually doom the entire effort.

Following desertions and some unfortunate deaths, the final tally stood at about 180 colonists, including the Talons, and these individuals eventually established a permanent settlement on Garcitas Creek just inland from Matagorda Bay. From there, La Salle searched in vain for the Mississippi River's mouth, but lack of accurate maps and instruments had initially led the group too far west and left them on New Spain's frontier. By January 1687, only about 45 of the 180 remained alive, requiring La Salle to seek vital assistance from New France. He and seventeen men thus departed for the other Fort Saint Louis in the Illinois Territory in hopes of gaining supplies from Canada. The journey proved a murderous affair, claiming even the life of La Salle himself. In the end, only three finally arrived at Fort Saint Louis in New France.[21]

Sharing in all of these disasters were the Talons who, as a family and as individuals, underwent Herculean ordeals that forged their uniquely New World identity and created an unbreakable family bond among them. The Talon family offers insight into that creolization process as their original

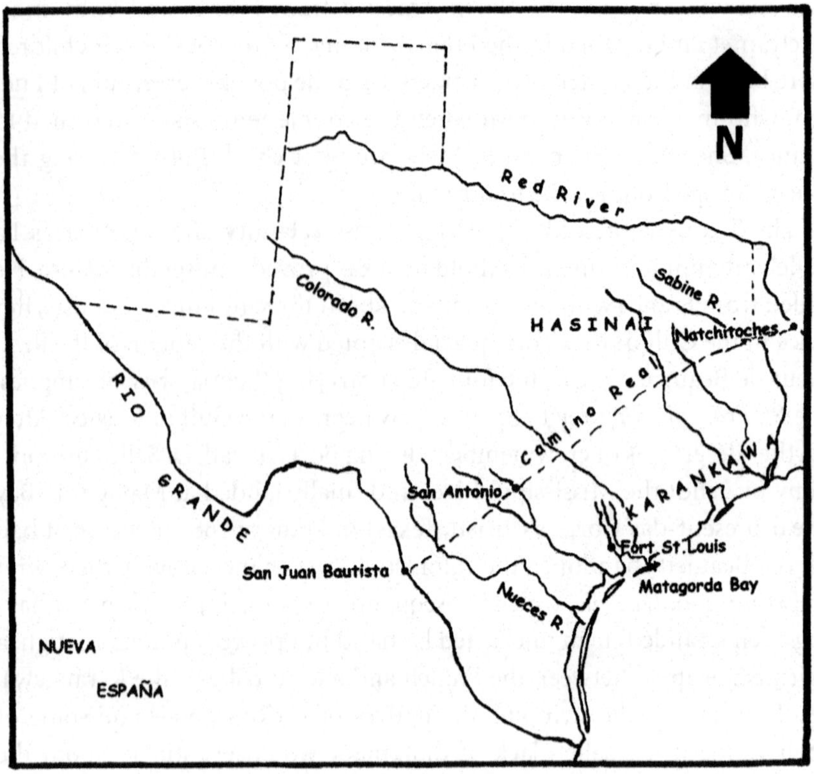

The Talons' North American saga began at Fort Saint Louis in 1684. By 1714, the odyssey brought two of the siblings to the French outpost of Natchitoches on the Red River. From there, they led Saint-Denis to San Juan Bautista.

French identity grew more blurred with each passing year and with each tragic ordeal; however, the survivors never lost sight of one another. Arguably, the children are the heroic characters. They had no other choice but to accompany their parents on an arduous and potentially deadly journey across the Atlantic Ocean and Gulf of Mexico. Once on shore, the children lost their father, Lucien, who went out with a hunting party but never returned. Soon after, in the winter of 1686, the eldest sister, Marie-Elizabeth, succumbed to an illness, leaving behind a grieving mother and her five children.[22] As the colony's death toll mounted and La Salle recognized the urgency of the situation, the struggling family was to say goodbye to yet another member. La Salle ordered the eldest son, Pierre, to live among the Caddo to learn their language and, it was hoped, forge friendly relations so that the remaining colonists could obtain the goods that they desperately needed.[23]

La Salle's feeble attempt at diplomacy came too late and perhaps was aimed at the wrong people. Had he demonstrated similar consideration with the Karankawa when first landing at Matagorda Bay, his enterprise may have been less costly. As it was, the losses proved staggering. When La Salle departed the colony in February 1687 with hopes of reaching New France, only about twenty-eight colonists remained at the settlement. Among them were the surviving Talons—the mother, Isabelle, along with the children Marie-Madeleine, Jean-Baptiste, Lucien, and Robert. By March, La Salle was dead, and Pierre Talon was living with the Caddo. By Christmas 1688, the Karankawa supposedly sought retribution for La Salle's disrespect and thus attacked and destroyed what was left of Fort Saint Louis. All colonists were murdered with the exception of the Talon children and one other child. Thus began their remarkable journey.[24]

According to the testimony of Jean-Baptiste and Robert Talon, given about ten years later, a band of Karankawa men and women stormed Fort Saint Louis and massacred its inhabitants, including the infants. Among the dead was Isabelle, whom the Karankawa dispatched in front of her children. According to the two brothers, their lives would have certainly been taken had it not been for the intervention of certain Karankawa women who pleaded with the warriors to spare the children: "They were saved by some savage women who, touched with compassion by their youth, loaded them on their backs and carried them into their cabins while their husbands massacred the rest, after the said Talons had seen their mother fall before their eyes."[25]

Whereas much may be owed to the sympathy of the native women, it was not unusual for Native Americans in general to spare and then carry into captivity those who may have been considered of value to the tribe (i.e., to replace fallen warriors, as slaves, or for ransom).[26] Regardless, the young Talons' initiation into the world of the "other" was most violent and traumatic. Their experiences mimicked that of countless other Europeans who fell victim to Native American raids. Once abducted from their familiar surroundings, they were stripped naked and subjected to abuse. Over time, the captives were forced to prove their fortitude, physical strength, and utility to the group. Those who endured were often ceremoniously adopted as blood kin; those who lacked vitality were killed or abandoned to die. Usually, and often very quickly, the captive would come to identify with the captor culture to such degree that the two—Indian captor/European captive—became indistinguishable. In the case of the Talons, the youngest children even lost the ability to speak and understand their native French language. Repeated and prolonged exposure to the sun darkened their white skins and the bodily markings of tattoos and piercings completed the physical metamorphosis. The Talons recalled that they "were obliged to do like them because they [the Indians] are so desirous that others imitate and resemble them in everything."[27]

Modern psychology has attempted to describe this psychological melding as the *Stockholm syndrome*, so named following a 1973 bank heist in Stockholm, Sweden, that resulted in the hostages so thoroughly identifying with their captors that the former came to sympathize and assist the latter.[28] In the opinion of experts, it is an innate survival technique. In the case of the Talons, this is difficult to diagnose considering the lack of first-person testimony; even their deposition is in the third person, dictated by the French transcriptionist. Those who first encountered them within several months after their abduction (Alonso de León was among the first to locate the remains of the settlement in 1689) did describe the Talon siblings, for all practical purposes, as completely conformed to their captor's cultures, even the oldest among them. The case of Pierre Talon offers a useful contrast that may suggest that trauma does not necessarily lead to conformity. He was never violently abducted. And although he did witness the murder of his leader, La Salle, it appears the Caddo welcomed him. He also could have accompanied Henri Joutel and the others who ventured on to New France after La Salle's demise, but he stayed behind to live with the Caddo—"he returned to the Cenis village, where he always stayed."[29] Although not necessarily easy, life among the Caddo was perhaps preferable to the unknown territory and hazards that confronted the French travelers. The family that he was forced to leave behind at Fort Saint Louis may have weighed heavily on Pierre's mind. One theme that permeates the Talon transcripts scattered throughout the archives is the strength of familial bonds.

In the absence of parents and given the distance from his siblings, Pierre perhaps found a new family that offered some solace. He resided among a people who had created the Hasanai Confederation (sometimes referred to by the French as the Cenis) that spanned East Texas and the Red River Valley regions of Louisiana and was composed of about ten nations. Europeans often described Caddo as the "most civilized" of all the American societies, subsisting largely on an agricultural economy with corn as the principal staple.[30] The Caddo were a handsome people, light complexioned, stocky, swift, and possessed of a friendly disposition. Pierre Talon described his Indian hosts as living in camps of wood huts covered with straw, and that he "always [lived] with their chief."[31] Eleven-year-old Pierre was introduced to a life quite different from his European heritage. Although politically patriarchal with a Gran Xinesi as the political and religious chief, the society was matrifocal, affording females respect and privilege. Their clothing consisted of tanned buffalo and deerskin hides. Both men and women displayed tattoos and piercings applied at an early age.[32]

Pierre discovered that life was highly ritualized and that the Caddo mythologies, on the surface, were quite different from Catholic doctrine. Because the Caddo were agriculturalists, their mythical imageries were steeped in planting metaphors—the moon sprouted from the earth; man emerged from the great father above; a man brought a drought and then a flood; a snake woman distributed seeds to people.[33] The Caddo also participated in rituals for war and for hunting. Perhaps most disturbing to Pierre was how the women aborted children whose father had deserted them. They also killed (by burying alive) any newborn that showed the slightest deformity. Among the birthing rituals, those infants found acceptable were quickly bathed in the nearest river and the mothers made incisions that scarred the flesh. Apparently, the Caddo subjected Pierre to a similar birthing ritual, signifying his acceptance into the tribe.[34]

A few hundred miles south of Pierre's location, the other four Talons experienced life with an indigenous people much different from the Caddo

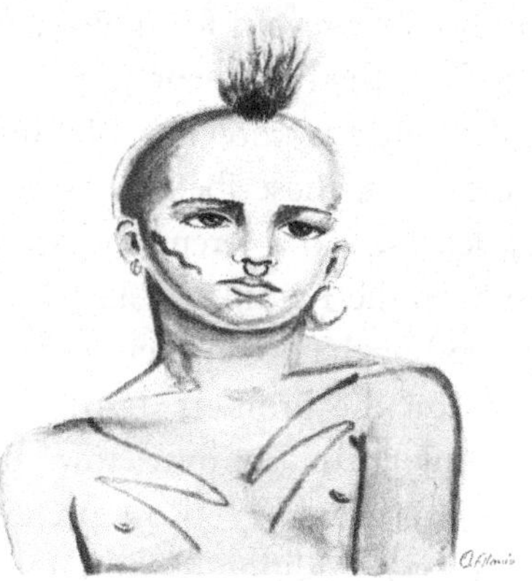

Depiction of what young Pierre (about eleven years old) may have resembled as a Caddo. The markings are typical of Caddo society, and they purposely exposed Pierre to the sun in order to darken his skin. (Artwork courtesy of Olga Alanis.)

and described by the brothers as "a people much more cruel and barbaric than the Cenis or any other tribe."[35] The Karankawa inhabited the coastal regions of Texas and subsisted as hunter/gatherers rather than agriculturalists. Five principal groups made up the nation—Carancaquases, Cocos, Cujanes, Guapitas, and Copanes. Some Talons most likely resided with the Copanes who inhabited the southernmost region near present-day Corpus Christi at the site of the French fort. Evidence suggests that all five groups regularly comingled, but Jean-Baptiste indicated that he lived among the Carancaquases (Karankawa proper). Physically, these people were unusual in that they obtained nearly six feet in height and possessed strong, robust bodies. Perhaps their diet was a factor that contributed to their physique because they subsisted for the most part on high-protein foods, including redfish, trout, catfish, whitetail deer, and oysters.[36] The Karankawa were often nomadic, moving inland to hunt during summer then relocating along estuaries and coastlines for fishing during fall and winter. They taught the Talons how to catch fish with a bow and arrow, although at times the Karankawa also used bamboo cages as traps.[37]

Unfortunately, we do not have Marie-Madeleine's account of her life with the Karankawa, but it undoubtedly would have been somewhat different from that of her brothers. Females fulfilled the role of gatherers, whereas males were hunters. As a female of sixteen, she most likely would have been expected to procreate. Jean-Baptiste described that the Karankawa "had greatly desired to abuse [from his perspective] their sister . . . who was already tall . . . quite pretty, and well built."[38] Karankawa (and most Native American) sexual practices unnerved patriarchal/patrifocal Christian sensibilities unaccustomed to matrifocal societies. The brothers told the French interrogators that Indian women acted as prostitutes who possessed no regard for honor and did so without experiencing any jealousy from their male cohorts.[39]

Very little is known of Karankawa rituals, although Europeans such as the Talons described the use of tobacco, a black drink made of yaupon leaves, and a ceremony associated with the moon. According to the brothers, the Karankawa also ritualistically bathed in the nearest stream or pond or the ocean every morning, the men more so than the women. Based on the brothers' testimony, these Indians also practiced a form of cannibalism, but only "toward their savage enemies . . . as they never ate a Frenchman."[40] Also reprehensible to European sensibilities was the Karankawa tradition of tattooing and piercing. Like their brother, Pierre, the other Talons were decorated according to Karankawa custom. The Talons described this as a very painful process in which walnut wood was burned to charcoal, which was then inserted into the skin using sharp thorns. The Talons' indelible tattoos marginalized them once they were reunited with their European compatriots.

Overall, though, the Talons would have most likely settled into a life that they may have discovered more preferable to that of European society. Since Columbus first landed in the Bahamas in 1492, countless numbers of Europeans either willingly fled to or were captured by Native Americans, and many captives, even when presented with an opportunity to return home, opted to remain with the Indians. Perhaps the Stockholm syndrome may help explain some of the expatriation, but it cannot adequately account for it all, especially when considering the numbers who willingly "went native" after deliberately fleeing their European kinsmen. Perhaps most of them discovered that life among the Indians proved liberating as opposed to a life in the rigidly stratified European societies that locked a majority of people into wretched conditions and servitude to the elite. Captives such as the celebrated Cabeza de Vaca described how, once adopted by the Indians, they enjoyed freedom.[41] Those who contributed to the survival of the tribe often found affection, gratitude, and, in some cases, a position of status—something European commoners would have never realized in the Old World.[42]

Having experienced the life of a child as a European and then as a Caddo or Karankawa, it is most probable that the Talons preferred the nurturing manner of their captors to the harsh discipline of their kin. Most descriptions of Native American child rearing indicated strongly that Indian children were seldom ever reprimanded or disciplined. The

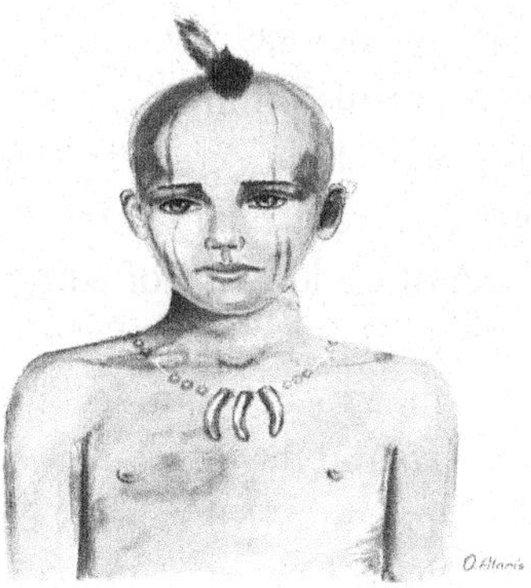

Depiction of what young Jean-Baptiste (about eight) may have resembled as a Karankawa. As a Karankawa matured, the vertical charcoal tattoos would have extended down the body. Females such as Marie-Madeleine would have been decorated with tattoos across the chest. (Artwork courtesy of Olga Alanis.)

Talons' recollections testify to their captors' gentle manners. According to the scribe,

> the Talons affirm that they were always treated by these savage people with the greatest kindness in the world, without ever having been maltreated with blows or otherwise. On the contrary, they love them tenderly and appeared to be very angry when anyone displeased them [the Talons] in any way and took their [the Talons'] part on these occasions, even against their [the Indians'] own children.[43]

The Talons went on to reveal an affinity for their former captors who "liv[ed] among themselves in marvelous union, never . . . quarrel[ing], and never striking each other."[44] The brothers described how easy it was for Europeans to trade with the Indians, and told the French authorities that their captors were "of such great simplicity, so credulous and so sensitive to the friendship offered them."[45]

Despite the Talons' admiration for the Caddo and Karankawa, their stay proved short lived. Thanks to some deserters from Fort Saint Louis at Matagorda Bay who eventually fell into Spanish hands, word of French encroachment on Spanish claims reached all the way to Mexico City and to the viceroy of New Spain, Condé de Monclova (governed 1686–88), who dispatched a reconnaissance party to ascertain the veracity of the rumors. Several expeditions along the Gulf Coast and overland commenced in 1687. By spring 1689, General Alonzo de Leon, Governor of Coahuila, and his scouting party, guided by one of La Salle's deserters, finally wandered into the remains of Fort Saint Louis. Hearing tales that other survivors of the French colony may have resided with the local Indians, Leon sent Indian messengers to nearby camps in hopes of finding the French. In 1689, two survivors appeared—L'Archevêque of Bayonne, one of La Salle's murderers, and Jacques Grollet, who had deserted Fort Saint Louis about one year before its destruction. Both indicated other Frenchmen remained behind. By May 1690, the Spaniards encountered a group of Caddo, one of whom was Pierre Talon. Leon soon discovered the remaining siblings—Robert, Marie-Madeleine, and Lucien—among the Karankawa. It required yet another year before Jean-Baptiste finally decided to join the Spaniards who had carried his siblings to Mexico City for interrogation by Viceroy Conde de Galve (governed 1688–96).[46]

Few clues exist concerning the Talons' thoughts and perceptions of the

Spaniards. Although some survivors such as L'Archevēque recorded his desire to return to Christendom, indications are that the Talons greeted the Spaniards with some trepidation and ambivalence. Pierre hesitated to join the Spaniards based on the belief that it was they who attacked and massacred the remaining colonists at Fort Saint Louis.[47] Leon recorded that the youngest Talons (Robert and Lucien) trembled in his presence.[48] Of course, they had good reason. Leon had just abducted the two boys and their older sister during a violent skirmish with their Karankawa captors. Regardless of the means, however, Leon was determined to secure the Talons and the other French compatriots and escort them to Mexico City for debriefing by the Spanish authorities. One can imagine how this event forced the children to relive their last traumatic abduction, which ended with the murder of their mother. Violence proved the norm for the Talons. Once relocated to Mexico City, the family experienced the 1692 Corn Riots, brought about by a severe drought that depleted grain stores and left the population starving. The mob set the Palacio Real (Royal Palace) in Mexico City ablaze, forcing the viceroy, his wife, and the Talons to flee for safety.[49]

During these turbulent episodes, one thing proved most comforting and stabilizing—the presence of family. Leon described how Robert and Lucien clung to their sister Marie-Madeleine.[50] It was Pierre who pled with Leon to help obtain the release of his siblings from the Karankawa so "that he [Pierre] might have the consolation of seeing them brought with him and among Christians."[51] Following their residency with the viceroy in Mexico City when they fell into the hands of the French in 1697, again Pierre and his brother Jean-Baptiste expressed an urgent desire to "[return] to Europe, that they might be able to go to Spain to rejoin their other brother and sister [who had traveled there with the viceroy's wife], the separation from whom they still felt severely."[52] Although their affections for one another brought some comfort, perhaps at no other time did they feel so welcomed as when living among the Indians. Jean-Baptiste, who had stayed behind for another year, related how the Karankawa "wept bitterly" when the Spaniards took the other three siblings and that they "mourned them for a month afterward."[53]

There is some consolation in this tragic tale. When carted off to Mexico City to live with the viceroy, all the siblings were, at last, together. From 1692 to 1697, when the viceroy retired and departed for Spain, the five Talons resided at his palace as "household servants" but were

treated "with great kindness and all sorts of good treatment."[54] There they learned the ways of the Spaniards, and when the three eldest boys reached the appropriate age, they were compelled to serve in the *Armada de Barlovento* that patrolled the Spanish Gulf. At this time, Pierre, Lucien, and Jean-Baptiste fell into the hands of the French when their ship, the *Santo Christo*, engaged the French warship *Bon*. Because Lucien was considered too young for service in the French fleet, he became a servant. To the others' dismay, the French government conscripted Pierre and Jean-Baptiste for service with the French military. Dashed was their greatest hope to be reunited with Marie-Madeleine and Robert—their fate determined yet again by the will of others.

Once in French hands, the Talons came to the attention of Minister of Marine Louis Pontchartrain, who ordered Pierre and Jean-Baptiste to provide the deposition on which this study relies. Their value to French plans of settling the Mississippi Valley was at once recognized by Pierre Le Moyne, sieur d' Iberville, who was to lead the colonization effort. In the meantime, the Talon brothers came to serve in a Canadian company commanded by Louis Juchereau de Saint-Denis; by January 1700, the Talons arrived in Biloxi Bay to begin service as soldiers and guides for the French colonists. Years later, they returned to France to search for their sister who, by that time, had married Pierre Simon of Paris and given birth to a son in 1699. Whether the brothers actually reunited with their sister is unknown, but according to Weddle's research, Pierre and Jean-Baptiste landed in a Portuguese prison for undisclosed reasons.[55]

Pierre and Robert later reappear in the records having returned to serve in Saint-Denis's company and, in 1714, they led him to San Juan Bautista from the French outpost of Natchitoches on the Red River. Weddle points out that the Talons' tattoos served as passports through the Caddo and Karankawa lands and most likely assured the French of safe passage.[56] Ironically, it was these tattoos that Spaniards attempted to scrub from the Talons' skin, but the indelible marks would eventually prove valuable to the French. After the journey into New Spain's frontiers, the Talons fade into obscurity. Weddle surmises, based on snippets of information, that Jean-Baptiste settled in Louisiana; Pierre most probably returned to France; Robert resided at Mobile; Marie-Madeleine most likely returned to Canada with her son; and Lucien simply disappeared.[57]

We want to know more about these remarkable people who survived every imaginable calamity and endured a series of captivities—first with

La Salle (the children were in essence captives to the will of their parents and La Salle), then by the Caddo and Karankawa, followed by the Spaniards, the French, and, for a time, the Portuguese. My initial goal was to offer these tragic characters a voice that, with as much accuracy as possible, could shed light on their very personal tale and the completion of their heroic journey. Pierre and Jean-Baptiste related their story in a deposition, but as far as we can ascertain, the others failed to leave surviving narratives, although they may have left oral histories to their children.

Given that the Talons were always pawns in the larger contest for imperial prerogatives, they were probably relieved that government transcriptionists lost track of their whereabouts. We know about the Talons only because the elite of that generation considered them important to either French or Spanish colonial policies. Lévi-Strauss once observed that after studying the origins of writing, one can only conclude that its sole purpose was to enslave the individual.[58] Interestingly, when the Talons appear in colonial records, they are slaves one way or another to the larger society. We can hope that the inability of the bureaucracy to record the Talons' final years meant that, at last, they found the freedom to control their own destinies.

Weddle's research suggests that perhaps the Talon siblings lived apart for the remainder of their lives. If so, this is the saddest chapter of their saga. As captives, their only consolation and freedom came in the form of their familial bonds. Considering their importance to one another during their trials and tribulations, one can perhaps imagine the emptiness they experienced from the separation. Perhaps some comfort came when they went on to marry and rear families of their own as they settled into a more tranquil life, but we simply do not know. At present, we can only assess their lives as subjects—pawns—who assisted in the imperial chess game that played out along the Texas Gulf.

Even so, there are indications that the Talons, like so many other captives, shared an enlightenment of sorts as they straddled the divide between two very different cultures. Pierre and Jean-Baptiste's testimony demonstrates fondness and affection for those considered "savages" by a majority of contemporary Europeans. The Talons, better than most, realized the depths of Indian humanity that usually surpassed that of the Talons' European compatriots. Ironically, although Europeans eyed the Native Americans as savages, the Talons described how the Indians considered Europeans to be partly divine—"sons of the sun" and that they "believe themselves unconquerable when they unite with the Europeans."[59] Couched within their deposition is a thinly veiled critique of European policies toward the Indians. We see this repeated throughout countless American captivity narratives and tales that span the colonial and postcolonial eras. Some, like Cabeza de Vaca, hinted that the "savage" Indians were in fact more Christian than the Christians.

In the end, we are left to ponder the Talons' struggle with identity. They entered North America as French, but by the time of their deaths they had been transformed into a creolized entity as they traversed French, Indian, and Spanish worlds. Their heroic journey brought them back to the point of cultural origin where they were forced to serve the larger mandates of the French monarchy in North American colonization efforts. Most likely, their hearts were never in it. They were reluctant participants who understood that they could never entirely return home, even if they actually had a clear indication of what "home" was. Their lives, in small part, added to the fabric of a new cultural tapestry—a creolized one—in the Western Hemisphere.

NOTES

1. Letter from Diego Ramon to the King, 22 July 1714, quoted by Robert Weddle, *San Juan Bautista: Gateway to Spanish Texas* (Austin: University of Texas Press, 1968).

2. Ramon placed Saint-Denis under house arrest until further instructions arrived from the Viceroy in Mexico City. The "incarceration" was more of a social affair. Both Saint-Denis and Ramon enjoyed each other's company, and Saint-Denis would later marry Ramon's granddaughter, Manuela Sanchez, and go so far as to help the Spaniards establish missions in East Texas. See Ross Phares, *Cavalier in the Wilderness: The Story of the Explorer and Trader Louis Juchereau de St. Denis* (Baton Rouge: Louisiana State University, 1952).

3. See David Buisseret and Steven G. Reinhardt, eds., *Creolization in the Americas* (College Station: Texas A&M University Press, 2000).

4. Studies of the hero archetype have proved to be of value to cultural anthropologists such as Claude Lévi-Strauss, *Anthropology and Myth, Lectures, 1951–1982*, trans. Roy Willis (Oxford: Basil Blackwell, 1987). The hero archetype's application to life's meaning has been explored by Joseph Campbell, *The Hero with a Thousand Faces* (New York: MJF Books, 1949), and Arnold van Gennep, *The Rites of Passage*, trans. Monica B. Vizedom and Gabrielle L. Caffee (Chicago: University of Chicago Press, 1960). I have found that captivity narratives and the captivity ordeal often parallel the journey of the hero. See Benjamin Mark Allen, *Naked and Alone in a Strange New World: Early Modern Captivity and Its Mythos* (Newcastle upon Tyne, UK: Cambridge Scholars, 2009).

5. See Allen, *Naked and Alone.*

6. James Axtell, *Beyond 1492: Encounters in Colonial North America* (New York: Oxford University Press, 1992), 3–22.

7. See Linda Tuhiwai Smith, *Decolonizing Methodologies: Research and Indigenous Peoples* (London: Zed Books, 2012).

8. Anthropologist Eric Wolf was among the first to challenge the concept that Europeans were the only ones who made history. He argued that those colonized cultures that lacked writing proved equally influential to European development. See *Europe and the People without History* (Berkeley: University of California Press, 1982).

9. Axtell, *Beyond 1492*, 12.

10. Professor Marcus Rediker, in a personal conversation with the author, opined how writing such studies is fraught with difficulties because our scholastic vocabulary has not yet evolved to adequately convey the ideas. "Webb Lectures," University of Texas at Arlington, March 2014.

11. Buisseret and Reinhardt, *Creolization in the Americas*, 6.

12. See Robert Young, *Colonial Desire: Hybridity in Theory, Culture, and Race* (London: Routledge, 1995).

13. Some have demonstrated how creolization and the captivity narrative influenced the development of societies like that of the United States. See Richard Slotkin, *Regeneration through Violence: The Mythology of the American Frontier, 1600–1860* (Middletown, CT: Wesleyan University Press, 1973); and Molly K. Varley, *Americans Recaptured: Progressive Era Memory of Frontier Captivity* (Norman: University of Oklahoma Press, 2014).

14. A recent contribution to scholarship serves as a model in which Native American voices are reconstructed from sparse sources through contextualization. See Dawn G. Marsh, *A Lenape among the Quakers: The Life of Hannah Freeman* (Lincoln: University of Nebraska Press, 2014). Marsh, in part, incorporated a methodology more tailored for the colonized as theorized by Linda Tuhiwai Smith, *Decolonizing Methodologies.*

15. I rely on the translation by Ann Linda Bell in Robert S. Weddle, ed., *La Salle, the Mississippi, and the Gulf: Three Primary Documents* (College Station: Texas A&M University Press, 1987), 225–58. The original is in the Archives Nationales of Paris, Outre-Mer, DFC, Louisiane 3.

16. See Robert S. Weddle, *The French Thorn: Rival Explorers in the Spanish Sea, 1682–1762* (College Station: Texas A&M University Press, 1991).

17. Peter Linebaugh and Marcus Rediker, *The Many-Headed Hydra: Sailors, Slaves, Commoners, and the Hidden History of the Revolutionary Atlantic* (Boston: Beacon Press, 2000), 2.

18. The Talons' background is described by Robert S. Weddle, "La Salle's Survivors," *The Southwest Historical Quarterly* 75 (1971–72): 413–33.

19. In 1996, archaeologists excavated *La Belle* from Matagorda Bay. See James E. Bruseth, *From a Watery Grave: The Discovery and Excavation of La Salle's Shipwreck,* La Belle (College Station: Texas A&M University Press, 2006).

20. According to Henri Joutel, one of the few survivors who found his way back to New France, the blame for the antagonistic relationship fell on those sent by La Salle to negotiate with the Karankawa. Joutel described how they "had more passion than sense." See Joutel, *Journal*, in William C. Foster, ed., *The La Salle Expedition to Texas: The Journal of Henri Joutel, 1684–1687*, ed. William C. Foster, trans. Johanna S. Warren (Austin: Texas State Historical Association, 1998), 91.

21. These three were Henri Joutel, Abbé Jean Cavelier, La Salle's brother, and Fray Anastasius Douay, a Recollect friar. For an account of La Salle's murder and the journey to New France, see Joutel, *Journal*, 191–202.

22. Weddle, *La Salle, the Mississippi, and the Gulf*, 211.

23. Joutel, *Journal*, 153.

24. The Talon Interrogations, in Weddle, *La Salle, the Mississippi, and the Gulf*, 237.

25. Ibid.

26. See Fernando Operé, *Indian Captivity in Spanish America: Frontier Narratives*, trans. Gustavo Pellón (Charlottesville: University of Virginia Press, 2008), and James F. Brooks, *Captives and Cousins: Slavery, Kinship, and Community in the Southwest Borderlands* (Chapel Hill: University of North Carolina Press, 2002). For comparison, see Evan Haefeli and Kevin Sweeney, *Captors and Captives: The 1704 French and Indian Raid on Deerfield* (Boston: University of Massachusetts Press, 2003).

27. The Talon Interrogations, 231.

28. Arthur A. Slotkin, "The Stockholm Syndrome and Situational Factors Related to Its Development" (Ph.D. diss., University of Louisville, 1997).

29. The Talon Interrogations, 236.

30. The Talons indicated that the Caddo were the "most gentle and most civil of all the nations they [had] known." Ibid., 229.

31. Ibid., 238.

32. See William J. Griffith, *The Hasanai Indians of East Texas as Seen by Europeans, 1687–1772* (New Orleans: Tulane University, 1954).

33. For a survey of Caddo myths, see George A Dorsey, *Traditions of the Caddo* (Washington, DC: Carnegie Institution of Washington, 1905).

34. The Talon Interrogations, 254.

35. Ibid., 229.

36. See Robert A. Ricklis, *The Karankawa Indians of Texas: An Ecological Study of Cultural Tradition and Change* (Austin: University of Texas Press, 1996).

37. The Talon Interrogations, 255.

38. Ibid., 252.

39. Ibid., 253.

40. Ibid., 238.

41. Alvar Nuñez Cabeza de Vaca's *La Relación* (1542) is one among several captivity accounts that indicate how Europeans came to respect and admire their Indian captors, even after experiencing brutal treatment. Once the captive proved of some value to the tribe, the Indians ceremonially adopted the captive, after which the one-time captive experienced affection, respect, and freedom.

42. Frederick Turner suggests that European captives often willingly adopted Indian culture because it offered a much stronger spiritual bond with nature than what could have been achieved in a Judeo-Christian society. See *Beyond Geography: The Western Spirit against the Wilderness* (New Brunswick, NJ: Rutgers University Press, 1994), 231–54.

43. The Talon Interrogations, 239.

44. Ibid., 253.

45. Ibid., 252.

46. Robert S. Weddle, *Wilderness Manhunt: The Spanish Search for La Salle* (College Station: Texas A&M University Press, 1999), 18–203.

47. The Talon Interrogations, 241.

48. Weddle, *Wilderness Manhunt*, 212.

49. The Talon Interrogations, 244. See also María Pilar Gutiérrez Lorenzo, *De la Corte de Castilla al virreinato de México: el conde de Galve (1653–1697)* (Madrid: Excelentísima Diputación Provincial, 1993).

50. Weddle, *Wilderness Manhunt*, 212.

51. The Talon Interrogations, 241.

52. Ibid., 248.

53. Ibid., 242.

54. Ibid., 247.

55. Weddle, *French Thorn*, 187.

56. Weddle, ed., *La Salle, the Mississippi, and the Gulf*, 221.

57. Ibid., 223.

58. Claude Lévi-Strauss, *Tristes Tropiques*, trans. John and Doreen Weightman (New York: Penguin Books, 2012 [original publication 1955]).

59. The Talon Interrogations, 251.

SELECTED BIBLIOGRAPHY

Allen, Benjamin M. *Naked and Alone in a Strange New World: Early Modern Captivity and Its Mythos.* Newcastle upon Tyne, UK: Cambridge Scholars, 2009.

Bannon, John Francis. *The Spanish Borderlands Frontier, 1513–1821.* Albuquerque: University of New Mexico Press, 1997.

Barr, Juliana. *Peace Came in the Form of a Woman: Indians & Spaniards in the Texas Borderlands.* Chapel Hill: University of North Carolina Press, 2007.

Bruseth, James E. *From a Watery Grave: The Discovery and Excavation of La Salle's Shipwreck,* La Belle. College Station: Texas A&M University Press, 2006.

Buisseret, David, and Steven G. Reinhardt, eds. *Creolization in the Americas.* College Station: Texas A&M University Press, 2000.

Cunningham, Debbie S. "The Diego Ramón Diary of the 1716 Expedition into the Province of the Tejas Indians: An Annotated Translation." *Southwest Historical Quarterly* 110, no. 1 (2006): 38–62.

Dodge, Meredith D., and Rick Hendricks, eds. *Two Hearts, One Soul: The Correspondence of the Condessa de Galve, 1688–96.* Albuquerque: University of New Mexico Press, 1993.

Gatschet, Albert S. *The Karankawa Indians: The Coast People of Texas.* Cambridge, MA: Peabody Museum of American Archaeology and Ethnology, 1891; New York: Kraus, 1967.

Giraud, Marcel. *A History of French Louisiana.* Vol. 1, *The Reign of Louis XIV, 1698–1715.* Translated by Joseph C. Lambert. Baton Rouge: Louisiana State University Press, 1953; reprinted 1974.

Joutel, Henri. *Journal.* In *The La Salle Expedition to Texas: The Journal of Henri Joutel, 1684–1687,* edited by William C. Foster. Translated by Johanna S. Warren. Austin: Texas State Historical Association, 1998.

Marsh, Dawn G. *A Lenape among the Quakers: The Life of Hannah Freeman.* Lincoln: University of Nebraska Press, 2014.

Ricklis, Robert A. *The Karankawa Indians of Texas: An Ecological Study of Cultural Tradition and Change.* Austin: University of Texas Press, 1996.

Smith, Linda Tuhiwai. *Decolonizing Methodologies: Research and Indigenous Peoples.* London: Zed Books, 2012.

Talon, Pierre, and Jean-Baptiste Talon. "Voyage to the Mississippi through the Gulf of Mexico, 1687." In *La Salle, the Mississippi, and the Gulf: Three Primary Documents,* edited by Robert S. Weddle, 225–58. Translated by Ann Linda Bell. College Station: Texas A&M University Press, 1987.

Weddle, Robert S. *The French Thorn: Rival Explorers in the Spanish Sea, 1682–1762.* College Station: Texas A&M University Press, 1991.

________. "La Salle's Survivors." *The Southwest Historical Quarterly* 75 (1971–72): 413–33.

________. "The Talon Interrogations: A Rare Perspective." In *La Salle, the Mississippi, and the Gulf: Three Primary Documents,* edited by Robert S. Weddle, 209–24. College Station: Texas A&M University Press, 1987.

________. *Wilderness Manhunt: The Spanish Search for La Salle.* College Station: Texas A&M University Press, 1999.

3

"Home Away from Home"

The Cameroon Diaspora in the United States

Emmanuel M. Mbah

INTRODUCTION

The 1990s ushered in remarkable socioeconomic and political transformations in Cold War world relations. For African states, the fall of the Berlin Wall and the collapse of the Soviet Union gave hope to nationalists determined to transform the political landscape in their respective countries. Calls for multiparty democracy were echoed throughout the continent. This happened at a time when the future of the continent was becoming more uncertain. A combination of factors including endemic collapse in socioeconomic and political structures resulted in economic hardship, insecurity, human rights abuses, political witch-hunting, chaos, and dysfunction in most parts of Africa. Consequently, many Africans left the continent for security reasons, or in search of economic opportunities in the developed Western and Northern Hemispheres. To be fair, the new African diaspora—the economic and/or politically induced out-migration of Africans from the continent—started during the period of colonial rule; the structural collapse of 1990s, however, resulted in a heightened peak in the number of people leaving the continent for economic and political reasons. Cameroon was not exempt from this migration epidemic.

Before 1990, only a small number of Cameroonians lived in the United States permanently. Prior to 1990, Cameroonians came to the United States mainly for higher education purposes, and they often left after completion of studies. Cameroon's economy was not yet in shambles; thus, returning graduates often found high-paying employment back home. Beginning in 1990, and as a result of the socioeconomic and political malaise that plagued Africa at the time, more Cameroonian migrants to the

United States sought to reside there permanently. After pursuing further education, many now buy houses, marry Americans, have children, and are forging a semblance of the Cameroon-style family, community, and ethnicity in the United States. As part of their attempt to create a "Home Away from Home," many have continued to maintain and even extend their connections and influence back in Cameroon. Through email, faxes, Internet, Skype, and telephones, they have successfully maintained a presence and participation in numerous sociocultural, economic, and political discourses at all levels in Cameroon—family, village, community, ethnic group, and country. Many spearhead development projects, others contribute money to pursue lawsuits over private, family, or village/community land, and yet others are in the fore in the search for genuine democracy in Cameroon. A majority of these Cameroonians are permanent residents or citizens of the United States, with established homes in their adopted country, away from their original home in Africa.

But can the experience of creating a "Home Away from Home" be as smooth as it sounds? My findings have shown that this is a tall order; in the long run, Cameroonians and many other Africans in the United States are never fully comfortable in either of their homes—the one in the United States and the one in Cameroon. First, whereas the United States might be home for the children of these immigrants, it is never truly home for many Cameroonian migrants so long as they perceive wide-scale inadequacies and deficiencies in sociocultural experiences, connections, and interactions. There is as well the constant reminder from extreme right-wing groups that others (mostly those who are not Anglo-Saxons) do not truly belong here.[1] Second, the Cameroonians left behind are never truly accepting of expatriates who are financially privileged and who attempt to juggle two different lifestyles and homes on two different continents. In many cases, financial wherewithal gives them the ability to dominate economic, sociocultural, and even economic spaces in Cameroon despite their absence from the country. The example of Ndedi Eyango, discussed in the final section, is a testament to this intransigence from Cameroonians back in the home country.[2] The above notwithstanding, the struggle to create a "Home Away from Home" continues to grow among Cameroonians residing in the United States.

This chapter examines how members of the Cameroon diaspora in the United States have struggled to forge their "Home Away from Home." Specifically, it investigates the experiences, successes, and problems encountered by Cameroonians in the United States during this process and addresses four major issues. First, it investigates reasons for migration, differentiating economic from political migrants, especially as they have different experiences before and during the period of departure. Next, it examines their experiences in the United States from the perspective of US immigration law, economic difficulties, and issues of adaptability in the US sociopolitical setting. Third, it examines their successes and setbacks in the United States, and finally, it assesses their connections and influences back in Cameroon. At the same time, the study of the Cameroon diaspora in the United States highlights many salient topics such as race, ethnicity, class, gender, language, sexual orientation, and religious beliefs and explores their injection into sociopolitical discourse in the United States as well as in Cameroon.

PERSPECTIVES ON AFRICAN MIGRATION

Throughout humankind's history, international migration has been a recurrent phenomenon. Societies with a long-standing immigration tradition such as Australia, Canada, and the United States have continued to receive immigrants from Asia, Africa, and Latin America. After 1960, all Western European countries became industrial and commercial magnets that drew migrants from Africa, Asia, the Caribbean, and the Middle East. By the 1980s, countries in southern Europe (Italy, Spain, and Portugal) that had been countries of out-migration a decade or two earlier also opened up to migrants from Africa, Asia, and the Middle East. In Asia, Japan also increasingly sought immigrant workers from South America and other parts of Asia to sustain a labor force that had been substantially curtailed by low birthrates and a rapidly aging population. As the wave of international migration continues to heighten, urban and even some rural areas of receiving countries in the developed world have been (and continue to be) rapidly transformed into "multiethnic societies."[3]

International migration is also a very complex phenomenon when studied from the perspective of motives or reasons for migration; this is especially so because no single theory has served to adequately respond to the issue of motives. Some of the theories advanced so far include the following: First, the neoclassical economic theorists emphasize country differences in wages and conditions of employment; to them, the decision to migrate is a personal calculation and hinges on perceived income to be earned. Second, there are proponents of the "new economics of migration" who perceive migration as a response to different market conditions and not just labor conditions. Next is the dual labor market theory that sees the motives of migration in the structural needs of the economies of today's industries. Finally, there is the world systems theory that "sees immigration as a natural consequence of economic globalization and market penetration across national boundaries."[4] The four theories advanced in the foregoing restrict international migration to economic motives. Of course, we know that is not the case because there are serious political reasons that undergird international migration, as I discuss in the case of African emigration.

All four theories explain international migration as the result of push or pull factors. The push factors may involve force, as was the case during the transatlantic slave trade (circa 1415–1815) when millions of Africans were forcibly shipped across the Atlantic into slavery. The old African diaspora, as this phenomenon has been labeled, was oppressive and the immigrants (slaves) had little or no say about the process and its outcome. A few freed slaves eventually made it back to Africa during the period of European colonization of the continent only to find societies that "had been dramatically altered by new systems of control that not only bore little relation to romantic notions they may have formed about the Africa of the past but constrained whatever contributions they may have pledged themselves to make to uplift the land."[5] The push aspect may also be the result of sex trafficking; it may be conflict induced, as is the case with hundreds or thousands of Africans who flee their homeland every year as a result of conflict.[6]

The pull factors are mainly economic, psychological, and sociocultural, or what Philip D. Curtin has termed "an apparent response to perceived self-interest"[7] and are responsible for much of the new wave of out-migration from Africa, which usually starts with rural urban migration in search of economic opportunities in cities before progressing to international migration. According to Curtin, the availability of economic opportunities in African urban areas and mining towns and in industrialized western and northern countries continues to attract waves of job seekers.[8] In advancing the world systems theory, Paul Zeleza has tied external migration to opportunities offered by today's globalization and its ability to move international job seekers from all walks of life to vibrant foreign economies in search of workers.[9] In the psychological and sociocultural realm, many African children grow up fantasizing about a white Christmas with a Santa Claus, an abundance of material wealth, and good living abroad.[10] These images of paradise in the West were, and continue to be, reinforced by secondary, high school, and university professors who studied there. Before long, many young Africans start romanticizing about living abroad. For many Cameroonians, the first step for migrants is to relocate to a major Cameroon city before they make an attempt at international migration. Other pull factors influencing African migration include changes in immigration laws in recipient countries and changes in economic and technical trends in both Africa and the northern recipient countries. For example, a decreasing birthrate in Europe creates opportunities for migration, whereas economic collapse and unemployment are deterrents to migration.[11]

Initially, this new wave of emigration (the new African diaspora) took migrants to the countries of their former colonial masters, with African migrants making up 33 percent of all migrants to France in 1990. But from the 1980s, the United States, Canada, Germany, northern European countries, and even China and other East Asian and South American countries opened up.[12] Between 1965 and the end of 1990, African emigration rose from 10.6 to 13.1 percent.[13] Although the reasons for this hike are not clear, economic failures, the high rate of unemployment resulting from the economic crises of the 1980s and 1990s, and the post-independence state collapse in Africa from the 1960s have all contributed significantly. What is clear in Africa generally, and in Cameroon in particular, is that in the past four decades mass emigration has increasingly become a serious problem as younger Africans no longer want to be stuck with a traditional livelihood of basic survival in nations that are predatory, corrupt, and disrespectful of their citizens. Recent estimates have revealed that the total number of Africans that have migrated to the United States since 1990 surpasses the number that was forced in as slaves before the United States outlawed the slave trade in 1807.[14]

MIGRATION OF AFRICANS/CAMEROONIANS TO THE UNITED STATES: REASONS AND MOTIVES

Many young (and even some old) people in Cameroon nurture dreams of migrating to the United States. Those who make the attempt, however, face enormous problems during the journey. Some make it to US ports of entry but are arrested for lack of proper documentation and are either returned immediately to Cameroon, or are detained in one of the numerous immigration jails scattered throughout the United States. The plight of those who end up in immigration jails in Europe and the United States is, sadly, one of the many disturbing examples about how humankind treats its fellows. As mentioned earlier, wide-scale immigration from Africa is, above all else, symptomatic of the political, economic, and social conditions there.

Political and Social Reasons

The sociopolitical reasons for African emigration include the elusiveness of constitutional democratic governance, national leadership crises, military interventions in governments, civil wars, and all other forms of conflict resulting in violence, flight, and the refugee problem. For example, a combination of some or all of these reasons for emigration did result in the collapse of governance structures that began in the 1990s in Somalia, the Democratic Republic of Congo (DRC), Rwanda, Liberia, Sierra Leone, Zimbabwe, Côte d'Ivoire, Sudan, Mali, and Central African Republic (among others), resulting in both a refugee crises and heightened emigration rates from the affected countries.

Policy failures and wasteful human and natural resource exploitation, coupled with the presence of corrupt leaders who have relied on patronage and other predatory forms of dictatorship over the years, have deprived many ordinary Africans of a livelihood and have compelled some to emigrate. With too much debt and insufficient operating capital, much of which is misappropriated, African governments cannot deliver even the most basic of services such as health care, education, and infrastructure maintenance.[15] Consequently, dysfunction and leadership failures ensue, and these result in recurrent conflict wherein the victims are usually innocent civilians. For some, emigration is the rational choice; this is particularly true in countries of the Horn of Africa, where natural calamities including drought are a constant threat.[16] The sociopolitical problems of postcolonial African societies have been succinctly summarized by Isidore Okpewho:

> But how can anything be set right when a nation has lost its sense of mission in its blind pursuit of power and privilege: When the government abandons its responsibility to provide the resources for

> quality education in its schools and universities and instead diverts them to grandiose, meaningless schemes both inside and outside the country? When the nation's leaders fund private research initiatives in the United States—thus opening up avenues for siphoning public money into their private accounts abroad—rather than situate the same initiatives in institutions inside their own country? When writers, scholars, and journalists are thrown into jail or relieved of their appointments simply because they dared to criticize political leaders and their misguided acts? When, indeed, a journalist could lose his life for exposing the abuses of leaders, and no efforts are made to apprehend or locate the culprits? So, what intellectual would want to remain in a country where the honest pursuit of truth is either derided or discouraged?[17]

In Cameroon, since the reintroduction of multiparty politics in the 1990s, the political climate has deteriorated as the quest for democracy continues to be elusive and the opposition has been stifled through constitutional and electoral manipulation, corruption, and intimidation. Many Cameroonians who staked their lives hoping for the change that never came were branded dissidents, intimidated, and persecuted by government security forces.[18] Generally, in much of Africa, "those who have been lucky enough to escape with their lives, or have simply decided that they needed to carry on their careers in less threatening conditions, have opted to flee the land and live in exile."[19] To these aspiring migrants, the United States epitomizes a land of freedom and plenty; therefore, for many Cameroonians in this category, it constitutes the final destination on their route, no matter how long this takes. For many Cameroonians in the United States who migrated for political reasons, the concept of "Home Away from Home" is a tall order, at least during the initial years of residence abroad. The more explosive the circumstances for leaving home were, the more difficult it is to maintain connections with the homeland.[20]

Economic Reasons

Poverty and deteriorating living conditions over the years have led to very low living standards. Thus, although the Human Development Index for much of sub-Saharan Africa has been improving since 2000, the rate of improvement is still very slow.[21] For example, education, basic health care, and infrastructure in many African countries are deplorable; even when money is allocated for these needs, contractors bribe the responsible officials and pocket much of it. Excessive greed begets corruption; when this happens, patriotism becomes elusive.[22] Patronage and excessive corruption have transformed African countries into private enterprises of a select few that are connected to privilege and power. In that regard, Ogbu Uke Kalu argues, "the summons to participate in nation building has ceased to be convincing, and the patriotic rhetoric about a jointly-owned mother/father land has lost its purchase."[23] When the culture of corruption is the rule among civil servants, the military, political elites, and members of government, as it has been the case in Cameroon and elsewhere in Africa since the 1990s, living conditions for ordinary citizens plummet. As the government becomes predatory, the option to migrate also becomes appealing to many, as Okpewho again summarizes:

> If conditions at home deteriorate to such an extent that you can no longer guarantee to yourself and your family the basic needs of life: when the water does not run for weeks, so that conditions in both the kitchen and bathroom become hazardous; when toilet facilities in the grade schools break down completely so that, in their dire need to relieve themselves, your children pick up diseases floating freely in the severely endangered environment; when the clinics can no longer provide prescribed medications because their budgets have been deeply slashed or suspended, and families are left to buy unregulated drugs from open shelves, thus putting their lives at risk; when salaries are not paid for months, so that parents cannot afford even the unregulated drugs, let alone sufficient food for the table; now who, under these conditions, would resist the urge to seek employment outside the country just so the family can at least stay alive?[24]

Patronage and excessive and rampant corruption by African predatory regimes mean there is little money left for academic research in the universities. The inability to conduct research means professors cannot be promoted. Therefore, the African university now also faces its own socioeconomic crisis/dysfunction derived from economic problems that are more or less the result of excessive patronage and corruption.[25] University professors cannot teach successfully when they are not paid for months. Although some use extracurricular methods to survive (sale of grades, pamphlets), others have chosen to leave. Within the past two or three decades, hundreds of university professionals in Africa have left for greener pastures overseas. Meanwhile, recent African graduates overseas are less likely to return to the mess in their respective countries. In short, the African university that is supposed to generate solutions to problems such as curbing massive emigration and the brain drain increasingly lacks the ability to perform those functions. Interestingly, however, Cameroonians in the United States who migrated for economic reasons quickly attempt to forge a "Home Away from Home" with financial security.[26]

THE DEPARTURE

There are three issues associated with the departure: the first has to do with acquiring the necessary genuine or fraudulent travel documents; the second involves putting together the financial resources to cover travel and other unforeseen costs during the journey and upon immediate arrival in the host country; the third involves the travel route and all associated problems encountered during the journey. I begin with the first issue.

Travel Documents

It is difficult to travel without a passport, be it fake or genuine. Migrants also need documentation to show the reason for migration (sometimes shown on the passport) and that they will be admitted to their host countries. There is great demand in Africa and in transit locations abroad for fake passports, visas, and other documents that could catapult African migrants to the United States and other parts of the world. In some cases, African security forces at the airports are collaborators in the scam for fake documents. Securing these documents, especially those that have to originate in Africa, has opened up fraudulent business opportunities for crooks, scammers, and some government security officials. The corruption involved in securing a new passport in Cameroon, even if it is for legitimate travel, is alarming; the bribe is often more than 100 percent of the official cost of issuance of the passport. This adds considerably to the total cost of travel. The amount of the bribe rises steadily because government officials have been successful at creating an artificial scarcity of passport booklets. Therefore, migrants feel lucky to pay any price for one of the few passports that are available. In 1998, this author spent a total of 75,000.00 francs CFA to secure a passport that would have normally cost

35,000.00 francs CFA; the cost has since gone up with the increased number of Cameroon travelers and prospective migrants (bush fallers, as they are popularly known in the English-speaking parts of the country); some put the cost of a new passport today at 200,000.00 francs CFA. However, there is an even bigger problem here: by transforming the issuance of passports into a business, the police have negated their original duties associated with the issuance of passports, that is, eliminating identity fraud and making sure these documents do not fall into the hands of criminals. In some cases, the immigration police have partnered with crooks/scammers who are passport entrepreneurs, making genuine or fake passports and other travel documents for desperate travelers. Therefore, in Cameroon and other African countries, it is not uncommon for some people to have multiple passports and other documents under different names.[27]

The reason for migration into the host countries is characterized in various ways. A small number of African migrants with professional skills may secure direct employment abroad through the work visa (H-1B visa, in the case of the United States). The US diversity lottery (Green Card) visa also facilitates entry of some Africans and their families into the United States. In many African countries, playing the Green Card lottery, winning it, and relocating to the United States is a big business that involves fake and genuine operators, all of whom are exploitative. Those who emigrate on student exchange or fellowship programs have become permanent migrants, unwilling to return. Some of these are also genuine, but some are fakes. Many of those with genuine exchange/fellowship visas have sought permanent status abroad. Some have abandoned higher education programs in Europe (especially in Germany) and elsewhere and deserted to the United States. Then, of course, there are economic migrants who migrate as visitors. Those lucky enough to convince foreign embassies to grant them visitor visas constitute the majority of Africans in transit; these, together with those who have secured fraudulent visas from scammers, have no intention of returning to the continent in the foreseeable future. They have to figure out ways of either legalizing their status or staying underground in the host country. Finally, there are those who claim political asylum status, and this includes many in the foregoing categories, with the exception of those who are admitted on family-related or lottery Green Card visas (as in the case of the United States). Cameroonians in the United States have used all the categories listed here and more for admission.[28]

The entire process of securing foreign visas serves to ridicule many Africans and calls into question the issue of embassy/consular reciprocity: Do African consular officials humiliate foreigners seeking African visas in a similar manner in foreign countries? In the case of the humiliation of Nigerians at foreign embassies in Nigeria, Kalu writes,

> Sociologists need to study the patterns of visa politics: the locations and procedures of foreign embassies, fees, screening, the regimen, and the limits placed on the numbers of various categories of visa. It could be a harrowing experience because foreign embassies in Nigeria compete in inventing devices for disgracing the indigenes. The American Embassy turns down the application of over 97% of applicants in Nigeria after each has paid a fee of one hundred dollars.[29]

The difficulty, frustration, and humiliation involved in acquiring passports, visas, and other travel documents contribute negatively to the immigrant experience and complicate international security. In the United States, many Cameroonians who had humiliating experiences at the US embassy romanticize about home, especially when similar patterns of humiliation are witnessed in the host country; for these, "Home Away from Home" becomes the ideal after attaining financial stability abroad.[30]

Financial Cost of Travel

The financial cost of travel abroad for economic and political migrants from Africa is high. Many of them come from poor families, but the hope of poverty alleviation—the result of immigrant success stories abroad—is very attractive both for the prospective migrant and the entire family: "Families sell off their household goods and mortgage family land. Others raise the capital by joining robbery gangs, defrauding banks and employers, or raising loans."[31] In Cameroon, many prospective migrants are underpaid civil servants, especially teachers at all levels; they use their civil service employment to save, borrow, or steal the money required to cover the cost of documentation, transportation, and initial stay abroad (family members of many of these continue to collect their salaries back home). The cost of travel has a significant role to play on the immigrant psyche, as well as the prospects for their return home. For example, immigrants will only willingly return home when they have the ability to pay back their families, banks, and other lenders for the cost of travel. How will immigrants pay back these loans if they do not make it financially or are deported? After enduring the heavy physical, mental, emotional, and financial costs of travel, some African migrants, especially those in the United States, either give up on home completely or may prefer to maintain only a minimal connection with home; for these migrants, "Home Away from Home" remains elusive.

The Travel Route

African migrants include men, women, and children. Gabon has become an exit hub from which West African migrant children can be smuggled into Europe.[32] The length of the journey and the travel route depend heavily on financial ability and documentary preparedness, "and both will shape the patterns of adjustment at the destination."[33] For some, the journey from Africa to greener pastures could take years and may occur in stages, with North Africa, the Middle East, Europe, or Asia serving as rerouting points to a final destination in the United States. Social networks that include ethnic/village/family members and friends residing at specific parts of the route or in the destination countries serve to facilitate immigrant travel and readjustment in the host societies. The use of fraudulent visas, discussed earlier, during all or part of the route could also be part of the process. Those who travel through North Africa recount horrible and sordid experiences. Many migrants deplete their resources, fall sick, or are arrested or simply abandoned by their guides who have already been paid for the entire trip. Those who die are buried in the sand.[34]

Women make up a significant number of African migrants, and the experiences that some have to go through, Kalu observes, provide a cautionary tale to prospective and unprepared female migrants:

> The feminine dimension of migration is a sordid story of its own. There was a time when African smugglers used migrant women's bodies in the transportation of illicit drugs. Today, women constitute a significant portion of immigrants on this route. These women are called *commodities* just as they served as *troop comforters* during the civil war. Many survive by linking themselves to a group of men who protect and provide for them, or a pimp who uses them to fund his own trip. Others pay their way through prostitution. But there is another sex trade route that goes directly by air to Italy. A number go

> on that adventure willingly; pimps recruit others for prostitution in Europe. Stories abound on the networks that recruit from Edo State, especially Benin City, for the Italian market. The early ones came home with lots of money. Nicknamed *Italos*, they flaunted wealth in a manner that became the envy of village girls.[35]

Recently, Italian officials arrested and deported many *Italos* after they incurred serious abuses by pimps, including some who had decided to become entrepreneurs in their own right, having spent close to $45,000 in setting up their own prostitution business. That amount may have included payoffs to pimps who brought them to Italy. Some NGOs, including Girls' Power Initiative, the International Organization for Migration, the National Agency for Prohibition of Trafficking in Persons, and the Committee for the Support of Dignity of Women, have come to the aid of some of the deported women.[36]

In the United States, getting a Green Card through fake marriage for women may involve short-term or long-term financial payments and/or unwarranted sexual relationships with US citizens, many of them African American men. Because these women may be desperate, the men blackmail them for regular sex throughout the period that US immigration is processing the paperwork. In some cases, the men threaten not to show up for interviews if the women refuse to have sex with them.[37]

In North Africa (Algeria, Morocco, Libya), many migrants, including women, are harassed by security officials; consequently, some African migrant women take cover in camps under very difficult conditions.[38] For those who make it to the shores of the United States and Europe, the endless wait for asylum approval or any other method of securing legal documentation begins, but many are unsure whether they will be granted legal status or deported/repatriated, or whether they will ever cover the cost of migration. Meanwhile, back home in Africa, family members, friends, and other loved ones are already awaiting money transfers/remittances through Western Union, MoneyGram, and other avenues.

The more harrowing the experience is en route, and in the destination countries, the more romanticized home becomes.[39]

LIFE IN THE UNITED STATES

Regardless of how African migrants end up in the United States, their first problem is that of adjusting to some legal status, permanent residency, and eventually citizenship. This is not a difficult process for those who obtain a visa through the US Diversity Immigrant Visa Program lottery, or for those who come in via family sponsorship as spouses, children, and other relatives of US citizens.

The process is also less problematic, at least in the short run, for those who enter as students on F1 visas, provided they can take care of their tuition and lodging at the US college/university they are attending. But because many Africans on F1 visas are prospective immigrants, that is, they have no intention of leaving the United States, the problems of adjustment of status to permanent residency becomes a major preoccupation once they get to the United States or just before completion of studies at the US college/university. Upon entering the country, many realize how expensive it is to live and study in the United States, and so their strategy changes. Some immediately start pursuing avenues for adjustment of status through marriage or asylum; others attempt to navigate a passage underground, engaging in legal and sometimes illegal activities to make ends meet, while strategizing ways of becoming legal. Some are caught and sent to immigration detention centers scattered throughout the United States.

A majority of Africans/Cameroonians less than fifty years of age who come in as tourists on visitor's visas (B1 and B2) have no intention of going back to Africa. These people have either escaped Africa for political reasons or are here as economic migrants. For them, marriage and/or refugee status are the options they have for permanent residency in the United States. But US immigration rules, procedures, and required evidence to gain asylum status or adjust to permanent residency and eventual citizenship are difficult and sometimes complicated. Some of these migrants have been longtime refugees back on the continent, from the Horn of Africa, Liberia, Sierra Leone, the DRC, and other areas, even before arriving or before being granted asylum in the United States. This has a negative impact on the immigrant psyche.[40]

Recently, there has been much discussion about immigration policies and procedures in the United States, especially since 2008 with the economic downturn that caused much unemployment among US citizens;

as a result, migrants "are caught in the middle of the re-negotiation of the concepts of melting pot, assimilation, diversity and multiculturalism."[41] The result has been an increase in deportations and a stricter enforcement of employment verification for immigrants. For many African immigrants in the United States, the lack of legal documents means they may not be able to find work to sustain themselves in their host country. With the exception of expedited processing, immigrants in the United States take many years, sometimes more than five, to become legal residents. The situation is worse in Europe where it is commonplace for migrants to adopt unconventional survival tactics, including fraud and theft.[42]

The question for Cameroonians and other Africans is thus: What does citizenship in the United States mean to your "sentimental commitment"[43] to Cameroon? Of course, US citizenship has immense advantages here in the United States, and holding the passport facilitates travel abroad, even to your own African country. But what about the emotional trauma of giving up your nationality and, in some sense, your identity? Does that heal easily, or ever? These and other issues are addressed at the end of this chapter. But before addressing these, I will first examine how Cameroonians/Africans have attempted to adapt to the US socioeconomic and political setting.

Adaptability to US Socioeconomic and Political Setting

The ability to sustain a livelihood in the United States, especially during the early months/years of migration, depends on a number of factors: the method of migration, with legal migrants adjusting faster; the presence of established family and friends in the United States, who might help new migrants adjust faster, both economically and socially; and the level of educational attainment prior to migration, with the more educated, skilled, and experienced migrants being able to adjust faster and secure legal documentation more easily.[44] Migrants who relocate with some money could easily start small businesses (some Africans who embezzled from government or home-based banks have fared well here). A greater number of professionals such as medical practitioners succeed in the United States because of their skills; some with similar skills do not make it. It all depends on the agility of the individual migrant with a profession.

A majority of Cameroonian migrants in particular and African immigrants in general in the United States are highly educated. As per 1997 data from the US Census Bureau, for example, "African immigrants had the highest education accomplishment. In the age range, from 25 and above, 48.9% of migrants had a bachelor degree and above, compared to Asians with 44.6%, Europeans with 28.7% and Latinos with 5.6%."[45] By elevating their own status, African migrants of the new diaspora have also benefited the United States generally, through their contributions in higher education, health care, technology, sports, and in many other fields. Many of them have found places in almost all the major professions that require higher education; but racism and other sociocultural barriers such as problems with educational equivalency (the lack of recognition of certificates from African universities) have not made life any easier for them.[46] As Kalu observes, "African migrants must struggle hard to gain access to good paying jobs, to secure valid documents, and pay the cost of retraining. They suffer racism and sexism as any other black; many immerse themselves in strenuous strivings to live. All this makes the ambiguous relationship between African Americans and Africans a cruel irony."[47]

Even worse is the fact that some African Americans have premised their current relations with African immigrants on assumptions about the transatlantic slave trade, arguing that their own ancestors were most likely sold into slavery by Africans themselves. Sadly, this perception is increasingly popular in the African American community among young people, despite the fact that the transatlantic slave trade ended two centuries ago.[48] Other factors that have strained relations between the two include unsuccessful "Green Card" marriages; lifestyle differences; competition for jobs; the pretentious, pompous, and ambitious attitude of African men toward work and family; the elevated level of self-esteem they have; and the very high educational success rate of many Africans and their children. As to the last, some African Americans have argued that recent African immigrants and their children have succeeded mostly because they migrate and start life anew, free of any baggage, at the right ages and "arrive better prepared for college than their African American counterparts."[49] Such stereotypical perceptions of African immigrants by African Americans have compromised prospects of black unity in the United States. According to Opkewho, "African Americans would rather be outnumbered by Europeans and others than by Africans, who would only improve the black demographic profile in American society."[50] Thus, it is not uncommon for African American (and even some Middle Eastern) men to adopt condescending attitudes toward Africans.[51]

African migrants are not received any better by some sections of the white Anglo-Saxon community or by other ethnic groups such as Hispanics, as Okpewho points out:

> We are black people, and however qualified or competent we are in our fields of endeavor, some whites who judge everything in human relations by Manichean principles have not hesitated to put us in the same place they have reserved for African Americans throughout their history. It does not take long for us to be shocked by a rude curtailment of that old self-assurance that we could get anywhere we had a mind to. Some of us may eventually attain our goals; the rest are broken by despair. Those who succeed are never entirely spared the feeling that they owe their success to someone else's token nod, not the strength of their own hard work.[52]

Forging "Home Away from Home": The US Connection

Cameroonian/African migrants are generally hardworking, conscientious, and ambitious. They send a portion of money they earn back home to take care of family members and friends and assist in varying forms of development initiatives. They are involved in numerous transatlantic and home-based formal and informal professions and businesses such as health care, education, cosmetology, transportation, food processing, and security. Many of their private businesses, such as restaurants, hair salons, and grocery stores, are small, targeting mostly consumers of African products. They are located in many urban settings in the United States and are advertised in the numerous newspapers and Internet sites that have emerged in the United States and Cameroon.[53] Those involved in the import/export sector, for example, have enabled Cameroonians and other Africans in the United States and other areas outside of Africa to forge "Home Away from Home" by providing local food, drinks, clothing, shoes, and other sociocultural appurtenances in a transatlantic web that takes these products to the United States and Europe and elsewhere (Asia, Australia, and the Middle East). Some collect/buy new and used cars, electronics, and spare parts from the United States, Europe, and Asia, and sell them in Africa (Cameroon), fostering transatlantic trade connections. In forging such socioeconomic connections, Cameroonians are able to create a semblance of home in the diaspora.

For many West Africans in particular, and sub-Saharan Africans in general, preservation of their identities is one area in which they have struggled to maintain a "Home Away from Home" in the United States. According to Kalu, "The immigrant condition has forced the Africans to nurture a 'diasporic consciousness' through a welter of associational life as survival networks. Associational life is beyond survival but enhances identity and provides avenues for political engagement."[54] African professional groups such as those involving physicians, nurses, and students, for example, bring African migrants together in forums in which the issues discussed go well beyond their professional activities in the United States; these forums are also used to promote varying initiatives both in Africa and in the United States. In the Dallas/Fort Worth metropolitan area, for example, the Cameroon Nurses Association meets once a month and, during these meetings, Cameroonian dishes, drinks, and ideas are shared among the nurses and their guests. They hold discussions on how to improve the health-care scene in Cameroon.[55] National associations such as the Cameroon Students Association (CAMSA), alma mater associations such as the Bali Old Boys Association (for former students of the Cameroon Protestant College in Bali, Cameroon), and dozens of other such groups with branches all over the United States are other forums in which a shared homeland identity is exhibited and where the experience of "Home Away from Home" flourishes.

African ethnic and/or clan-based associations in the United States are sources of identity affirmation and avenues for reliving home experiences. Ghanaians in Chicago, for example, have eleven ethnic associations grouped under a national council to foster sociocultural, economic, and political ties with the motherland. Organizations based on ethnic/clan loyalties such as the Igbo and the Yoruba are stronger and hence offer broader experiences of home. Cameroon ethnic associations such as the Moghamo Cultural and Development Association (MEDA) and scores of others (Bali, Manyu, Ejagham, Babanki, Meta, Mankon, Santa, etc.) have particularly enhanced shared experiences of "Home Away from Home" for Cameroonians because of their close-knit ethnic and cultural outlook.[56] Because of the family-like closeness of shared experiences, attendant upon ethnic bonds, it is not uncommon for ethnic disputes back in Africa to be replayed in various degrees abroad in the United States.[57] For example, Kenyans in the United States rallied along ethnic lines during the eruption of violence that ensued after the presidential elections of 2008.

Branches of African political parties now operate in many countries abroad where African migrants have settled. Cameroon migrants in the United States, for example, have created branches of the two major political parties back home, the Cameroon People's Democratic Movement (CPDM) of President Paul Biya and the Social Democratic Front of Ni John Fru Ndi. But because of the fragile and explosive political situation in Africa, this political correspondence within the diaspora replicates some of the chaos and dysfunction that are part of African politics—a negative aspect of "Home Away from Home." Finally, religious affiliations/African churches have mushroomed all over the United States. There are Cameroon Christian Churches in the Dallas/Fort Worth metropolitan area, in Houston, in Minnesota, and in Maryland, among others. Home pastors and parish priests visit their parishoners and vice versa.

Forging "Home Away from Home": The Cameroon/African Connection

African migrants have sought to maintain varying degrees of connections with the homeland by keeping in touch with family, friends, and other interests regularly through instantaneous forms of communication, such as Facebook pages, Skype connections, and phone calls. The proliferation and use of cell phones in Cameroon have particularly helped Cameroonians in the diaspora, including those in the United States, to maintain connections with family and friends back home. This was not the case before the 1990s, when letter writing was the main form of communication, and it took months for correspondence to travel between the United States and Cameroon. The new forms of communications have also enabled Cameroonians in the United States to sustain an economic presence through remittances to family and friends and through investments in housing and other business initiatives, usually with some supervision from family and friends in Cameroon.[58]

Instantaneous communications also mean Cameroonians in the diaspora are able to receive information firsthand about sociocultural, economic, and political initiatives and may choose to fly home on short notice to participate in these. For example, Cameroonians in the United States fly home on short notice when family members are sick, for funerals, for death celebrations, to participate in cultural/traditional dances and political campaigns, and to vote during elections. Those who are financially well off can participate in these and other activities as if they had never left Cameroon; meanwhile, their relatives, acquaintances, and friends continue to benefit from remittances, technology, the spread of ideas, charity contributions, and the promotion of education.[59] The Ndedi Eyango example (discussed in the following section) seems to suggest that some home-based Cameroonians are uncomfortable with the constant presence of the diaspora in many home-based functions.

THE IRONY OF AFRICAN MIGRATION

Failures/Setbacks

Although African migration has numerous success stories, many stories of gloom and doom also abound. For some, the psychological traumas of the journey, peer competition, and the difficulties of living in the diaspora have forced them to engage in destructive behavior such as envy, deceit, and fraud. For example, in February 2014 in Maryland and Washington, DC, prosecutors charged twenty-five people with Medicaid fraud, an overwhelming majority of them Cameroonians; they were "accused of making claims based on fake symptoms and personal home care that was never performed."[60] These Cameroon Americans were allegedly defrauding American taxpayers to the tune of millions to embrace upscale lifestyles, the result of peer competition both in the United States and in Cameroon. Many of them may lose everything and end up spending decades in prison. In fact, such forms of peer competition and other attributes are responsible for the rising rate of divorce among Cameroon/African immigrants in the United States.[61]

With the exception of the few African migrants who have embraced a life of scamming the system, qualified and skilled Africans have become permanent residents or US citizens and have progressively settled into good and high-paying careers, thereby escaping the deplorable conditions back in Africa. The story is, however, not the same for many who have been psychologically and socially scarred by the negative experiences of migration. The irony of migration means that these Africans would have been better off staying home than emigrating. I adduced this sentiment from the questionnaires and from the interviews that I conducted with many Cameroon migrants in the United States, where their frustrations and sentiments of "Had I known" come to light. Many did not succeed despite working hard back home. In the United States, they face some of the same obstacles, even more than they endured in Cameroon. Looking back to Cameroon after a number of years abroad, they see how much progress some of their peers have made—living comfortable lives, building luxurious homes, amassing land, starting farms, and opening businesses—and they resort to unhealthy work patterns and sometimes to illegal methods of catching up. Even some who have had economic/financial success abroad spend their last decades trying to compete or measure up to peers back home; this constitutes one major reason they struggle to maintain a home in Cameroon at all cost, regardless of the fact that their children may never settle there or that the home is unoccupied for most of the year, sometimes for many years. Meanwhile, for those Cameroonians who have the necessary documentation to live abroad, but have not succeeded financially, Africa becomes uninteresting; many are unprepared for the ridicule that comes with returning home the same way one left decades ago—financially broke.

The Problem of Brain Drain and Gain

Despite many individual African immigrant success stories and the gains in remittances that the continent receives yearly, the brain drain from Africa—a situation in which the continent's professionals migrate to Western and other industrialized nations for economic opportunities as a result of the negative/hostile sociopolitical and economic environment back in Africa—is one of the major setbacks of migration. As professionals leave the continent, the problem of lack of qualified staff compels African governments to recruit more foreign professionals, usually from the West. Most affected are university professors and medical and other science-related professionals. For example, some accounts have put the number of Nigerian medical doctors working and living outside the country at more than eight thousand. Many Africans trained abroad do not return home to bridge the brain-drain gap in the universities and other professions. The long-term effect is that a majority of academic heads of university departments are home trained by the same university that employs them; as a result, ideas remain the same, with little or nothing new injected from outside.[62]

WHERE IS HOME FOR AFRICAN MIGRANTS?

To leave home by self-exile abroad is a complicated issue with psychological repercussions. Kalu has argued that the possibility of returning home "has remained ambiguous in the literature even though the rate of repatriation of 'aliens' has increased and some return out of disillusionment and out of a desire to retire at home."[63] Once removed from home for long periods, it becomes difficult to maintain and sustain connections and alliances back home. One becomes increasingly more committed to one's host country.[64] African migrants and their offspring are caught in a desperate situation—the inability to determine where home is. For many Africans, and in this case, Cameroon migrants, it is difficult to completely go home; they can only attempt to balance both homes through occasional or frequent visits back to Africa, "so as to keep alive the umbilical cord connecting them to the earth of their ancestors."[65] According to Okpewho, even "those who are reduced to making these tentative returns have become victims of a schizophrenia that is ultimately the price they pay for taking the decision to separate themselves from their home."[66] For those who have gone home to settle upon retirement, after a very long stay abroad, it has not been easy; the Ndedi Eyango saga illustrates this succinctly. Eyango who lived in the United States for about fifteen years, during which he secured US citizenship, returned to his home country of Cameroon on retirement. In 2013, he campaigned for the position of president of the Cameroon Musical Corporation (SOCAM) and won. He clearly had financial advantage, having made much of his money while residing in the United States. Before long, the question of dual citizenship and nationality was brought up by those who lost; they engaged in a campaign of sabotage that eventually labeled Eyango as a foreigner and a fraud. Despite the fact that he was voted Cameroon Musician of the Year in 2007 (while a US citizen, but living in Cameroon), his peers did not want him as president of the well-financed SOCAM, to the point that there is talk of deporting him to the United States.[67] Had he not challenged an institution noted for corruption, no one would have cared what he did in Cameroon.[68]

What about the children of African immigrants? What happens to those born abroad or taken abroad by their parents at a young age? Okpewho has argued that Africa is not home for these children:

> Some of us who brought our families to live in America may continue to insist, against all countervailing evidence, that we are still Africans to the core. But what about our children, who, delighted to be exchanging the depressing physical conditions in Africa for a

> life of ease and comfort in America, have a weaker grasp than we do of the deeper losses that expatriation brings? In time, of course, living in America reduces the romance of the place for them, and they may come to see—thanks to the moral deficit of America's conduct under some of its leaders—that there is something to be said, after all, for the Africa they left behind. But their appreciation of that Africa and its values are now filtered through eyes that are no longer indigenously African, conditioned as they now are, to some extent at least, by the comforts and securities of their new environment. In the final analysis, there is something about them that may not so easily "go home again."[69]

Fear for the uncertainty of their children's future only heightens the psychological trauma of African migrants. Many want their children to know and like the Africa of their ancestors. But because of the high cost of airfare, not many are able to take these children on frequent visits to Africa; yet they still hope and dream that after their passing, their children would one day return home to Africa. For many of these children, the passing of a parent who insists on being buried at "home" may be the only time they visit Africa, that is, if they make the trip at all. And for those who make the trip to bury a parent, the financial cost and the traditional/cultural demands of an African funeral attendant with much ritual and rites of passage may scar them for life, making that visit their last. In fact, the reality that loved ones—your own children—may not be there to visit, clean, and pray by your grave on the anniversary of your death has swayed some migrants with children to opt for burial in their adopted countries abroad.[70]

CONCLUSION

In conclusion, therefore, I ask the question again: So where is home for African migrants of the new diaspora? The answer remains elusive. Many African migrants are "in-betweens": they have two homes but are satisfied with neither. They hope Africa remains home, but influences such as economic and political necessity and/or exigencies and, of course, children blur their hope. For many with children, the answer is even more elusive; home may eventually be where you raise your children—abroad in a distant and foreign country, an ocean away from your ancestral homeland.

NOTES

1. Adduced from responses to my questionnaire, "'Home Away from Home': The Cameroon Diaspora in the United States of America," which was completed by more than fifty Cameroonians currently residing in the United States. The questionnaire is reproduced at the end of the chapter.

2. Augustine Acha, interviewed on March 10, 2014, in Mansfield, TX. Mr. Acha is a Cameroonian American who has been commuting between his home in Cameroon (during vacations) and his home in the United States. (The author also shares this point of view.)

3. Douglas S. Massey, Joaqu n Arango, Graeme Hugo, Ali Kouaouci, Adela Pellegrino, and J. Edward Taylor, "Theories of International Migration: A Review and Appraisal," *Population and Development Review* 19, no. 3 (1993): 431–66, 431.

4. Ibid., 432.

5. Isidore Okpewho, "Introduction: Can We 'Go Home Again'?," in *The New African Diaspora*, ed. Isidore Okpewho and Nkiru Nzegwu (Bloomington: Indiana University Press, 2009), 4–6.

6. See Ogbu Uke Kalu, "Patterns of African Migration and Immigrant Condition," in *African Pentecostalism: Global Discourses, Migrations, Exchanges and Connections*, vol. 1 of *The Collected Essays of Ogbu Uke Kalu*, ed. Wilhelmina J. Kalu, Nimi Wariboko, and Toyin Falola (Trenton, NJ: Africa World Press, 2010), 190.

7. Philip D. Curtin, "Migration in the Tropical World," in *Immigration Reconsidered: History, Sociology, and Politics*, ed. Virginia Yans-McLaughlin (New York: Oxford University Press, 1990), 23.

8. Ibid., 33–34.

9. Kalu, "Patterns of African Migration," 190.

10. See Kalu, "Patterns of African Migration," 191.

11. Ibid., 186.

12. Ibid., 191.

13. Ibid.

14. See Okpewho, "Introduction," 7.

15. Maurice N. Amutabi, "NGOs, Civil Societies, and Development in Africa: The Case of Kenya," in *Globalization and the African Experience*, ed. Emmanuel M. Mbah and Steven J. Salm (Durham: Carolina Academic Press, 2012), 105–31.

16. See Kalu, "Patterns of African Migration," 189. For more on the political and socioeconomic challenges that Africa has faced recently, see Toyin Falola and Emmanuel M. Mbah, "Introduction: Change and Continuity in Contemporary Africa," in *Contemporary Africa: Challenges and Opportunities*, ed. Toyin Falola and Emmanuel M. Mbah (New York: Palgrave Macmillan, 2014), 1–19.

17. Okpewho, "Introduction," 8.

18. Emmanuel M. Mbah, "Cameroon: The Elusiveness of Democracy," in *Democracy in Africa: Political Changes and Challenges*, ed. Saliba Sarsar and Julius O. Adekunle (Durham: Carolina Academic Press, 2012), 113–33.

19. Okpewho, "Introduction," 7.

20. Adduced from responses to questionnaire.

21. Toyin Falola and Emmanuel M. Mbah, "Conclusion: Africa That Works," in *Contemporary Africa: Challenges and Opportunities*, ed. Toyin Falola and Emmanuel M. Mbah (New York: Palgrave Macmillan, 2014), 245–51.

22. See Kalu, "Patterns of African Migration," 189.

23. Ibid., 185.

24. Okpewho, "Introduction," 10.

25. Kalu, "Patterns of African Migration," 189–90.

26. Adduced from responses to questionnaire.

27. Adduced from responses to questionnaire.

28. Adduced from the responses to questionnaire; see also Kalu, "Patterns of African Migration," 193.

29. Kalu, "Patterns of African Migration," 193. The feeling of humiliation is the same for many Cameroonians who completed the questionnaire.

30. Adduced from responses to questionnaire.

31. See Kalu, "Patterns of African Migration," 194.

32. Ibid., 197.

33. Ibid., 186.

34. Ibid., 195–97.

35. Kalu, "Patterns of African Migration," 195.

36. Ibid.

37. Adduced from responses to questionnaire.

38. See Kalu, "Patterns of African Migration," 197.

39. Adduced from responses to questionnaire.

40. See Kalu, "Patterns of African Migration," 198.

41. Ibid., 188.

42. Ibid., 188–98.

43. Okpewho, "Introduction," 11. Cameroon does not allow dual citizenship. By becoming a US citizen, one automatically and completely gives up one's Cameroonian nationality.

44. Adduced from responses to questionnaire; see also Kalu, "Patterns of African Migration," 198.

45. Kalu, "Patterns of African Migration," 190.

46. Adduced from responses to questionnaire.

47. Kalu, "Patterns of African Migration," 198.

48. See Okpewho, "Introduction," 11.

49. Ibid., 12. This is not true. See computer use or the lack thereof, frequent power failures, ill-equipped schools, and all other problems attendant to the African continent. The answer may lie here in US immigration laws and the selectivity of African immigrants to the United States. In most cases, only the best or academically promising are allowed to immigrate legally into the United States.

50. Ibid., 12.

51. Kalu, "Patterns of African Migration," 198. As an African-born immigrant

who has been teaching in the United States for about a decade now, I have witnessed numerous occasions in which African Americans would rather take a class from an Anglo-Saxon colleague than from an African.

52. Okpewho, "Introduction," 11.

53. See Tanure Ojaide and Akin Ogundiran, "Knowledge Circulation and the Diasporic Interface," in *The African Diaspora: Slavery, Modernity, and Globalization*, ed. Toyin Falola (Rochester, NY: University of Rochester Press, 2013), 255–81, 259.

54. See Kalu, "Patterns of African Migration," 200.

55. Marieclaire Mbah Acha, interviewed on March 10, 2014, in Mansfield, TX.

56. Adduced from responses to questionnaire.

57. See Kalu, "Patterns of African Migration," 200–205.

58. Adduced from responses to questionnaire.

59. Ibid.

60. Tom Howell Jr., "Feds: Medicaid Fraud Reached 'Epidemic Levels' in D.C. Region," *Washington Times*, February 20, 2014.

61. Adduced from responses to questionnaire.

62. Kalu, "Patterns of African Migration," 188.

63. Ibid., 186.

64. Adduced from responses to questionnaire; see also Okpewho, "Introduction," 10.

65. Okpewho, "Introduction," 10.

66. Ibid.

67. See "Ndedi Eyango Is a Fraudster," *Cameroon360*, January 19, 2014, http://kamer360.wordpress.com/2014/01/19/ndedi-eyango-is-a-fraudster/; see also Dibussi Tande, "The Ndedi Eyango Dual Nationality Saga: When the Stranger Is Cameroonian," *Scribbles from the Den*, January 24, 2014, http://www.dibussi.com/2014/01/the-ndedi-eyango-dual-nationality-saga-.html

68. Adduced from responses to questionnaire.

69. Okpewho, "Introduction," 10–11.

70. Adduced from responses to questionnaire.

BIBLIOGRAPHY

Amutabi, Maurice N. "NGOs, Civil Societies, and Development in Africa: The Case of Kenya." In *Globalization and the African Experience*, edited by Emmanuel M. Mbah and Steven J. Salm, 105–31. Durham: Carolina Academic Press, 2012.

Curtin, Philip D. "Migration in the Tropical World." In *Immigration Reconsidered: History, Sociology, and Politics*, edited by Virginia Yans-McLaughlin, 21–36. New York: Oxford University Press, 1990.

Falola, Toyin, and Emmanuel M. Mbah. "Introduction: Change and Continuity in Contemporary Africa." In *Contemporary Africa: Challenges and Opportuni-*

ties, edited by Toyin Falola and Emmanuel M. Mbah, 1–19. New York: Palgrave Macmillan, 2014.

Falola, Toyin, and Emmanuel M. Mbah. "Conclusion: Africa That Works." In *Contemporary Africa: Challenges and Opportunities*, edited by Toyin Falola and Emmanuel M. Mbah. New York: Palgrave Macmillan, 2014.

Howell, Tom, Jr. "Feds: Medicaid Fraud Reached 'Epidemic Levels' in D.C. Region." *Washington Times*, February 20, 2014. http://www.washingtontimes.com/news/2014/feb/20/top-prosecutor-announces-largest-hea

Kalu, Ogbu Uke. "Patterns of African Migration and Immigrant Condition." In *African Pentecostalism: Global Discourses, Migrations, Exchanges and Connections*. Vol. 1 of *The Collected Essays of Ogbu Uke Kalu*, edited by Wilhelmina J. Kalu, Nimi Wariboko, and Toyin Falola, 185–209. Trenton, NJ: Africa World Press, 2010.

Massey, Douglas S., Joaquin Arango, Graeme Hugo, Ali Kouaouci, Adela Pellegrino, and J. Edward Taylor. "Theories of International Migration: A Review and Appraisal." *Population and Development Review*, 19, no. 3 (September 1993): 431–66, 431.

Mbah, Emmanuel M. "Cameroon: The Elusiveness of Democracy." In *Democracy in Africa: Political Changes and Challenges*, edited by Saliba Sarsar and Julius O Adekunle, 113–33. Durham: Carolina Academic Press, 2012.

"Ndedi Eyango Is a Fraudster." *Cameroon360*, January 19, 2014. http://kamer360.wordpress.com/2014/01/19/ndedi-eyango-is-a-fraudster/

Ojaide, Tanure, and Akrin Ogundiran. "Knowledge Circulation and the Diasporic Interface." In *The African Diaspora: Slavery, Modernity, and Globalization*, edited by Toyin Falola, 255–81, 259. Rochester, NY: University of Rochester Press, 2013.

Okpewho, Isidore. "Introduction: Can We 'Go Home Again'?" In *The New African Diaspora*, edited by Isidore Okpewho and Nkiru Nzegwu, 3–30. Bloomington: Indiana University Press, 2009. 3–30.

Tande, Dibussi. "The Ndedi Eyango Dual Nationality Saga: When the Stranger is Cameroonian." *Scribbles from the Den*. http://www.dibussi.com/2014/01/the-ndedi-eyango-dual-nationality-saga-.html

QUESTIONNAIRE

"Home Away from Home": The Cameroon Diaspora in the United States of America

1. When did you come to the United States of America (USA)?
   a) Before 1980
   b) 1980–1990
   c) 1990–2005
   d) After 2005

2. Do you consider yourself an economic, political or social migrant?

3. Which of the following best describes your reason for coming to the USA? Circle all that applies to you:
   a) Economic hardship
   b) Insecurity
   c) Human rights abuses
   d) Political witch-hunting
   e) Chaos and dysfunction throughout
   f) Education
   g) Healthcare
   h) Marriage/love
   i) All of the above
   Explain your answer in question 2 beginning with the most important reason:

4. What was your occupation in Cameroon?

5. What was your salary?

6. Describe what you currently do for a living:

7. What were your previous occupations in the USA?

8. Level of education before leaving Cameroon:
   a) Primary school certificate

b) Ordinary levels
c) Advanced levels
d) Bachelor's Degree
e) Master's Degree and above
f) Not applicable (explain)

9. Current educational level in the USA
a) Professional Degrees and/or certificates (list them)
b) Academic Degrees and/or certificates (list them)
c) None of the above (explain)

10. Do you own your own home in the USA?

11. Do you own a home in Cameroon? If yes, why?

12. How often do you visit Cameroon?

13. Are you married?

14. Did you meet your wife here or back in Cameroon?

15. Do you have children? Were they born here or in Cameroon?

16. What expectations do you have for your children?

17. How integrated are you in the US community? (Politics, culture, economics etc.)

18. Comment on your experiences in the US with regard to the following:
a) Your immigration status and US immigration law (how difficult/complex/easy was the process?
b) Have you faced economic difficulties? Explain:
c) Was it easy to adapt to the US sociopolitical setting? Explain:
d) Comment on your successes and setbacks in the US:

19. Comment on your experiences with the following in your day-to-day interactions in the US with ordinary Americans:
a) Race and racial equality

b) Class and gender
c) Language and equality/inequality
d) Sexual orientation
e) Religion

20. Do you attend your village/ethnic meeting in the USA? If not, explain.

21. Do you contribute to fundraising for village/ethnic development projects? List projects and explain:

22. Do you have your Cameroon alma mater in the United States? If yes, Name:

23. Do you contribute to projects for that alma mater? List projects and explain.

24. What connections do you maintain in Cameroon? (Family, friends, village, etc.)

25. How often do you send money to Cameroon and to whom?

26. Approximately how much do you send to family and friends in Cameroon?

27. What projects do you have in Cameroon (business, etc.)?

28. How often do you use the following in your communications with Cameroon?
a) Email
b) Fax
c) Internet
d) Skype
e) Telephone

29. Comment on the forms of sociocultural attachments you maintain in Cameroon

30. Comment on the forms of economic attachments/interactions you maintain in Cameroon.

31. Comment on the forms of political attachments/interactions you maintain in Cameroon.

32. Comment on the forms of family attachments/interactions you maintain in Cameroon.

33. Comment on the forms of village/community/ethnic interactions you maintain with others in Cameroon.

34. Comment on the forms of development projects you are involved with in Cameroon.

35. What causes do you contribute money to in Cameroon?

36. Comment on your role in the search for genuine democracy in Cameroon.

37. Do you plan on eventually going back to Cameroon? When?

38. Do you miss Cameroon? What do you miss the most about Cameroon?

II

Commodities

4

"The Second Fallen Adam"

William Adam and Nineteenth-Century Transatlantic Reform

Julie L. Holcomb

In June 1840, the British and Foreign Anti-Slavery Society commissioned artist Benjamin Robert Haydon to produce a painting to commemorate the World Anti-Slavery Convention. This international gathering of abolitionists brought more than four hundred British, American, and other delegates to London that month. Completed in 1841, Haydon's historical painting, which now hangs in the National Portrait Gallery in London, features more than one hundred identifiable portraits, including the only extant portrait of the Orientalist William Adam who is identified in the painting's accompanying key as "Prof. Adam," a reference to his position on the faculty of Harvard University. British abolitionist Thomas Clarkson and freed slave Henry Beckford of Jamaica are the focal point of Haydon's painting. Clarkson and Beckford are surrounded by rows of disembodied heads, including that of Adam who occupies the liminal space between the more prominently featured male delegates, located in the center and foreground of the painting, and the female observers arranged on the far right and in the background of the canvas. Adam's profile is barely visible behind the bonnet of the woman next to him in the painting. Despite his placement, it is significant that Adam was among those delegates included in Haydon's portrait, suggesting Adam's importance in the transatlantic anti-slavery movement.[1] After full emancipation occurred in the West Indies in 1838, British and American abolitionists turned their attention east to British India. The subject of British India appeared in the pages of the *Liberator* nearly one hundred times between 1838 and 1842; the subject appeared on the front page eight times in 1840 alone.[2] Adam, who moved to the United States in 1838 after a twenty-year sojourn in India, was an important source of information about India and its land and labor conditions. On the second day of the convention, Adam delivered a highly anticipated lecture to the delegates about the continued existence of slavery in British India.[3]

Born in Scotland in 1796, Adam was educated there and in England in the classics, theology, and classical and vernacular Asian languages. In 1815, Adam was accepted by the Baptist Missionary Society and sailed for India two years later to join the Baptist mission at Serampore. Adam's disassociation from the Baptists in 1821 led his former evangelical friends to describe him as "the second fallen Adam."[4] After his infamous conversion to Unitarianism, Adam, who was cut off from Baptist funding, worked a number of jobs to support his family. In 1838, Adam and his family moved to Boston where he joined the Harvard faculty, serving as the university's first Orientalist. In Boston, he met American abolitionist William Lloyd Garrison, who convinced Adam to join the immediatist cause. On a brief trip to London in 1839, Adam met George Thompson, Garrison's British counterpart. Adam quickly gained the respect of Garrison and Thompson, as well as other American and British abolitionists, for his intimate knowledge of and his commitment to reform in India.[5]

Adam is a neglected historical figure. References to him are scattered throughout the historiographies of transatlantic abolitionism and British India. Unlike many of his contemporaries, however, particularly Garrison and the Indian reformer Rammohun Roy, Adam has not been the subject of significant biographical study. Two challenges confront anyone interested in learning more about Adam. First, the lack of sources poses a significant obstacle. Adam's few extant letters are scattered in a number of archives in the United States and Britain. The second challenge is the wide range of Adam's reform interests. As a Baptist missionary, Unitarian convert, minister, newspaper editor, educator, researcher, author, abolitionist, and women's rights advocate, Adam personified the cosmopolitan slogan of Garrison's *Liberator*, "Our Country is the World—Our Countrymen are All Mankind." Adam refused to acknowledge allegiance to any existing government, though he did pledge to "obey the laws of the country" in which he resided so long as "the laws of [that] country" did not require him "to violate any moral principles."[6] In addition to India, Scotland, England, and Boston, Adam lived in Northampton, Massachusetts, as one of the founders of the Northampton Association of Education and Industry; in Toronto and Chicago, where he served briefly as a Unitarian minister; and in New Orleans, where he spent six months for unknown reasons. Adam was, as one historian has observed, "one of those much neglected individuals whose activities and ideas almost surreptitiously find their way into any history of the period."[7] He was "a man of considerable talent, resourcefulness, and courage, who, nevertheless, never quite succeeded at what he set out to do."[8] Adam fought passionately for the major social issues of the nineteenth century; yet, much of what he fought for ultimately failed.

Adam's speech at the World Anti-Slavery Convention placed Indian slavery at the center of a new, universal conception of global anti-slavery activism, one that fit well with British abolitionists' new transatlantic focus. Between 1839 and 1841, Adam lectured and wrote about his experience in British India.[9] Adam's speeches and writings differed from earlier treatments of Indian slavery that downplayed its severity and highlighted its indigenous roots. He challenged traditional arguments about the character and the source of Indian slavery by claiming that East Indian slavery was as extensive and as horrific as African slavery had been in the West Indies. Adam called for renewed abolitionist effort to end slavery in British East India, thus completing the abolition of slavery in the British Empire. Convention delegates received Adam's speech with approval; yet, many convention delegates, including Thompson, were more concerned with establishing India as a source of free-labor goods than reform of land and labor conditions in India.[10] Adam did not share Thompson's optimism that cotton cultivation in India would lead to the abolition of slavery in the American South. Unlike the majority of British and American delegates interested in East Indian reform, Adam sought reform in India for the sake of Indians. Thus, for Adam, any impact on slavery elsewhere, including the American South, would be "*collateral*."[11] For Adam, lasting reform of the transnational economy had to include significant changes in the existential conditions of Indian bondsmen and -women. If we examine Adam's life experience in India as a missionary, an editor, and an educator, we appreciate how those roles influenced the development of his complex understanding of native Indian culture and British rule in India. Moreover, Adam's story tells us much about the challenge of creating a global economy based on justice and humanity rather than profit and loss.

The Baptist mission to India began in 1793 when British shoemaker William Carey arrived in Calcutta. He had not obtained a license from the British East India Company (EIC) whose royal charter allowed this joint stock company first to trade with and, later, to rule India. Carey settled temporarily in northern Bengal where he managed an indigo manufacturing operation. He was soon joined by Joshua Marshman a schoolmaster, and William Ward, a printer. Their status as Dissenters (non-Anglicans) led EIC officials to question the Baptists' loyalty and purpose. Moreover, as unlicensed Europeans in EIC-governed territories, the missionaries were subject to be sent back to England. In 1799, under pressure from the EIC, the three men moved the Baptist mission from British territory to Dutch-ruled Serampore. Although the Baptists relocated their mission, they continued to have problems with the EIC, problems that were exacerbated by the 1806 revolt of the EIC's Indian sepoys at Vellore, which resulted in the death or wounding of nearly two hundred British soldiers. Although the revolt was the result of multiple grievances, EIC officials blamed the missionaries for the uprising. The Vellore Mutiny set in motion a number of crises in India and in England that continued until renewal of the EIC's charter in 1813, which brought about a series of compromises between the EIC and the missionaries in India.[12]

Although the Charter Act's renewal allowed the Baptists to begin establishing missions in areas of India controlled by the EIC, it did not resolve all of the problems between the government and the missionaries. By providing for the establishment of a bishopric in Calcutta, the Charter Act reinforced tensions that had existed between Anglicans and Dissenting Baptists from the earliest days of the mission in India. For example, in 1805 the Baptists, represented by Carey, and the Anglicans, represented by Claudius Buchanan and later David Brown, disagreed over the disbursement of funds and the authority to approve various translations of the Bible.[13] In the 1810s and 1820s, the missionary effort expanded in India, increasing competition among the various missionary groups. Between 1819 and 1822, for example, the Baptist Missionary Society, the London Missionary Society, and the Church Missionary Society established presses in Calcutta. These three groups eventually formed the Religious Tract Society, which later became the Calcutta Christian Tract and Book Society, to publish inexpensive Christian works in the vernacular languages of India.[14] The competition between the Baptists and the Anglicans also reflected long-standing theological differences between the two sects.[15]

Rival factions among the Baptists, centered in Serampore and Calcutta, developed in the early nineteenth century. The Serampore Trio—Carey,

Marshman, and Ward—urged the Baptist Missionary Society (BMS) in London to support them in their contention that new Baptist missionaries should limit their efforts to working with Indians, rather than Europeans, and to remain in Serampore rather than moving to the more cosmopolitan city of Calcutta. The Serampore Trio also resisted efforts by the BMS to assert more control over their mission. In 1817, William Yates, John Lawson, W. H. Pearce, and Eustace Carey (a nephew of William Carey) left Serampore and established an autonomous mission in Calcutta. The Serampore mission remained independent from the BMS and the Calcutta mission, which retained close ties to the BMS.[16] The two missions remained, as one historian notes, "independent and antagonistic" until 1837.[17]

When Adam left for India in 1817, he sailed into the middle of these internecine disputes over converts and control of funds and biblical translations. Initially, Adam joined the mission at Serampore; however, just three months after arriving in India, Adam left Serampore to join the Calcutta mission.[18] In 1820, Adam and Yates were asked by Rammohun Roy to assist in creating a new Bengali translation of the Gospels to replace those produced by William Carey and the Anglican John Ellerton, who had each produced translations that were widely criticized for being inaccurate and unidiomatic.[19]

Rammohun has been referred to as the "Father of Modern India."[20] (Rammohun is the preferred short form because, in the nineteenth century, Roy was seen as a title, not a name.)[21] He embraced the Western-influenced modernity associated with Indian nationalism. In India, Western impact produced three distinct patterns of reaction in Bengali Hindu society. Conservative Bengalis fought to uphold the social and religious status quo while radicals, generally young men, rejected Hinduism altogether. Reformers, like Rammohun, sought compromise between old and new, meeting the Western challenge not by rejecting or holding fast to Hinduism, but instead by reinterpreting Hinduism in light of contemporary knowledge and criticism. Rammohun worked from within Bengali Hindu society to create a climate of reform, challenging, for example, the practice of sati, or widow burning, which he believed was practiced and tolerated under the name of religion but in reality was used to obtain the widow's property. Rammohun supported education. He also criticized British censorship of the Indian press and the exclusion of Indians from British juries. Rammohun was fluent in English, Greek, and Hebrew, as well as Sanskrit and Persian. He published widely in Bengali, English, and Hindustani.[22]

Born in 1772 in British-ruled Bengal, Rammohun belonged to the Brahman caste, the highest ranking of the four varnas, or social classes, in Hindu India. Little is known of his early life, education, and religious training. Raised within the Hindu tradition, Rammohun was exposed to the Islamic tradition at an early age. In the 1810s, he became interested in Unitarianism.[23] In 1845, Adam noted that while Rammohun had been raised an "idolater," he came to the belief that idolatry was inconsistent with "the truth of God and the laws of nature" and that idolatry was "a fruitful source of degradation, vice, and misery, personal, social, and national."[24] Historian Lynn Zastoupil, who has written extensively on Rammohun, describes Rammohun's religious views as "a vexing issue." Rammohun moved between Islamic, Hindu, and Christian rationalist traditions, localizing his religious ideas based on the character of his audience: Muslim, Hindu, or Christian. Zastoupil explains that when Rammohun "argued for the unity of God and rational forms of worship, or warned that all organized religions tended to divide and mislead, he did so in ways tailored to the mental universe of each distinct audience." Rammohun's ability to speak with confidence from within each of these religious traditions helps explain his deep engagement with Unitarianism. Significantly, this confidence proved critical in his controversy with the Baptist missionaries in the early 1820s.[25]

While Adam, Yates, and Rammohun were at work on a new Bengali translation of the Gospels, Rammohun published *The Precepts of Jesus, the Guide to Peace and Happiness* (1820). *The Precepts of Jesus* presented selections from the Gospels of Matthew, Mark, Luke, and John. Rammohun omitted the doctrinal passages and the miracle stories, presenting Jesus as a standard for ethical conduct rather than a means of salvation. By "separating from the other matters contained in the New Testament, the moral precepts found in that book," Rammohun believed the sayings of Jesus were "more likely to produce the desirable effect of improving the hearts and minds of men of different persuasions and degrees of understanding."[26] The Baptist response to *The Precepts* was immediate and harsh.[27] According to the editor of the Boston weekly the *Christian Register*, "instead of being hailed as the harbinger of a new era of light and happiness to the benighted Hindoos [*sic*]," Rammohun "was violently attacked and censured by the [C]hristian missionaries of that region."[28] Marshman denounced *The Precepts*, claiming it had been produced by "an intelligent *Heathen* whose mind is as yet completely opposed to the grand design of the Saviour's becoming incarnate."[29] The controversy raged for three years. The Baptists, represented chiefly by Marshman, published widely in the religious press in India, Britain, and the United States. Rammohun defended *The Precepts* with increasingly sophisticated biblical exegeses, publishing three successive *Appeals* to the public, which were also widely disseminated in India, the United States, and Britain.[30] Adam was one of the chief defenders of Rammohun, claiming that the Baptists had by their conduct in this case demonstrated their mission in India was "not to spread Christianity but to retard its progress."[31]

In 1820 and 1821, Adam worked with Rammohun on the Gospel translation project and defended his colleague against the charges of the Baptists. During this period, Adam experienced a spiritual crisis. In 1821, he decided to end his connection with the Calcutta Baptist Mission. He later claimed it had to do with a difference of opinion regarding the missionaries' objectives. The Calcutta Baptists preached primarily to the poor and illiterate whereas Adam believed the missionaries should focus on "the wealthy and the learned."[32] Interestingly, Adam did not deny or affirm that his decision had anything to do with Rammohun or the controversy surrounding *The Precepts of Jesus*. In this same period, Adam suffered another, more severe crisis, which led him to reject the doctrine of the Trinity. Adam's doubts about the Trinity began during his translation work with Yates and Rammohun. Writing in May 1821, Adam noted he had for some time studied the Scriptures, seeking divine guidance. Unable to reconcile himself to the doctrine of the Trinity, Adam converted to Unitarianism.[33] In an open letter to his brother, Adam defended his conversion, saying he had been "influenced by nothing but a regard for truth and conscience." Adam noted the high price he had paid for his decision, describing his estrangement from his friends and family and noting the false reports that had circulated about him, his conversion, and the role of Rammohun. "I have had to suffer reproach and public afflictions, the illness of Mrs. Adam, and the death of our only child, with scarcely a friend to cheer my spirits, or a hand stretched out to my assistance," Adam wrote.[34] In September 1821, Adam preached his first Unitarian sermon. Two days later, the Circular Road Baptist Church excommunicated him.[35]

Following his separation from the Baptists, Adam criticized missionary efforts in general, which he believed were misguided, even naive. In the early nineteenth century, missionaries in India, Baptists and Anglicans alike, saw themselves as bringing enlightenment to a benighted world. Missionaries ignored the indigenous tradition, or assumed it had nothing of value on which they could build. For Adam, Rammohun's controversy with the Baptists was evidence of the missionaries' unwillingness to consider the native point of view. Of the numerous Christian tracts produced for the native population, Adam noted in 1824, "scarcely one is fit to be put into the hands of a native of understanding and reflection." Translations of the Bible suffered similar flaws. The Baptists had attempted to create too many translations of the Bible too soon. Their hasty work and unfamiliarity with the language rendered the translations unusable. Christian missionaries focused their efforts on educating the native population to prepare Indians for conversion. That objective proved unsuccessful in winning souls to Christianity, however, in large part because missionaries assumed the indigenous population would accept, as Adam noted, "without the offer of proof and scarcely even the permission to object," the binary that because Christianity is true, Hinduism is false. Moreover, Adam explained, the missionaries "expected to find a *table rasée* ready to receive the doctrines of Christianity laid down by them as self-evident truths which only required to be known to be once adopted."[36] The evangelical view failed to consider the vitality and the strength of native culture and to encourage native participation in reforming Indian society.

In the 1820s, Adam and Rammohun expanded the Unitarian community in India. In 1821, the two men formed the Calcutta Unitarian Society. Adam, cut off from the financial support of the Baptists, struggled to support his family. In 1826, the newly established British and Foreign Unitarian Association appointed Adam as its only missionary in India. The Calcutta Unitarians agreed to provide additional funds. In 1827, Adam began full-time work as a missionary. Disagreements soon erupted. Native members of the Calcutta committee would not support Bengali lectures because they were given in a vernacular language. In 1828, the Calcutta Unitarian Society dissolved. Rammohun and other Hindu Unitarians left to form the Brahmo Samaj. There is no evidence in the historical record to suggest that the end of the Calcutta Unitarian Society meant the end of the friendship between Rammohun and Adam.[37] Indeed, in his 1845 lecture on Rammohun, Adam spoke of him with great respect: "I would say that . . . in friendly and confidential converse with him . . . I was in the presence of a man of natural and inherent genius, of powerful understanding, and of determined will, a will determined with singular energy and uncontrollable self-direction to lofty and generous purposes."[38]

Rammohun's controversy with the Baptists and Adam's conversion to Unitarianism received great press coverage in the early 1820s. Both Rammohun and Adam had used the press to shape public opinion, defend their views, and criticize their opponents. Given the importance of print culture for Adam, it is not surprising that he would turn to newspaper work in the 1820s as he searched for a means to support his family.

The earliest vernacular printing presses in Bengal were set up by the Baptist missionaries at Serampore. Until that time Bengali culture had been largely an oral one. The few written Bengali texts were popular verses and long narrative poems and ballads, based primarily on local religious tales. As Anindita Ghosh argues, "The range and resilience of existing cultures ensured that the absorption of print by the reading population could be neither immediate nor all pervasive."[39] Nonetheless, by the late 1810s, print culture in Bengal had grown substantially, aided in large part by the development of newspaper publications in the vernacular languages. By using printed works as a source of income and a source of employment for their Indian protégés, the missions played an important role in the expansion of print culture in India in the first quarter of the nineteenth century.[40]

In 1825, Adam became editor of the *Bengal Chronicle*, a newspaper owned by James Sutherland. The British colonial government had attempted to suppress the newspaper. A compromise agreement allowed the newspaper to continue with Adam as its editor. However, he soon had a disagreement with Sutherland.[41] In 1827, Adam became co-owner of the *Calcutta Chronicle*. He spoke out against the Calcutta Stamp Act, drawing criticism from the Chief Secretary to the Government, who described Adam's comments as "highly disrespectful to the Government" and in violation of "the Regulations regarding the press." Despite a conciliatory response from Adam, the *Chronicle*'s license was revoked.[42] In 1829, Adam tried once again, this time becoming editor of the ultraradical *India Gazette*, a position he held until 1834. At the *India Gazette*, Adam continued his outspoken views "undeterred by any fear of displeasure or authority or anxiety for the applause of the multitudes." Among the unpopular views espoused by Adam was the falseness of the English assumption that the native population was illiterate and uncivilized. Adam insisted that Indians were largely self-taught and civilized.[43]

In this period, Adam wrote an article for the *Gazette* supporting indigenous education. In the late 1820s and early 1830s, debates about education in India had settled into a debate between the Orientalists and the Anglicists. Although both agreed that the chief purpose of education was the promotion of useful knowledge, in other words Western knowledge, the two sides disagreed over means. The "overcautious" Orientalists refused to recognize many Bengali Hindus' increasing interest in English education. In contrast, the "overzealous" Anglicists were obsessed with the notion that everything in the East was bad and everything in the West was good; thus, the Anglicists were impatient in their demands for a wholesale replacement of Indian learning by Western learning. The Orientalist-Anglicist controversy revolved around the question of whether Western knowledge would be taught in classical Oriental languages or in English. Both groups refused to consider education in the vernacular languages, believing those languages inadequate for the transmission of new ideas and new knowledge.[44] Rammohun had been critical of the British government's policy toward education, especially its plans to establish the Sanskrit College in Calcutta. As the Orientalist-Anglicist controversy unfolded, Rammohun was at the center of the debate.[45] Adam's article for the *India Gazette* originated out of his long-standing interest in education and his friendship with Rammohun.

Adam had come to the conclusion that the expenditure of public money on Sanskrit and Arabic literature and schools was not a mistake when the majority of the Indian people were eager for education in their own languages. Moreover, Adam was certain that if education was to lead to moral regeneration of Indian society, it could not be limited to the education in English of a few men of the upper and middle classes. Rather, education had to permeate the entire social structure. In 1829, Adam first approached Lord William Bentinck, Governor-General of India, and again in 1834, he requested an opportunity to research the state of education in India. Bentinck approved Adam's plan in January 1835.[46]

Adam spent the next three years conducting his education survey. He traveled extensively throughout Bengal, meeting with members of both high and low castes, coming into close contact with the people, and assessing the actual condition of education in the villages he visited.[47] His travels deepened his convictions that in rural areas native culture remained vibrant and vital. Adam produced three reports, each recommending the use of existing vernacular languages as the basis of the Indian educational system. The Government Committee of Public Instruction (GCPI) rejected Adam's scheme as too costly and too impractical.[48] Adam's radicalism may have also contributed to the rejection of his recommendations. The notoriety of his conversion to Unitarianism, his editorship of radical newspapers in Calcutta, and his denunciations of missionaries and Anglicists alike may well have prejudiced the GCPI against him.[49]

In the meantime, in 1834 Adam's wife and children had moved to the United States. In 1838, after submitting his final education report and realizing that his recommendations would be ignored, Adam left for the United States as well. Adam's reform career might well have ended there had it not been for changes in the political climate in Britain. In 1833, Parliament passed the Emancipation Act, abolishing slavery on August 1, 1834, and establishing an interim apprenticeship system that would end in 1845. Five years later, under tremendous public pressure, Parliament amended the Emancipation Act and ended apprenticeship as of August 1, 1838. The following April, British abolitionists, invigorated by the victories of 1833 and 1838, established the British and Foreign Anti-Slavery Society (BFASS), which boldly proclaimed its commitment to universal abolition. Within weeks, British abolitionists proposed an international anti-slavery meeting for the following year in London, sending out a broadly worded invitation to "the friends of the slave of every nation and every clime."[50]

In addition to the BFASS, British abolitionists established the Aborigines' Protection Society. The society, organized by Thomas Fowell Buxton and other British reformers, developed out of the turmoil of famine in India, trade disputes with China, and the recent migration of Indian labor to the West Indies. Though events in India, in particular, were important in leading to the founding of the society, the association focused on the condition of indigenous populations throughout the British Empire.[51] In the summer of that year, George Thompson and Joseph Pease helped with the publication of a circular that outlined conditions in India that was distributed to members of Parliament and the Aborigines' Protection Society. Thompson was also engaged to present a series of lectures to inform the public of the need for reform in India.[52] In January 1839, Thompson and Adam met during the latter's visit to Britain. Adam convinced Thompson, Pease, and his daughter Elizabeth Pease that an association was needed to seek reform on behalf of the people of India. Although he was a logical choice to take a leadership role in the new society, Adam left that spring to return to the United States because he had already accepted a teaching appointment at Harvard.[53]

In March 1839, a provisional committee was appointed to formally organize the British India Society (BIS). The Peases and Thompson attended the London Yearly Meeting of the Society of Friends (Quakers) where Thompson outlined the goals of the BIS.[54] Quakers were the primary supporters of abolitionism in Britain; thus, it was important to gain their support for the BIS. The first formal meeting of the BIS in June 1839 was celebrated on both sides of the Atlantic. In a series of speeches, British reformers urged the reformation of conditions in India for the benefit of the indigenous population, the prosperity of British business, and the emancipation of the slave. Improving labor conditions would provide opportunities for expanded agricultural development in India, which would increase Indian supplies of cotton for British mills and, in turn, would increase Indian demand for British manufactures.[55]

Abolitionists in the United States, including Garrison and Adam, urged support for reform in British India. Garrison edited a volume of Thompson's India speeches to promote the cause.[56] Garrison also used the pages of the *Liberator* to keep his readers informed of events in India. The subject of British India appeared in more than one hundred articles published in the *Liberator* from 1838 through 1842; British India appeared on the front page of the *Liberator* eight times in 1840 alone, sometimes to the exclusion of almost all other news.[57] Although Adam did not share Thompson's "sanguine expectations" that reform in India would affect slavery in America, he still agreed to give a series of lectures about his experiences in British India.[58] Elizabeth Pease, although excluded from membership in the BIS, used her extensive correspondence with American abolitionists to maintain a steady flow of information about the BIS to the United States. Pamphlets, reports, and letters sent by Pease to American abolitionists were, as Quaker abolitionist Lucretia Mott's son-in-law Edward M. Davis noted, kept in "constant motion."[59]

On the second day of the World Anti-Slavery Convention, Adam delivered a lecture to the delegates that highlighted the continued existence of slavery in the territories of the EIC. Abridged from the series of open letters Adam had written to Buxton and published in Boston and in London earlier that year, Adam's lecture challenged traditional arguments about the character and the source of slavery in British India. The EIC had failed to abolish slavery and had given tacit sanction to its continued presence.

"[S]lavery in India does not rest on law but custom," Adam remarked, "and this illegal custom has been invested by the British government in India, with the desecrated forms and sanctions of law and justice." Moreover, slavery in India was not as benign as previously claimed. Using a rhetorical strategy from the abolitionist movement, Adam emphasized specific instances of physical cruelty, alluding to "the unnatural and atrocious barbarity" practiced on slave eunuchs, for example. Female slaves, he added, were kept "for licentious purposes" and often subjected to "mutilation and murder." Although Adam admitted that slavery was not the worst social evil from which India suffered, he maintained that Indian bondage was far from harmless. Highlighting the horrors of slavery, Adam contradicted earlier assumptions that Indian slavery was "divested of all the cruel features which characterized the African trade." He called for a renewed abolitionist effort to end slavery in British India, thus completing the abolition of slavery in the British Empire. "Nothing has been done to mitigate the condition of the slaves, or to lead to the extinction of slavery," Adam told the delegates. "You have, therefore, strong, clear, defined ground upon which to proceed; and I earnestly hope that you will proceed."[60]

The delegates received Adam's speech with approbation, noting that the political compromises of the Emancipation Act of 1833 had limited action against slavery in India. "We have long talked of the evil [of slavery in British India], but what have we done to remove it?" Joseph Pease asked. The delegates appointed a committee that included Adam, Pease, Thompson, and Charles Stuart to consider Adam's lecture and deliver to the convention a resolution or resolutions based on it. Joseph Sams, a Quaker bookseller from Darlington, urged the committee to do more than consider Adam's report. Instead, he urged the committee also to consider the subject of free labor. If "we as a nation were to use only free labour produce," Sams said, "it would be one of the severest blows which could possibly be given to slavery." R. R. R. Moore, a political economist from Dublin, objected: "We shall gain nothing by mixing up the subjects," Moore claimed. Thompson agreed. The delegates unanimously approved the resolution, limiting the committee's review to the information contained in Adam's report.[61]

On the eighth day of the convention, Stuart introduced a "free-produce" resolution, recommending "the disuse of slave-labour produce, and instead of it the use of free-labour produce, as far as practicable."

Stuart, a native of Jamaica and a retired army officer, had been active in anti-slavery in the United States and the West Indies. In the 1830s, Stuart was unsuccessful in his attempts to introduce a free-produce resolution at the annual meetings of the American Anti-Slavery Society. At the World Anti-Slavery Convention, Stuart's resolution triggered an intense debate. Those critical of the resolution noted the challenge of abstaining from slave-labor goods, particularly in the United States. "Slave-labour, in some form or other, enters into nearly all the substantial articles of commerce, that are in ordinary use, and ranked as necessaries," American abolitionist James G. Birney remarked. Other delegates debated the meaning of the phrase "as far as practicable," asking whether the resolution should be reworded or the phrase omitted altogether. American abolitionist and Unitarian minister George Bradburn claimed the phrase "as far as practicable" amounted to "nothing." "Great diversity of opinion will be entertained as to what *is* practicable," he said. Several delegates were concerned that the consequences of the boycott had not been fully considered. Noting the importance of cotton to British industry, one delegate believed any free-produce resolution would impede the abolitionist cause. "I think we ought to pause, and to deeply consider the consequences of this motion," he warned. Delegates who supported a free-produce resolution noted the thousands of Americans who abstained from slave-labor goods. "Americans . . . eschew every article of slave produce, and would pay fifty cents instead of five, if it were required, to put down American slavery," bragged one American delegate, whereas another claimed hundreds more abstained in the United States than in Britain. Thompson believed passage of the resolution, or a modified version of it, "would strengthen the hands of abolitionists very materially." In the end, the delegates refused to endorse Stuart's resolution. Instead, delegates agreed to form a committee to examine possible sources for free-labor goods.[62]

Immediately after the free-produce debate, Adam introduced the resolutions drafted by the committee charged with examination of his report on East Indian slavery. The committee presented a series of eight resolutions, highlighting the nature and extent of slavery in India. The resolutions, which restated the key points of Adam's lecture, passed unanimously. The resolutions did not reference free labor or identify India as a potential source of free-labor goods.[63]

After the World Anti-Slavery Convention, British reformers struggled to continue the British India Society. In August 1840, Manchester replaced

London as the center of the Indian reform movement. Five months later, the association established the *British Indian Advocate*, edited by Adam, who had relocated to Britain from Massachusetts after the convention. The *Advocate* was short-lived, however. In 1841, the BIS entered into a formal alliance with the Anti-Corn Law League (ACCL). In an effort to increase free trade, the ACCL sought repeal of British laws restricting the importation of foreign grain. Although many British and American abolitionists supported free trade and the ACCL, many others worried the movement would distract attention from abolitionism, particularly after Thompson agreed to set aside agitation for the BIS temporarily in order to work for the ACCL. Thompson, Joseph Pease, and the leadership of the BIS agreed to the alliance. In return, the leaders of the ACCL promised to throw the weight of their influence behind Indian reform once the Corn Laws had been repealed. The leaders of the BIS thought they had negotiated a good bargain; however, the alliance proved disastrous for the BIS. The British India Society lost all public momentum for the cause and gained the enemies of the ACCL. By the time the Corn Laws were repealed in 1846, Indian reform and the British India Society were nearly forgotten, and Adam himself had moved on to other reforms.[64]

In 1841, after the British India Society dissolved and the *British Indian Advocate* ceased publication, Adam found himself adrift once again. He paid a deposit on land in Australia before giving in to his family's demands to return to America. Adam and his family initially planned to purchase a farm in Pennsylvania; however, after making initial inquiries about the utopian community Brook Farm, Adam and his family ended up in Northampton, Massachusetts, where he joined George W. Benson, Erasmus Darwin, Joseph Conant, Earl Dwight Swift, Theodore Scarborough, and Hiram Wells in a plan to establish a new community, the Northampton Association of Education and Industry (NAEI). Benson, Hudson, and Adam were abolitionists; Conant and Swift were silk manufacturers; Scarborough, a farmer; and Wells, a mechanic. The NAEI incorporated in 1842 as a community based on a community-owned-and-operated silk mill. The members of the NAEI challenged prevailing social attitudes, creating a society in which "the rights of all are equal without distinction of sex, color or condition, sect or religion." For Adam, the NAEI seemed the ideal expression of his cosmopolitan ideals for social reform.[65]

The NAEI occupied 470 acres situated about two and one-half miles from the center of Northampton, on a site that "included farm- and woodland, a four story, brick silk factory, a boardinghouse, various outbuildings, and several private houses." The factory building included manufacturing space, as well as a dormitory, a common kitchen and dining room, and schoolrooms. Members worked at a variety of trades in addition to the community's primary activity, raising silkworms and manufacturing thread. Membership was based on the purchase of stock. As NAEI resident William Bassett explained, "Our association is based on the principle of a community of interests—not on that of a community of property. Each person is credited with the amount he invests, and on withdrawal he is entitled to receive the amount to his credit." From its incorporation in 1842 until its dissolution in 1846, the community attracted 240 men, women, and children, including black abolitionists David Ruggles and Sojourner Truth. William Lloyd Garrison and Frederick Douglass also were involved in the group's activities.[66]

Adam served as secretary and director of education for the NAEI. His daughters provided music and dancing lessons. In 1843, Adam was criticized for being too academic and resigned as director of education. Throughout 1843, Adam's frustrations with the members of the NAEI community grew, and in the fall he withdrew as secretary and moved his family into Northampton. After leaving Northampton, Adam made a brief attempt to offer classes in Boston, but that effort soon failed because his lectures were, as one friend candidly noted, "dull & uninteresting."[67]

Little is known about the rest of his life. At the suggestion of abolitionist and Unitarian minister Samuel J. May, Adam moved his family to Toronto, where he became the city's first Unitarian minister in 1845. Financial difficulties with the congregation made his position there untenable. He then moved to Chicago where he assumed ministerial duties in 1846. After leaving Chicago, he moved briefly in New Orleans for reasons unknown. In 1851, he apparently returned to Chicago. Four years after that, he returned to England without his family. By 1861, he had renounced Unitarianism. He died in 1881. His estate was left to his former grammar school to establish a university scholarship, stipulating that funds should be distributed "irrespective of sex or creed or no creed, parentage, color, or caste, nationality or political allegiance."[68]

Adam was a restless and complex individual. He certainly believed in the superiority of Christianity. Adam had also given a great deal of thought to the ways in which a whole society might be reformed by education, and he supported both women's rights and the abolition of slavery. During his time in India, Adam became convinced that the indigenous population had to be included in the reform process in order to understand what they were capable of accomplishing on their own and could achieve in cooperation with British officials. Adam understood that radical reform entailed other social changes and that any change would have to be gradual.[69] Adam was, by all accounts, a difficult man. At some point during his time in Chicago, Adam's wife, Phebe, and children moved to Boston without him. She and her daughters lived there through the 1880s. In 1887, according to one account, a Bengali gentleman spent a pleasant afternoon visiting and reminiscing with Phebe Adam in her Boston home.[70] Regardless of his personal and professional failures, Adam helped shape abolitionists' plans for India as a source of free-labor goods. Recognizing Adam's role in shaping public discourse about British India in the 1830s and 1840s is an important step toward understanding the complicated role of British India in the boycott of slave-labor goods.

NOTES

1. Benjamin Robert Haydon, *Description of Haydon's Picture of the Great Meeting of Delegates; Held at the Freemasons' Tavern, June 1840, for the Abolition of Slavery and the Slave Trade throughout the World; Thomas Clarkson, President* (London: Printed by Charles Reynall, 1841); Catherine Hall, "The Lords of Humankind Re-visited," *Bulletin of the School of Oriental and African Studies* 66 (October 2003): 472–85; David Higgins, "Art, Genius, and Racial Theory in the Early Nineteenth Century: Benjamin Robert Haydon," *History Workshop Journal* 58 (Autumn 2004): 17–40. In 1880, the British and Foreign Anti-Slavery Society donated Haydon's painting to the National Portrait Gallery, London. See Benjamin Robert Haydon, *The Anti-Slavery Convention, 1840,* 1841, NPG 599, Primary Collection, National Portrait Gallery, London; *Key to The Anti-Slavery Convention, 1840, List of Sitters in the Painting by Benjamin Robert Haydon,* 1880, NPG D20517, Reference Collection, National Portrait Gallery, London; John Alfred Vinter, after Benjamin Robert Haydon, *"The Abolition of the Slave Trade" (The Anti-Slavery Society Convention, 1840),* c. 1846–64, NPG D20516, Reference Collection, National Portrait Gallery, London, all available online from http://www.npg.org.uk/

2. Ninety-two articles related to British India were published in the *Liberator* between 1839 and 1842, peaking in 1840 and 1841 with 42 and 34 articles, respectively. See also Elizabeth Kelly Gray, "Whisper to Him the Word 'India': Trans-Atlantic Critics and American Slavery, 1830–1860," *Journal of the Early Republic* 27 (2008): 385.

3. British and Foreign Anti-Slavery Society, *Proceedings of the General Anti-Slavery Convention Called by the Committee of the British and Foreign Anti-Slavery Society and Held in London from Friday, June 12th, to Tuesday, June 23rd, 1840* (London: British and Foreign Anti-Slavery Society, 1841), 77–86. See also Andrea Major, *Slavery, Abolitionism and Empire in India, 1772–1843* (Liverpool: Liverpool University Press, 2012), 321–24.

4. Dermot Killingley, *Rammohun Roy in Hindu and Christian Tradition: The Teape Lectures, 1990* (Newcastle upon Tyne, UK: Grevatt and Grevatt, 1993), 143.

5. S. C. Sanial, "The Rev. William Adam," *Bengal Past and Present: The Journal of the Calcutta Historical Society* 8 (1914): 251–72; Christopher Clark, *The Communitarian Moment: The Radical Challenge of the Northampton Association* (Ithaca: Cornell University Press, 1995), 26–28.

6. William Adam, "Reminiscences," *Liberty Bell*, January 1, 1844, 74.

7. Joseph DiBona, *One Teacher, One School: The Adam Reports on Indigenous Education in Nineteenth Century India* (New Delhi: Biblia Imprex Private, 1983), 6.

8. Clark, *Communitarian Moment*, 26.

9. William Adam to Maria Weston Chapman, November 5, 1839, in *British and American Abolitionists: An Episode in Transatlantic Understanding*, ed. Clare Taylor (Edinburgh: Edinburgh University Press, 1974), 86–87. For Adam's lecture tour, see William Adam to Maria Weston Chapman, November 5, 1839, in *British and American Abolitionists*, 86–87; William Adam to Maria Weston Chapman, December 5, 1839, MS.A.9.2.12.107, Anti-Slavery Collection, Boston Public Library, Boston. Adam's speech before the Massachusetts Anti-Slavery Society was included in the meeting's report published in the *Liberator*, February 5, 1840. The text of Adam's lecture was printed in the *Liberator*, February 14, 1840, and reprinted in the *Christian Register and Boston Observer*, March 7, 1840. See also William Adam, *Slavery in India: Paper Presented to the General Anti-Slavery Convention* (London: Thomas Ward and Co., 1840); William Adam, *The Law and Custom of Slavery in British India, in a Series of Letters to Thomas Fowell Buxton, Esq.* (London: Smith, Elder, and Co., 1840).

10. British and Foreign Anti-Slavery Society, *Proceedings*, 77–86, 90.

11. William Adam to Maria Weston Chapman, November 5, 1839, in *British and American Abolitionists*, 86–87. Emphasis in original.

12. S. Cromwell Crawford, *Ram Mohan Roy: Social, Political and Religious Reform in Nineteenth Century in India* (New York: Paragon House, 1987), 48–49; E. Daniel Potts, *British Baptist Missionaries in India, 1793–1837: The History of Serampore and Its Missions* (London: Cambridge University Press, 1967), 169–204.

13. Potts, *British Baptist Missionaries*, 23–26, 54–58, 169–204; Lynn Zastoupil, "Defining Christians, Making Britons: Rammohun Roy and the Unitarians," *Victorian Studies* 44 (Winter 2002): 226.

14. Anindita Ghosh, "Between Text and Reader: The Experience of Christian Missionaries in Bengal, 1800–1850," in *Free Print and Non-Commercial Publishing since 1700*, ed. James Raven (Burlington, VT: Ashgate, 2000), 163.

15. Potts, *Baptist Missionaries in India*, 54–61.

16. Potts, *Baptist Missionaries in India*, 23–26, 54–58, 169–204, 233–35; Killingley, *Rammohun Roy in Hindu and Christian Tradition*, 108.

17. Zastapouil, "Defining Christians, Making Britons," 226.

18. Sanial, "Rev. William Adam," 251.

19. Ghosh, "Between Text and Reader," 171–72; Sophia Dobson Collett, *The Life and Letters of Raja Rammohun Roy*, ed. Dilip Kumar Biswas and Prabhat Chandra Ganguli (Calcutta: Sadharan Brahmo Samaj, 1962), 121; William Adam, *Correspondence Relative to the Prospects of Christianity* (Cambridge: Hilliard and Metcalf, 1824), 7–11.

20. See, for example, Hem Chandra Sarkar, *Rammohun Roy, the Father of Modern India* (Calcutta: Sreemati Sakuntala Rao, 1910); Satis Chandra Chakravarti, *The Father of Modern India: Commemoration Volume of the Rammohun Roy Centenary Celebrations, 1935* (Calcutta: Rammohun Roy Centenary Committee, 1935); Bruce Carlisle Robertson, *Raja Rammohun Ray: The Father of Modern India* (New Delhi: Oxford University Press, 1995).

21. My usage of Rammohun Roy's name follows that of Lynn Zastoupil, who notes: "Rammohana Raya is the modern transliteration of [Rammohun Roy's] name, but I have left it the form which Rammohun used when signing his name in English, as do many scholars today. Current usage also favors 'Rammohun' as the short form, since, in his day, Roy or Raya was still seen as a title, not a name." Lynn Zastoupil, "'Notorious and Convicted Mutilators': Rammohun Roy, Thomas Jefferson, and the Bible," *Journal of World History* 20 (September 2009): 399.

22. Zastoupil, "'Notorious and Convicted Mutilators,'" 401; A. F. Salahuddin Ahmed, *Social Ideas and Social Change in Bengal* (Leiden: E. J. Brill, 1965), 26–35; William Adam, *A Lecture on the Life and Labours of Rammohun Roy*, ed. Rakhal-Das Haldar (Calcutta: Sadharan Brahmo Samaj, 1977), 7–10.

23. Lynn Zastoupil and Martin Moir, eds., *The Great Indian Education Debate: Documents Relating to the Orientalist-Anglicist Controversy, 1781–1843* (New York: Routledge, 1999), 15.

24. Adam, *Lecture on the Life and Labours of Rammohun Roy*, 3.

25. Zastoupil, "'Notorious and Convicted Mutilators,'" 402. See also Zastoupil, "Defining Christians, Making Britons," 220–24.

26. Rammohun Roy, *The Precepts of Jesus, the Guide to Peace and Happiness, Extracted from the Books of the New Testament Ascribed to the Four Evangelists. To Which Are Added, the First, Second, and Final Appeal to the Christian Public in Reply to the Observations of Dr. Marshman, of Serampore* (London: Unitarian Society, 1824), xxvii.

27. The discussion of the controversy surrounding Rammohun Roy, the Baptists, and *The Precepts of Jesus* is extensive. For some of the more helpful works, see Crawford, *Ram Mohan Roy*, 49–51; Killngley, *Ramohun Roy in Hindu and Christian Tradition*, 120–42; Potts, *British Baptist Missionaries in India*, 235–44; David Weir, *American Orient: Imagining the East from the Colonial Era through the Twentieth Century* (Amherst: University of Massachusetts Press, 2011), 54;

Zastoupil, "Defining Christians, Making Britons," 215–43; Zastoupil, "'Notorious and Convicted Mutilators,'" 399–434.

28. *Christian Register*, December 7, 1821.

29. As quoted in Killingley, *Rammohun Roy in Hindu and Christian Tradition*, 142. Emphasis mine.

30. Zastoupil, "'Notorious and Convicted Mutilators,'" 408. In 1824, the Unitarian Society in London published *The Precepts* and the three appeals as a single volume. See Rammohun Roy, *The Precepts of Jesus, the Guide to Peace and Happiness, Extracted from the Books of the New Testament Ascribed to the Four Evangelists. To Which Are Added, the First, Second, and Final Appeal to the Christian Public in Reply to the Observations of Dr. Marshman, of Serampore* (London: Unitarian Society, 1824).

31. *India Gazette*, May 1824. Adam's letter has been reprinted in its entirety in Jatindra Kumar Majumdar, ed., *Raja Rammohun Roy and Progressive Movements in India: A Selection from the Records (1774–1845)* (Calcutta: Brahmo Mission Press, 1941), 56–70.

32. Adam, *Correspondence Relative to the Prospects of Christianity*, 16.

33. William Adam to N. Wright, May 7, 1821, Collett, *Life and Letters of Raja Rammohun Roy*, 123.

34. [William Adam], *Letter from the Rev. William Adam, a Baptist Missionary in India, to His Brother in Great Britain, in Defence of His Own Conversion to Unitarianism* (Charleston, SC: W. Riley for the Unitarians Book Society, 1826), 6–7.

35. Andrew Hill, "William Adam, Unitarian Missionary," *Transactions of the Unitarian Historical Society* 21 (January 1995): 32.

36. William Adam, *Correspondence Relative to the Prospects of Christianity*, 11–16; Killingley, *Rammohun Roy in Hindu and Christian Tradition*, 108.

37. Collett describes the parting of Rammohun Roy and William Adam as "inevitable," citing irreconcilable theological differences. Adam remained "a devout and sincere *Christian missionary*" while Rammohun retained his deep connection to Hinduism. See Collett, *Life and Letters of Raja Rammohun Roy*, 242–47. Killingley describes the two men as "an ill-matched pair" and their cooperation in the Calcutta Unitarian Society "an alliance of expediency." Rammohun's and Adam's replies to Ware, in response to his questions about the prospects of missionary work in India, reflect "profound differences of method between them, just as there were between Adam and the Calcutta Baptists. Rammohun's replies are brief and general, and deal with aspirations more than with facts. . . . Adam's replies, by contrast, are detailed, wide-ranging, informative and practical" (Killingley, *Rammohun Roy in Hindu and Christian Tradition*, 146). Finally, Anathnath Basu notes that Rammohun paid the rent for the space Adam used to conduct Unitarian services: "All through his life Rammohun Roy was a good friend of Adam, he even provided for Adam and his family in his will" (Anathnath Basu, *Reports on the State of Education in Bengal [1835 and 1838]. Including Some Account of the State of Education in Bihar and a Consideration of the Means Adapted to the Improvement and Extension of Public Instruction in Both Provinces by William Adam* [Calcutta: University of Calcutta, 1941], xix).

38. Adam, *Lecture on the Life and Labours of Rammohun Roy*, 15.

39. Ghosh, "Between Text and Reader," 163, 169.

40. Ahemd, *Social Ideas and Social Change in Bengal*, 79; Killingley, *Rammohun Roy in Hindu and Christian Tradition*, 30–32.

41. See Charles Lushington to William Adam and Villiers Holcroft, Proprietors of the *Calcutta Chronicle*, May 31, 1827, and William Adam to Charles Lushington, May 31, 1827, both reprinted in Basu, *Reports on the State of Education in Bengal*, xix; DiBona, *One Teacher, One School*, 7.

42. Basu, *Reports on the State of Education in Bengal*, xix–xxi; Ahmed, *Social Ideas and Social Change in Bengal*, 66–67; DiBona, *One Teacher, One School*, 7.

43. DiBona, *One Teacher, One School*, 8; Basu, *Reports on the State of Education in Bengal*, xxii.

44. Ahmed, *Social Ideas and Social Change in Bengal*, 136–138; Basu, *Reports on the State of Education in Bengal*, xvi.

45. Ahmed, *Social Ideas and Social Change in Bengal*, 137.

46. Basu, *Reports on the State of Education in Bengal*, xxiii.

47. Ibid., xxiv.

48. DiBona, *One Teacher, One School*, 9–11. DiBona reprints Adam's education reports in their entirety.

49. Zastoupil, *Great Indian Education Debate*, 59.

50. Douglas H. Maynard, "The World's Anti-Slavery Convention of 1840," *The Mississippi Valley Historical Review* 47 (December 1960): 452–55; Betty Fladeland, *Men and Brothers: Anglo-American Antislavery Cooperation* (Urbana: University of Illinois Press, 1972), 195–256; *Liberator*, October 11, 1839.

51. S. R. Mehrotra, "The British India Society and Its Bengal Branch, 1839–1846," *Indian Economic and Social History Review* 4 (Summer 1967): 131; Anne Stoddart, *Elizabeth Pease Nichol* (London: J. M. Dent and Co., 1899), 72; Kenneth D. Nworah, "The Aborigines' Protection Society, 1889–1909: A Pressure-Group in Colonial Policy," *Canadian Journal of African Studies* 5, no. 1 (1971): 79–81.

52. Stoddart, *Elizabeth Pease Nichol*, 73–79.

53. Stoddart, *Elizabeth Pease Nichol*, 85; John Hyslop Beel, *British Folks and British India Fifty Years Ago: Joseph Pease and His Contemporaries* (London: John Heywood, 1891), 61; DiBona, *One Teacher, One School*, 11.

54. Bell, *British Folks and British India*, 62–64; Stoddart, *Elizabeth Pease Nichol*, 89–90; *Speeches Delivered at a Public Meeting, for the Formation of a British India Society; Held at Freemasons' Hall, Saturday, July 6th, 1839* (London: Printed for the British India Society, 1839), 67. The British India Society was one of three organizations established by British abolitionists in 1839. The other two organizations were the British and Foreign Anti-Slavery Society and the African Civilization Society (ACS). Together these three groups clarified British abolitionists' decision, after emancipation in 1838, to focus their reform energies on the abolition of slavery in the United States. Buxton was the primary organizer of the ACS, which pledged to eradicate the foreign slave trade and promote legitimate commerce, education, and Christianity in Africa. See Clare Midgley, *Women against*

Slavery: The British Campaigns, 1780–1870 (London: Routledge, 1992), 121–22.

55. *Speeches Delivered at a Public Meeting, for the Formation of a British India Society*, 14.

56. *George Thompson, Lectures on British India, Delivered in the Friends' Meeting-House in Manchester, England, in October 1839, with an Introduction by William Lloyd Garrison* (Pawtucket, RI: William and Robert Adams, 1840).

57. Ninety-two articles related to British India were published in the *Liberator* between 1839 and 1842, peaking in 1840 and 1841 with 42 and 34 articles respectively. See Gray, "Whisper to Him the Word 'India,'" 385.

58. William Adam to Maria Weston Chapman, November 5, 1839, in *British and American Abolitionists*, 86–87.

59. Edward M. Davis to Elizabeth Pease, December 11, 1839, MS.A.1.2.8.89, ASC BPL.

60. British and Foreign Anti-Slavery Society, *Proceedings of the General Anti-Slavery Convention*, 77–86. See also, Major, *Slavery, Abolitionism and Empire*, 321–24.

61. Ibid., 90.

62. Ibid., 437–47. Emphasis in the original.

63. Ibid., 447–54.

64. Elizabeth Pease to J. A. Collins, undated; Elizabeth Pease to Anne Warren Weston, June 24, 1841; and Elizabeth Pease to unknown, February 28, 1842, all in *British and American Abolitionists*, 140, 154, 169–70. William Bassett to Elizabeth Pease, April 25, 1842, MS.A. 1.2.12.2.46, Anti-Slavery Collection, Boston Public Library; Mehrotra, "British India Society and Its Bengal Branch," 139–42; Malcolm Chase, *Chartism: A New History* (Manchester: Manchester University Press, 2007): 158–60.

65. Clark, *Communitarian Moment*, 15, 26–29.

66. Christopher Clark, "A Mother and Her Daughters at the Northampton Community: New Evidence on Women in Utopia," *The New England Quarterly* 75 (2002): 598; William Bassett to Elizabeth Pease, July 22, 1844, MS.A.1.2.14.44, Anti-Slavery Collection, Boston Public Library. See also Clark, *Communitarian Moment*; Christopher Clark and Kerry W. Buckley, eds., *Letters from an American Utopia: The Stetson Family and the Northampton Association, 1843–1847* (Amherst: University of Massachusetts Press, 2004).

67. Clark, *Communitarian Moment*, 130–32.

68. Andrew Hill, "William Adam," *Dictionary of Unitarian and Universalist Biography*, 2000, http://uudb.org/articles/williamadam.html

69. Zastoupil, *Great Indian Education Debate*, 61; Clark, *Communitarian Moment*, 29.

70. Hill, "William Adam, Unitarian Minister," 38–39.

5

"The Ties That Bind"

Dallas, Lancashire, and the Cotton Trade

Tom Aiello

Cotton, an innocuous member of the plant kingdom, proved to be both a boon and a curse to those who sought to profit from its production. For centuries, cloth produced from cotton fibers remained a sought-after luxury item. The advent of the Industrial Revolution changed all that, bringing phenomenal wealth to a few and backbreaking toil and misery to most. For the emerging capitalist industrial system, the mechanization of cotton cloth production was the key to successful industrialization. Great Britain led the way in this process and rode a tidal wave of cotton cloth production to the economic dominance of the globe in the nineteenth century. No other commodity played a greater role in the ultimate success of industrial capitalism. The transformation of the Lancashire cotton industry from the domestic system to the factory system beginning in the late eighteenth century had worldwide repercussions. The 1851 British census showed 250,000 workers in the cotton textile industry of the Lancashire district.[1] By 1911 this figure stood at 600,000, representing an increase of 71 percent in six decades. This vast increase in the industry called for massive amounts of raw cotton, amounts that the area around Dallas, Texas, stood ready to supply at the end of the nineteenth century.

The economic and cultural links created from the flow of cotton fiber to the Lancashire textile mills formed a transatlantic bond that helped to shape the Atlantic World and transformed the lives of millions in that world. In the latter stages of that process, a transatlantic link was forged between Dallas and the Lancashire mills. As a result, Dallas's Lancashire relationship transformed the region surrounding Dallas, caused a shift in the agricultural sector from food crops to cotton, and therefore oriented the North Texas economy toward the city and the transatlantic cotton trade. It also set Dallas on a different economic path from that of

Fort Worth, Dallas's chief urban rival in North Texas. Fort Worth went on to become the leading granary and beef-processing center in the region, whereas Dallas dominated the area's cotton trade.

This process changed the city as well as the lives of those who were in the city and the vast hinterland around the city. As one economic historian put it six decades ago, "The Anglo-American partnership transcended the facts of economic geography. The North Atlantic trade merely provided the underpinning for a complex structure of social relationships which bound together important elements in the northern United States and Great Britain into a single community."[2] Although this statement referred to the creation of the Atlantic World linking the communities bordering the Atlantic Ocean in the nineteenth century, it also applies to Dallas, far in the US interior, at a much later stage.

During the early period of the transatlantic cotton trade between the United States and Great Britain, the relationship rested on two interconnected economies. The central fact in the growth of the Atlantic community was an informal partnership between the American and British peoples. The American Revolution did not alter the fundamental economic and social relationship across the Atlantic. The American frontier was, in a very real sense, one of the frontiers of the British Empire.

The American cotton crop was worth £2 million in 1791. In the ensuing decades, the size of the crop increased five hundred–fold to £1 billion in 1860. During this period, the cotton crop accounted for half of the total value of American exports with no other commodity coming close.[3] Paul Mantoux, who undertook the first comprehensive study of the Industrial Revolution in the eighteenth century, noted that "the rapid transformation in the cotton industry, wrought by a succession of technical inventions, made it the earliest and also the classical example of modern large-scale industry."[4]

The United States assumed the role of Britain's main source of raw cotton by 1803. It then defeated successive attempts by Britain to develop alternate sources of supply. The United States used its overwhelming ability to export the best quality product, in massive quantities, and at the lowest price to drive all potential rivals out of the world market. This period involved two complementary economies. From 1820 to 1860, half of American exports went to Great Britain, whereas 40 percent of its imports came from there. Of the foreign tonnage entering US ports in 1860, 80 percent was British. The most important element of this trade was textiles, which, according to R. G. Albion, "towered above all else in the world commerce of the day."[5] In the middle of this period, following Texas independence in 1836, Southern planters and their slaves moved to Texas in large numbers, settling in the fertile land of the Brazos, Trinity, Colorado, and Red Rivers. For the next two decades, American newspapers described the enormous fortunes to be made in Texas cotton and encouraged what came to be known as "Texas Fever." Thousands of cotton planters caught the fever, selling their lands and moving to a new cotton frontier.

Dallas followed a long road to the top of the cotton spot market. It started down the path to joining Atlantic World in 1851, with the building of the city's first cotton gin. In subsequent decades, Dallas emerged as one of the great cotton centers of the world and from time to time the world's largest spot, as opposed to futures, market for that important commodity. Not a little of the success in eventually linking Dallas to international trade and fueling Texas fever was the early effort of boosters who touted the possibilities of economic development in Texas.

One individual stands out in this arena, Jacob De Cordova. Born in Spanish Town, Jamaica, in June 1808, he eventually moved to Philadelphia where he married into wealth. His good education served him well. He spoke English, Spanish, Hebrew, French, and German fluently, and possessed talents as a writer and public speaker. After starting his business career as a New Orleans merchant, he migrated to Galveston in 1837 where he eventually became a US citizen. De Cordova then moved to Houston, where he created a business and political empire. He served as the Harris County representative to the Second Legislature of Texas. While serving, he continued to amass landholdings and became influential first in the politics of the Republic, and later in state politics.[6] De Cordova was largely instrumental in building the first cotton mill in Texas at New Braunfels; he secured the spinners, weavers, and machinery for that mill, which operated for a number of years. At one time he owned more than a million acres of land in Texas. He was founder of the city of Waco, having laid out that city in 1849, and donated the land for a city park, several churches and offered city lots for sale at remarkably low prices.[7]

In February 1852, De Cordova published a series of articles entitled "Leaves from the Notebook of the Wanderer." Four years later, in 1856, he wrote to his brother about his new book: "I am publishing the Texian Immigrant and Travelers Guide Book to retail at 30 cts. each without the map. This Guide Book will be a re-hash of my old Book with considerable additional material. I intend to print of the first edition but a single thousand for I shall enlarge it very much in the second edition."[8] By 1858, Cordova was the recognized authority on Texas. In the spring of that year he delivered several lectures up and down the East Coast of the United States promoting the future of the state. One of these talks was given at the annual meeting of the New York Geographical Society. At this point, he emerged as a pioneer in the development of the cotton industry in Texas and as a pioneer in forging a link between Great Britain and Texas.

At the invitation of the Cotton Supply Association of Manchester, England, Cordova traveled to England in late September 1858 to present his lecture "The Cultivation of Cotton in Texas" at Manchester's Town Hall. It proved so popular that he stayed for another two weeks and presented it again in mid-October. Cordova later returned to talk to other English audiences about prospects in Texas. Largely as a result of these talks, British mills started buying 90 percent of the cotton grown in Texas. This created a template for post–Civil War development in Dallas among both city boosters and the members of the cotton trade.[9] While Cordova was making his transatlantic connections, the Texas population grew from 212,592 in 1850 to 604,215 in 1860, representing a 184 percent increase during the decade. Cotton production during the same period climbed from 58,161 bales to 431,463 bales, making for an astounding 642 percent increase.[10] This increase, however, still represented only a small portion of the country's total production, the center of which still lay in the black fertile soil, known as the Black Belt, of the American Southeast.

Textile exports made up 60 percent of the value of all British exports at that time. The cotton trade made New York the pre–Civil War apex of the famous cotton triangle and was responsible for Liverpool's economic preeminence in Atlantic trade for the bulk of the nineteenth century. Cotton goods salesmen from Lancashire established as export-import merchants in New York "took the chief hand in shaping the pattern of transatlantic commerce and shipping."[11]

By the time of the outbreak of the American Civil War in 1861, the proportion of the raw material exported from the United States to Britain grew to 80 percent. In that same year, the United States produced two-thirds of the world's cotton and supplied more than three-quarters of all the raw material in the world trade system. At this time, total cotton imports in Europe reached 4.84 million 400–pound bales, an average of

93,000 per week of which the United States supplied 4.01 million bales, or 83.9 percent of the total. A year later, after the start of the war, only 102,000 US bales reached Europe, accounting for only 7 percent of total European cotton imports. This collapse of the trade set the stage for both Texas and Dallas to enter the Atlantic World.

After the war, the worldwide flow of cotton resumed, but not without major changes in the market. Cotton farmers once again flocked to the Texas frontier, with production sweeping westward across the Grand Prairie, the Cross Timbers, and on to the Rolling Plains.[12] One of the most important developments proved to be the completion of the transatlantic telegraph cable, in 1866, which eased communication between the New York and British markets in Liverpool. The ability to communicate at rapid speed led the New York Cotton Exchange to specialize in the trading of cotton futures. The opening of the Suez Canal in 1869 in conjunction with the increased use of steamships for American export cotton reduced the number of bales at sea by increasing the speed of commerce, providing an example of what Karl Marx termed "the annihilation of space through time."[13]

At this time, growing foreign demand for cotton contributed to price speculation, which became so intense that speculators began buying cotton for future arrival as well as cotton on the spot. This led to the establishment of the futures market for cotton. The New York Cotton Exchange, founded in 1871, led the field for obvious economic reasons, being the financial center of the country. Many well-known financial firms gained their start in the cotton trade including Merrill, Lynch, Pierce, Fenner and Beane (later Smith). The firm started as Fenner and Beane, with its original offices in New Orleans and later Dallas in the 1920s. Lehman Brothers also began as a cotton-trading firm in the state of Mississippi before moving to New York. The increasing use of futures contracts and, most significantly, the reentry of King Cotton into the world market after the American Civil War, renewed the expansion of the Cotton Belt, especially to Texas, and led to a tripling of US cotton exports in the period 1872–91.

Despite a prolonged economic depression in the period 1873–90, this period also witnessed a growing connection between Dallas and Lancashire. By 1885, Dallas had become the major inland spot market and shipping point both in the Cotton Belt and the United States. Its dominance is partly explained by its close working relationship with Great Britain, as manifested by the presence of a growing number of Britons who moved to the city to take up cotton trading. The economic and cultural connection that resulted ensured that Dallas remained a major player in the international cotton trade linking the city to the Lancashire textile district in the heart of industrial Great Britain. Britain became the major beneficiary of the fall in the price of American cotton, which lost its power of attraction as an investment for capital. At the end of this depressed period, the state of Texas surged to the forefront of cotton production, with the city of Dallas playing a pivotal role.

On all sides of Dallas, farmers worked rich, productive soil. The soil of Dallas County and surrounding counties proved to be a most valuable physical asset. The productivity of the black waxy clay was high, partly because it was rich in lime. Here was the major source of prosperity in the four decades after the Civil War. Dallas served as the farmers' staging area for marketing and distributing their crops, especially cotton. Within a 150-mile radius these farmers were growing one-sixth of the entire world's cotton crop. In servicing its surrounding agricultural hinterland, Dallas became the world's leader in manufacturing cotton gin machinery, saddlery, and harness equipment.

Britons arrived early in the area's history and paved the way for the later success of the city and the cotton business. George Mifflin Dallas, who many believe is the man after whom the city was named, came from the village of Dallas in the Scottish Highlands.[14] George Dallas's journey to Texas prior to the Civil War augured a steady flow of British immigrants to the city after the war.

The first wave of British cotton traders in Dallas began arriving to foster the trade in the 1880s. Henry Lee Edwards was one of those who had a long-lasting impact in Dallas. Born in Presteigne, Wales, he was the son of a Welsh farmer. Several bad harvests led him to London, from which he emigrated to Texas ranchlands in 1880s.[15] He lived in Dallas for fifty-eight years after originally failing in his attempt to become a sheep rancher in Llano County. He turned to milking cows, peeling potatoes, and other ranch chores before moving to Paris, Texas, in Lamar County. While there, he managed an ice factory and studied the cotton business. Edwards first entered the cotton trade as a partner in the firm H. L. Edwards & Company of Greenville, Texas. The firm moved to Dallas in 1889. After that, he made annual trips to England and Continental Europe, and he was "well known in every foreign and domestic cotton market in the world."[16]

Edwards eventually joined the boards of directors of First National

Bank in Dallas, the Arthur A. Everts Company, and the Texas Bithulithic Company; he also became a member of the Liverpool Cotton Association and the New York Cotton Exchange. Moreover, he joined the Dallas Cotton Exchange, Dallas Manufacturers' Association, and the Dallas Chamber of Commerce. His brother, James Edwards, introduced him to the game of golf during one of his trips to England in the 1890s. He later became known as the father of golf in Dallas and is credited with inaugurating the game in the city. Along with R. E. Potter, he laid out the city's first golf course, a six-hole affair in the Oak Lawn neighborhood. They circled the greens with barbed wire to keep out livestock, buried tin cans for cups, and had balls shipped in from Boston. He also helped to pioneer the game of tennis in the city.

John Randolph Hoey, another British cotton agent, lived in Dallas for almost half his life.[17] Born in Liverpool in 1885, he joined the cotton firm of Merrifield Ziegler and Company prior to the outbreak of World War I. During the war, he served in France with King Edward's Horse Regiment. He returned to Merrifield Ziegler after the war and was sent to the firm's Dallas office as manager. When his company ceased operations in 1945, he joined the Dallas office of O'Donnell Brothers, a New York cotton firm. Because Hoey was a long-time member of the Dallas Cotton Exchange, the exchange honored him when his company closed by granting him full floor privileges.

By 1890, Texas was leading the nation in cotton production. This production remained the major development in the Texas economy from the end of the Civil War to 1914. By 1900, Texas produced one-third of the nation's crop and Galveston captured the lead as the nation's number-one cotton port. Dallas played a central role in these developments. Its population growth went hand in hand with its economic growth. In 1870, the city had 2,960 residents. By 1892, the population stood at 63,645, representing a twentyfold increase in the span of a generation.[18]

Following in the tradition of De Cordova, Dallas city boosters continued to extol and promote the economic growth of the city and the control of its surrounding region. City boosters played a major role in encouraging that growth and helped to strengthen Dallas's connection to the world cotton market. The 1892 *Memorial and Biographical History of Dallas County, Texas* smugly proclaimed that "it has been the pleasure of a few of these pioneers to behold their little village nestling on the east banks of the Trinity transformed into a most magnificent city . . . the metropolis of the Southwest."[19] That same year another booster, Paul Giraud, secretary of the Commercial club of Dallas, zealously proclaimed, "The growth of the City of Dallas the past two years is one of the wonders of the age."[20] He supported this prolix contention by noting that for the previous twenty-five years the city's population had doubled every four years and predicted continued phenomenal growth for Dallas. The booster's prediction of future success rested on its success in the agricultural sector, with the booster pronouncing, "First, the foundations of the City are laid in the center of one of the largest and richest agricultural areas in the civilized world."[21] By the 1895–96 cotton season, Texas held 28 percent of all the cotton acreage in the nation and produced 32 percent of all the cotton bales in the country.[22]

By this time, the area of North Texas centered on Dallas contained more than one-third of the state's population, produced more than one-third of the Texas cotton crop, and was responsible for the bulk of the corn, wheat, lumber, iron, and coal in the state. "Although data on investments are none too accurate," stated economist John S. Spratt, "probably as much as one-fourth of the state's $90,000,000 industrial structure for 1900 was invested in cotton."[23] By the end of the nineteenth century, an area that eventually encompassed more than 40 percent of the nation's cotton production formed in northeastern Texas, southeastern Oklahoma, southern Arkansas, and western Louisiana. At the center of this region, serving as its nerve center, sat the city of Dallas. Businessmen in the city established relationships with the cotton farmers, and then handled the marketing, sale, and shipment of the raw material. This served as a major catalyst for the development of the city's and the state's manufacturing base. With the development of the rich, black lands surrounding Dallas and the improvement of transportation and communication facilities, by the early 1900s Dallas vied with New Orleans, Memphis, Vicksburg, and other Mississippi Valley markets in importance as a marketing center of the money crop of the Southland on the international market.

At the same time, on the other side of the Atlantic, and for the previous 150 years, the Lancashire textile district held the same primacy in the cotton spinning and manufacturing trade as in the production of the raw material by the American Cotton Belt.[24] By 1906, Lancashire held 48,322,684 cotton spindles, 684,611 looms, and 90 new spinning mills with 8,026,356 spindles, of which 74 percent were devoted to processing raw cotton from the United States. The leaders of the Liverpool Cotton

Association dominated the sale of Dallas cotton to manufacturers, buying and selling for their clients every bale landed in Liverpool, it being said that "cotton cannot be discharged from a ship in that city unless it is to be disposed of through a broker member of that association."[25] One Dallas observer declared that cotton "in truth is the most important trade in the world, as well as the largest."[26]

Cause for continued optimism did not just stem from the exploitation of the area's natural resources and the concomitant industrial growth. It was also the result of the development of a rationalized North Texas cotton market. In 1905, only seven firms handled cotton trading in Dallas. This changed within two years, and the change brought forth a bonanza for those middlemen who bought the raw material from North Texas farmers and sold it to Lancashire. Although the Dallas-Lancashire link became firmly established, Lancashire's primacy in the British economy was waning. Even so, its textile production still amounted to more than a third of Great Britain's exports in 1906.

Dallas business leaders now benefited from developments elsewhere to put their relationship on a more equitable footing with Lancashire and other markets in the United States. Charges of unethical practices in cotton futures trading, especially on the New York Cotton Exchange, led to a number of government investigations into price-fixing. The unethical business practices uncovered by several US Department of Agriculture investigations helped to spur the creation of the Dallas Cotton Exchange in 1907. Although New York continued to lead the way overall, especially in futures trading, the Dallas Cotton Exchange eventually developed into the largest spot market in the world. It also contributed to the increasingly dense network of transatlantic ties that united the Atlantic World in the first quarter of the twentieth century.

The Dallas Cotton Exchange was originally composed of twenty-two full members and sixteen associate members, together with supporting elements of the shipping business—futures brokers, foreign exchange dealers, foreign buyers' representatives, and insurance specialists. The purpose of the exchange was to supply members with up-to-date market quotations, rules and regulations for the trade, weather reports, and other conditions affecting the cotton crop. These included estimates of acreage, production and consumption figures, and the establishment of affiliations with markets around the world. The transatlantic affiliation oftentimes proved contentious, and almost from the exchange's birth it became embroiled in disputes with its customers across the Atlantic. The Dallas Cotton Exchange, however, possessed a key advantage in establishing transatlantic business relationships and dealing with disputes, that is, many of its original members came from the exchange's most important market, Great Britain.

The Dallas Cotton Exchange had British roots. Arthur H. Cleaver, an Englishman, was one of four founding members of the organization. The exchange, created to rationalize the Dallas cotton market, also helped settle disputes about price and quality between Texas sellers of raw cotton and the chief consumer of that cotton, the Lancashire textile district across the Atlantic. Roger L. Dixon, another Briton, later made significant contributions to resolving some of these disputes, eventually succeeding to the presidency of the Dallas Cotton Exchange. Of all the English cotton men who came to Dallas, Cleaver remains perhaps the most important and the one who set the tone for those who followed. A native of Neston, Cheshire, England, he came to Dallas in 1906 and founded the firm of Campbell, Cleaver & Company.[27] Cleaver's firm, one of the first British cotton trading firms in Dallas, became one of the earliest to export cotton abroad from the city. In 1907, Cleaver, along with E. T. Webster, M. H. Wolfe, and Mike H. Thomas, saw the need for an organization to govern cotton trading. As a result of their deliberations, these four men, joined by twenty-five others, started the Dallas Cotton Exchange in the basement of the Old Scollard Court building. From those humble beginnings, the Dallas Cotton Exchange went from the basement room to a seventeen-story skyscraper in 1926 and from a buy-in fee for a seat on the exchange of $100 in 1907 to $2,500 sixteen years later.[28]

Dallas as the center of the "Magic Circle," 1892.

The cultural influence of the English arrivals became manifest within a few years of the founding of the exchange in the form of the sporting life. British members of the Dallas Cotton Exchange played "an interesting game between the teams of the Dallas Cotton Exchange Cricket Club," in 1913.[29] In a match between the Married Men's team and the Single Men's team, the singles trounced the married men 66 to 31. Cricket spread to other playing fields of Dallas in 1933, largely as a result of the English influence in the Dallas Cotton Exchange. In July of that year, members of the local cotton trade reintroduced the "traditional sport of the old country to Dallas."[30] Teams representing the Dallas Cotton Exchange and the Oak Lawn neighborhood two decades later met on July 9 in a cricket match at Southern Methodist University field on Turtle Creek Boulevard. The previous 1913 match seems to have been considered a "pick-up" match and the 1933 affair is thought to be the first official cricket match ever held in the city. The team representing Oak Lawn bested the Dallas Cotton Exchange team 40 to 33, despite the presence of many prominent members of the exchange team captained by J. R. Hoey. A rematch followed on July 16, and the events became a regular recreational staple for members of the Dallas cotton trade until the outbreak of World War II.

The period after the Great War witnessed a steady stream of British cotton traders into the city, including people such as Robert Hannay, from Delgany Ireland, who served as a captain in the Irish Guards of the British Army from 1915–19 and eventually came to Dallas.[31] He arrived in the United States in 1919 and worked in the cotton business in Memphis, Tennessee, and New Orleans, Louisiana, before settling in Dallas in 1920. He established the Hannay-O'Donnell cotton firm. An active member

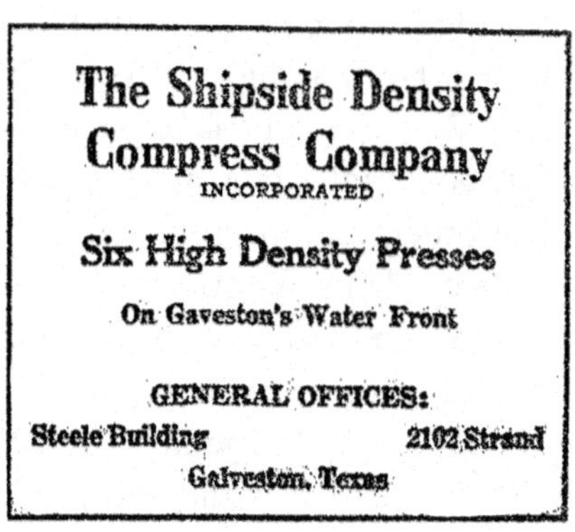

Galveston, Dallas's outlet to the Atlantic World.

of the Dallas Cotton Exchange, Hannay served as president of Hannay-O'Donnell before later establishing the Hannay Brothers cotton trading firm by bringing his brothers across the Atlantic to take part in the Dallas cotton boom of the 1920s. Hannay stayed in Dallas for the next four decades, rising to the presidency of the Dallas Cotton Exchange and later becoming president of the Dallas Cotton Shippers Association.[32]

Harry Holden, another veteran of the Great War, came to Dallas to pursue his fortune in 1919. Holden, born in Oldham, England, at the very center of the English textile industry, served in the Royal Flying Corps during the war and afterward went to work for the British Cotton Agency in Dallas. He spent the better part of two decades crisscrossing the Atlantic, buying Texas cotton and selling it in Lancashire. He later moved on to the firm of Affleck & Moss before entering into a partnership with the McClary & Holden Company, headquartered in Dallas.[33]

William E. Woolley, a native of Cheshire, England, experienced the war at sea, having survived the Battle of Jutland in 1916. After the war, he came to Dallas in search of work and utilized the already extant network of English businessmen in the city to enter the cotton trade. Another Briton and native of Liverpool recommended Woolley for the job of cotton classer, and he joined R. L. Dixon & Bros. in 1920.[34] He quickly rose to the position of cotton broker, serving in that capacity for fifteen years until 1935. In that year, he moved to São Paulo, Brazil, acting as a coffee exporter in the Dixon firm's new venture into another agricultural commodity. People such as Woolley thrived at the Dixon firm and helped to create the idea of the "English Colony in Dallas."

Men such as H. Arundel Bell also played an important role in both the cotton trade and the Dallas cultural scene in the 1920s. A native of Liverpool, Bell graduated from the University of Cambridge and came to the United States as a correspondent for a London paper to cover General John H. Pershing's 1916 expedition into Mexico to suppress Pancho Villa.[35] Bell also contributed some articles to the *Dallas Morning News* before going into the cotton business in Cleburne, Texas. He established Bell Brothers Company in Dallas during the late 1920s and maintained an active role in the firm for the next two decades. More important for the Dallas cultural scene, Bell helped organize the Dallas Little Theatre. He acted in many of its productions, playing such roles as Doolittle in *Pygmalion* and Scrooge in *A Christmas Carol.* Also a charter member of the Dallas Country Club and the University Club, Bell played a signifi-

The Dallas Cotton Exchange Building, circa 1912.

cant role in the success of Southern Methodist University and provides another example of the English influence on the development of Dallas society in the 1920s.

Harry A. Buff made a significant contribution to the city's cultural life. Buff, born in Preston, Cheshire, England, came to Dallas in 1907. He worked as a representative for the Liverpool cotton merchants Woods & Thorburn and crisscrossed the Atlantic in his capacity as an agent for the firm.[36] When World War I broke out, Buff returned to England and joined the West Lancashire Regiment, serving as a gunner in several major engagements. Buff returned to Dallas in 1919, where he took up the cotton business again, actively engaging in amateur dramatics. Buff, like H. Arundel Bell, helped establish the Little Theatre of Dallas and earned a prominent role in the long-playing *On Approval*, written by English dramatist Frederick Lonsdale.

Of all of these men's careers, perhaps none was more interesting than that of Roger L. Dixon. A native of Preston, England, Dixon was born into the transatlantic cotton trade. His father and two uncles made up the management team of Dixon Brothers of Liverpool.[37] This firm also maintained an office in New Orleans at the turn of the century. The Dixons, however, labored in the shadow of the McFadden firm that dominated the industry on both sides of the Atlantic at the time. Seeking greener pastures,

Roger L. Dixon, along with his brother Hugo and a cousin, Bill, moved to Dallas from Great Britain early in the twentieth century. They played a prominent role in the city's cotton trade and its social life while maintaining a foothold on the other side of the Atlantic. Dixon immigrated to the United States in 1910. He started his own cotton marketing business in Waco and in 1912 moved the business to Bowie in Montague County.[38] The outbreak of the Great War saw Roger answer his native country's call, and in September 1914 he returned to England and received an officers' commission in the Royal Artillery. Dixon later described his close call with death when "a fragment of the shell struck the floorboard between my knees and another through the lid of my service cap. I had a very close escape."[39]

Dixon's unit finished the war in Valenciennes, France, and from there he went to Cologne by train and joined the Army of Occupation. Because he had returned from the United States to join the army, the British government paid his fare from Texas to Liverpool and put him in line for quick demobilization. In February 1919, Dixon returned to England, traveling three days in a boxcar to Calais and then across to Dover by ferry. There he was demobilized, paid a £7 Separation Fee, and was sent on his way with a souvenir, noting, "I also carried back a very good German Mauser."[40] He traveled on a transport with three thousand troops who had the same experience. The mayor of New York and fireboats celebrated the ship's return. After spending a few days with his sister Hope in New York, he returned by train to Texas and the Dallas cotton business.

While Roger Dixon served in France, his brother Hugo spent four years in a German prison camp for enemy aliens after being trapped in Germany when war was declared in August 1914. The Dixon brothers' cousin Bill served in the Coldstream Guards during the war, and was invalided out of the service because of the effects of mustard gas. Determined to reestablish his cotton-trading firm, Roger returned to Liverpool in late 1919 to search for a competent cotton classer. While in Liverpool, he hired William Woolley, "a young man recommended to me who had been a signaler at Jutland."[41]

The brothers chose the booming cotton center of Dallas as the locale for R. L. Dixon and Bros. where they joined the Dallas Cotton Exchange. Accompanied by his brother Hugo, Roger Dixon returned to Texas in early 1920. In July 1920, the Dixons arrived in Dallas and stayed at the Adolphus Hotel while looking for an office to lease. While there, the Dixons made the acquaintance of Freddie Lloyd, a cotton trader from Liverpool who knew many people in Dallas. Lloyd gained the Dixons entrée into Dallas high society and endorsed their application to join the Dallas Country Club. When the brothers finally found a modest office for their firm that fit their meager budget, Roger Dixon described it as follows:

> Our first office was on the third floor over the Elite Café on Main St. There was a large room in front for a general office and another large room in the back with a skylight for a sampler room. There was a bay window in our office which looked up and down Main St. A dance hall occupied the second floor, and lovers [occupied] the stairs of our building.[42]

While trying to establish their business in such a morally challenging climate, the Dixons divided their duties, which Roger Dixon described as "Hugo in charge of the office and selling; I was in charge of buying and classing."[43]

The firm soon hired Edgar Kucera, who stayed with the firm for the next fifty years, eventually rising to become president of the company. Roger Dixon described Kucera as "very sound of judgment, he started at the bottom, moved on to bookkeeper, and then into higher jobs."[44] Dixon attributed the firm's ensuing early success to his previous wartime service. He noted, "I think because I moved back to England and joined the army, I received quite additional support from my customers in Liverpool. They sent me a good many orders which I was able to fill successfully, and I had a very good season."[45]

Although people from all over the world came to Dallas and Texas, it was the British connection that had the most impact on the city and state. The Dallas Woman's Forum sponsored a visit to the city by Sir John Foster Fraser in January 1920.[46] Fraser first visited the United States in 1918 to talk about his war experiences as part of aiding the Liberty Loan drive. A native of Scotland and for many years a globetrotting newspaper correspondent, Fraser lectured at the city's Unitarian Church on postwar international relations and his travels through the countries that had an important role in world affairs. The Woman's Forum sold tickets to the event through the city's major department stores as a means to raise funds for a completely new clubhouse on South Akard Street. Other city leaders also sponsored international visitors to Dallas.

Founded in 1920, the Little Theatre resulted from the British connection and became a Dallas cultural institution. Several times in the 1920s it won the national Belasco Cup, which was awarded to the best amateur theater company in the United States. Harold Brighouse, a distinguished English playwright, visited Dallas and San Antonio in 1928. Brighouse, whose father was a Manchester businessman, received his education at Manchester Grammar School before leaving at the age of sixteen to work in the cotton trade. His experiences in that business colored the rest of his prolific writing career. Brighouse wrote more than seventy plays, mostly comedies about the people and events of the Lancashire textile district where he had grown up and learned the cotton business. His best-known work, *Hobson's Choice* (1915), was the story of an irascible, self-pitying shop owner. He noted the enthusiastic support that the Little Theatre received, and he referred to an article in *Dallas*, the official publication of the city's chamber of commerce, to make the case that "a point is that in Dallas there is a vibrant community of Englishmen and women who support the arts." He asserted that such a state of affairs, "as every amateur society knows, is phenomenal."[47]

Brighouse recounted his journey for an English audience in the *Manchester Guardian*. He attempted to dispel the notion of backwardness fostered by the late Sir Edmund Gosse, who had alluded to Austin, the capital of Texas, as "a little town on the Mexican border and therefore an odd destination for an important library." He referred to Gosse's quote as only relevant to "the older Texas . . . the new Texas is Austin, Fort Worth, San Antonio, and Dallas which is modern, skyscraping, with factories and cotton mills." Of all the Texas cities, Dallas seemed to impress the English playwright the most. He commented, "Dallas was capable of inducing an inferiority complex in a Londoner coming to it from a foggy night in a Pullman." Brighouse remained confused, however, by Dallas's propensity for skyscrapers, asking rhetorically, "Why, in a state of spaces, they should it imitate an architecture made necessary by New York's physical condition, I cannot say." Brighouse went out of his way to visit the city not, however, for its architectural impressiveness, but for its growing importance as a cultural center in the Southwest: "What took me to Dallas, an eight-hour side trip from my westbound Southern Pacific route was precisely culture, and Dallas, if only for its Little Theater, has cultural significance."[48] The Little Theatre can be seen as "a springboard for the regional and community theater networks that emerged in later decades."[49]

As a result of Brighouse's strong support for the Little Theatre, a number of British amateur actors performed in its productions. G. N. Mathews, a former British Army officer and Texas manager for the Cunard shipping lines, appeared there in March and April 1930.[50] Mathews came to the United States in 1917 as training officer for the Royal Flying Corps. Stationed at Fort Hicks, near Fort Worth, for the greater part of World War I, Mathews returned to the area in 1924. He later played the role of "Gentleman Johnny" Burgoyne, the British general whose defeat at Saratoga, New York, helped turn the tide of the Revolutionary War in favor of the Americans, in the George Bernard Shaw play *The Devil's Disciple.* Other Britons followed in Brighouse's and Mathews's wake. The Dallas British community provided continued support for performances at the Little Theatre well into the 1930s.

The Dallas city government also involved itself in the transatlantic cultural exchange. In December 1924, Mayor Louis Blaylock issued an official invitation to Sir H. Perry Robinson, the chief editorial writer of the *London Times*, to visit the city. In early January 1925, Robinson's publication replied in a cablegram to the mayor, "Many thanks for your invitation. Our representatives will visit your section."[51] Robinson had already planned a February trip to Texas to gather material for a special thirty-two-page section about the annual convention of the Associated Advertising Clubs of the World scheduled for Houston in May 1925. A. B. Kay, a foreign correspondent for the *London Times*, accompanied Robinson to North Texas in mid-February 1925.[52] The two journalists visited Fort Worth for interviews and photographs of the city before arriving in Dallas, where they collected a large number of pictures and scenes for their special section for the *London Times* on the cities of Texas.

The establishment of a branch of the English-Speaking Union in Dallas probably did more to strengthen the Dallas-Lancashire cultural connection than anything else besides the cotton trade in the 1920s. It also reflected the views of the British elites and cannot have failed to affect the intellectual life of Dallas. The English-Speaking Union of the United States incorporated in 1920 with its national headquarters in New York City.[53] Its members sought to promote friendly relations, common interests, and peaceful cooperation between the American people and the rest of the world's English speakers. To that end, the organization cooperated with its sister society, the English-Speaking Union of the British Empire. The British society maintained its headquarters at London's Dartmouth

House, where members from branches the world over enjoyed room and board at discount rates along with the assistance of a travel, shopping, and general service bureau. Whenever members of the Dallas branch traveled to London, they received cards of introduction to be presented at Dartmouth House. Besides overseas branches in the United States, the English-Speaking Union retained branches in Adelaide, Melbourne, Perth, and Sydney in Australia; Auckland, Christchurch, and Wellington in New Zealand; Nassau, Bahamas; Hamilton, Bermuda; the island of Malta; and in the European cities of Biarritz, Florence, Naples, Paris, and Rome. The efforts of the local Dallas chapter resulted in a steady stream of visitors to the city from the British Empire.

The Dallas branch of the English-Speaking Union continued to host famed British icons as the 1920s wore on. Norman Angell, lecturer and author, appeared at the first meeting of the organization at the University Club in November 1926. Angell's theme, Anglo-American relations, included a number of racially tinged remarks with which business elites on both sides of the Atlantic agreed at that time. Angell predicted that the next Great War would not be between Europeans, the United States, or Japan, but "will be, if it comes, between the white races and colored races of the globe." He went on to defend British actions in their colonies, particularly in India, where he asserted, "No, England is not oppressing India. She is teaching India how to govern itself."[54]

In this variation of the "White Man's Burden" argument, Angell noted that Britain, by rendering this service, contributed a great thing to the United States and the world, maintaining that "if England then, can teach the peoples of India the science of government, the value of cooperation, and mutual effort instead of strife, she will have done much to avert a catastrophic conflict in the future." In that light, Angell called for the United States to work together with England "for the general good." If they did, they "might come to understand . . . their foreign policy and foreign problems are much the same and actuated by the same altruistic purposes."[55] The view of Britons such as Angell undoubtedly only reinforced the already prevalent white supremacist racial views of both the native born and immigrant in the Dallas ruling class.

Another Dallas-based organization with British roots, the Loyal Knights of the Round Table, held its four-day fourth international convention in the city in September 1927. Started five years earlier in Oakland, California, the organization spread through the United States and

Canada. In some respects, not unlike other luncheon clubs of the day, the Loyal Knights of the Round Table accepted members, including women, from various walks of life. It differed, however, from the usual clubs in its legendary background and ritualistic forms, such as limiting each club to 128 members, the purported number that originally sat at King Arthur's round table. The organization took its name, customs, rituals, and purpose from the English legend.[56]

Internationally renowned cultural figures continued to address Dallas audiences. In January 1928, Dr. E. H. Cary of Southern Methodist University introduced Richard Halliburton, a globetrotting author of *The Royal Road to Romance* and *The Glorious Adventure*, to the University Club.[57] Halliburton, born in 1900 at Brownsville, eventually went to Princeton University, where he entered with the class of 1921. Dissatisfied with his studies, Halliburton began a career as a travel writer and circled the globe largely by "working his passage" or by hitching rides. Newspapers around the globe featured Halliburton's adventures on their front pages and publishers translated his own accounts of his exploits into virtually every major language. His career, along with those of people such as Charles Lindbergh and Ernest Hemingway, aptly represented the 1920s and 1930s, two decades that constituted perhaps the last age of adventure and conquest in the modern era.

At the University Club, Halliburton regaled his wide-eyed audience with tales of swimming the Hellespont in imitation of his English hero, Lord Byron; climbing Mount Fuji in Japan; being jailed in the fortress of Gibraltar for taking illegal pictures; and feeding barley porridge to the four-year-old Dalai Lama of Tibet and rocking the child to sleep.[58] During his four-day stay in the city he also spoke to the Dallas Open Forum in the auditorium at City Hall and to three hundred members of the Dallas Woman's Club. Halliburton's Anglo-influenced adventures helped make Dallasites receptive to other types of British cultural influences.

In the same month that Halliburton visited Dallas, popular English singer Kathleen Robinson, the leading lady in the musical *Abie's Irish Rose*, arrived in the city. Dallas radio personality Glenn Rowell introduced Robinson for a Friday afternoon recital carried by WFAA radio, a station jointly owned by the *Dallas Morning News* and Sears, Roebuck and Company. The recital, broadcast from the station's studio at the Baker Hotel, "found the audiences appreciative." They, in turn, found that "in her speaking she has just enough of the peculiarities of the English-born to give the listening an added zest!"[59] A reviewer also found that Robinson's singing combined "all the thoroughness of the English, the talent of the Continental, and the spirit of the American," something of a living symbol of the transatlantic spirit.[60]

The British sport of polo also took hold in the city during the 1920s. The growing popularity of the sport led the Dallas Polo Association to build its own club grounds and inaugurate play on Lemmon Avenue, north of town, in December 1930. A match between newspapermen, including Harry Crozier of the *Dallas Morning News*, and members of the Junior Chamber of Commerce, ended in a 1 to 0 victory for the Jaycee foursome. More than five thousand people attended the match, which was announced over a field microphone by Major Jerry Haughton, formerly an officer in the British Army. Haughton, a veteran polo player, explained the finer points of the game to "a horde of Dallasites who were slightly at sea on a few points."[61] Mrs. Roger Dixon, a member of the house committee for the Polo Club, also attended the match. She, along with other prominent wives, poured coffee for the visitors in a manner that elicited a compliment that "the coffee-serving, may it be said, was nobly done."[62]

The prominence of Britons in Dallas cultural life continued into the late 1930s. Anna Neagle, a well-known British film star, and Herbert Wilcox, the director-producer of the motion picture *Nurse Edith Campbell*, arrived in the city during September 1939 for the film's premiere. They were met by the ubiquitous Roger Dixon, whom the *Dallas Morning News* declared "will represent the English colony here."[63] In that role, Dixon met Neagle and Wilcox upon their arrival in the city and attended a dinner given in their honor at the Baker Hotel's Mural Room prior to the film's screening at the Palace Theater. A number of out-of-town film critics, civic officials, local theater men, and members of the press also attended both functions. Neagle visited the same month that World War II broke out, but this new disaster for civilization failed to stop the stream of British visitors to Dallas.

Into the 1940s Dallas's "English Colony"—the term used repeatedly by both the *Dallas Morning News*, and the Dallas Chamber of Commerce—continued receiving reinforcements. In March 1941, 111 aliens appeared before federal judge William H. Atwell for swearing in as US citizens.[64] Former British subjects led the list with twenty-nine, followed by fifteen Germans and ten Mexicans. These English reinforcements, however, faced a changed Dallas cotton trade.

Beginning in 1919, the number of bankruptcies among farmers relative to those in other forms of business increased markedly. Before the Great War, bankruptcies among farmers represented about 5 percent of the total, whereas in 1922 they represented 17 percent of all bankruptcies. For the United States as a whole, the number of farm bankruptcies in 1922 was six times that for 1913.[65] The fortunes of the cotton economy were closely tied to the national economy. The negative trend for the entire US agricultural sector from the 1920s into the 1940s amounted to a veritable disaster.[66] For the period in question, US farm income fell by 69 percent whereas agricultural exports fell slightly more than 80 percent. For the Texas cotton industry, especially around Dallas, dependent as it was on exports to Europe, such statistics boded an economic tragedy for both the farmers and those involved in the cotton trade.

By the middle of the 1920s, although cotton was still the most important agricultural product exported from the United States, its relative importance in the agricultural export trade declined dramatically. During the prewar period, 1909–13, cotton constituted 53 percent of the value of agricultural exports; during 1921–23 cotton accounted for less than 35 percent of these exports. During the prewar period, 1910–14, the United States exported an annual average of 8,839,604 bales of cotton, but in 1923–24 the exports decreased to 5,898,713 bales.[67] The drop in exports led, inevitably, to overproduction and a market glut, as desperate cotton farmers sought to maintain their income. As the price per pound dropped, they planted more and more acreage. Already facing the problems of soil erosion and the depredations of the boll weevil, the farmers now faced a collapse of the market. Yet city leaders still touted "Cotton as King," whether out of habit or hope for a turnaround in the market.

On the other side of the Atlantic, Lancashire faced increased competition in textile production from the United States, India, Japan, and China. The district's old dominance faded along with the fortunes of the declining British Empire. A failure to invest in new factories and technologies combined with rising competition led to a disaster for the Lancashire mill workers that paralleled that of Texas cotton farmers. It was a situation in which there were "at least 400,000 men and women working less then thirty-five hours a week; No dividends; next to none, or not-easily-arrived-at dividends for the best part of two-thirds of the whole cotton industry."[68] In the period 1928–31, British imports of raw cotton dropped by 28 percent. In that same period, imports from the United

States dropped by 49 percent.[69] From its high point in 1913, when Lancashire accounted for 70 percent of the total world trade in cotton piece goods, its share of the export market dropped by a staggering 39 percent by 1927.

The advent of the Great Depression accelerated the decline. Cotton prices dropped by 50 percent during the Depression because of slack demand, and Texas farmers were encouraged to shift to other crops, resulting in a marked drop in the acreage devoted to cotton. The low prices during the Depression caused many small farmers to leave cotton farming altogether, especially in the East Texas prairies. Many of these farmers had been working their fields with horse teams and chopping and picking the cotton by hand. By decreasing the number of such marginal cotton farms, the Depression not only helped open the way for the large-scale mechanization of cotton farms but also exacerbated the basic ills confronting the industry. This process exemplified what the noted economist Joseph Schumpeter referred to as "creative destruction," that is, the process by which, under capitalism, old ways of doing things are continuously destroyed and replaced by the new. During the period 1927–39, total farm cash income in Texas dropped from approximately $760 million in 1927 to slightly over $400 million in 1939—a 47 percent drop in thirteen years.[70] By the end of this period, cotton had lost its dominance of Texas agriculture and the cotton trade fell victim to economic changes that marked the end of an era for both the Dallas English colony and the city. The outbreak of World War II completed the process.

Dallas and Lancashire had a good run, but all good things come to an end. Until oil was discovered at Spindletop near Beaumont in 1901, cotton was king in the state's economy, but the cotton farmer rarely got rich.[71] Neither did the Lancashire mill workers. Those in the Dallas Cotton Exchange, along with the Lancashire mill owners, usually did reap great rewards. Starting in the 1920s, however, production of the raw and finished material decreased for a variety of reasons, including damage by insect pests, changes in world markets, competition from other nations, decreased demand during the Great Depression, and competition from synthetic fibers. Changes in world cotton markets also affected Texas cotton farmers because of the vast percentage of the Texas cotton crop that was exported. What had served Dallas and the state well since the end of the nineteenth century now made them vulnerable to changes in the world market.

One important change occurred in the 1920s and 1930s, when the British stimulated production in the sterling bloc countries of India, Egypt, Sudan, and Brazil, which tied its exchange rate to the sterling bloc, to diversify their source of supply and perhaps lower the price. As a result, American cotton exports to Great Britain dropped by two-thirds over twenty years and the American percentage of British imports of cotton dropped from 84 percent to 38 percent.[72] This was indeed the end of an era. But for those people who had previously profited from cotton in Dallas, specifically the members of its "English Colony," their fortunes and influence were largely secure. Many of them remained influential in the business community. Dixon, in particular, maintained national influence in the cotton trade into the 1950s. He and others like him shaped the city's culture and strengthened the transatlantic link over the course of half a century. From cricket and polo to theater and radio, the cultural life of Dallas took on an English upper-class flavor. When he visited Dallas, English theater critic Harold Brighouse elevated the stature of the city's Little Theatre and attested to the importance of the "English Colony" in the city. Leaders such as Arthur H. Cleaver and Dixon played not only important economic roles but also social roles that contributed to this outcome.

Boosters on both sides of the Atlantic played an important part in the success of the socioeconomic process. Dallas city boosters reflected not only local enthusiasm for the cotton trade but also its national importance. As early as 1874, a congressional report stated: "There is no country upon this earth, so far as is known, that is equal to our own in the production of cotton, and no seed so good as that made here."[73] Four decades later, only two years after the founding of the Dallas Cotton Exchange in 1907, the US government still published statements such as the following: "The beneficence of the cotton plant as an agent of civilization can hardly

Dallas; cotton still king in 1923.

be overestimated. Its sudden development is almost unparalleled in the history of economic products, and [hence] its enormous importance to-day in the agricultural, commercial, and industrial life of the world. . . ."[74] These statements made over the course of several decades demonstrate the decades-long dominance of the cotton trade in the minds of the business community and government policy makers.

This cotton mind-set was reflected on the other side of the Atlantic as well. During this same period, an observer of the textile industry in Lancashire was asserting, "The Cotton Industry is the greatest manufacturing industry not only in Britain but in the whole world. Its importance is not confined to Lancashire, but concerns the whole of the British Isles and the British Empire."[75] At the zenith of the Empire's power in 1913, it was being said by a British government official that "Lancashire was arrogant, Lancashire talked cotton, thought cotton, dreamed cotton, to be the typical cotton man the Manchester Royal Exchange, the Liverpool Exchange and Paradise . . . ranked in that order!"[76] And the eyes of Britain continued to focus on the Lone Star State with hyperbolic statements emanating from Liverpool such as "Texas alone has sufficient area to raise a crop of 30,000,000 bales"[77]

The role of the transatlantic cotton trade in the long-term economic success of Dallas cannot be overstated. And although the numbers of English cotton men in Dallas were always relatively small, they played a significant role in molding the culture of the city. The historian C. Vann Woodward contends that foreign immigrants to the South played a role out of all proportion to their relatively limited numbers when compared with Northern urban centers. From George Mifflin's Dallas arrival through the arrival of the British cotton traders who forged the Dallas-Lancashire link over the course of half a century, Dallas became an outpost of the British Empire and was shaped by the experience. Woodward's contention certainly proved true in the case of Dallas, where Englishmen involved in the city's cotton trade helped create the Dallas "English Colony" that greatly affected the economic, social, cultural, and intellectual life of the city. In the process, they cemented Dallas's role as a key player in the Atlantic World.

NOTES

1. Alan Fowler, "British Textile Workers in the Lancashire Cotton and Yorkshire Wool Industries" (Metropolitan Manchester University, National Overview Great Britain, Textile Conference, November 2004), 6.

2. Frank Thistlewaite, "Atlantic Partnership," *The Economic History Review* 7, no. 1 (1954): 7.

3. Stuart Bruchey, ed., *Cotton and the Growth of the American Economy: 1790–1860* (New York: Harcourt, Brace and World, 1967), 44.

4. Paul Mantoux, quoted by Bruchy, *Cotton and the Growth of the American Economy*, 45.

5. Frank Thistlewaite, "Atlantic Partnership," 4.

6. J. M. Woods, *Jacob De Cordoba, Pioneer and Fraternalist* (Seguin: Past Grand Amity No. 60, San Antonio Lodge, No. 11, 1987).

7. Ibid.

8. James M. Day, *Jacob De Cordoba, Land Merchant of Texas*, letter from Jacob De Cordoba to Phineas De Cordoba, August 19, 1856 (Waco: Texian Press, 1962), 124.

9. Ibid., 129–30.

10. Ibid., 117.

11. Ibid.

12. "Texas Business Review," Bureau of Business Research, University of Texas. (Austin: University of Texas Press, 1966), 4.

13. Karl Marx, "Economic Manuscripts: Grundrisse," in *Grundrisse: Outlines of the Critique of Political Economy*, https://www.marxists.org/archive/marx/works/1857/grundrisse/ch10.htm

14. *Dallas Morning News*, September 5, 1926, sec. 4, 12.

15. "Henry Lee Edwards, 91, Cotton Factor Dies," *Dallas Morning News*, October 1, 1947, sec. 2, 1.

16. Ibid.

17. "Death Takes Cotton Agent John R. Hoey," *Dallas Morning News*, December 15, 1951, part 3, 11.

18. George Santerre, *Dallas' First Hundred Years: 1856–1956* (Dallas: Craft Books, 1956), 1.

19. Harvey J. Graff, *The Dallas Myth: The Making and Unmaking of an American City* (Minneapolis: University of Minneapolis Press, 2008), 3.

20. "Texas and Her Metropolis," *Dallas Illustrated* (*Dallas Times-Herald*, 1892), 6.

21. Ibid.

22. A. B. Shepperson, *Cotton Facts, A Compilation from Official and Reliable Sources of the Crops, Receipts, Exports, Stocks. Home and Foreign Consumption, Visible Supply, Prices and Acreage of Cotton* (New York: A. B. Shepperson, 1895). This work also included *The Reports and Condition of Growing Cotton Crops*, issued by the US Agricultural Bureau since 1879.

23. Michael Q. Hook, *The Struggle for Dominance: Urban Rivalry in North Texas, 1870–1910* (Austin: University of Texas Press, 1979), 70.

24. William Whittam Jr., Special Agent for the US Department of Agriculture, "Foreign Markets for Cotton Products," *Report of the Commissioner of Corporations on Cotton Exchanges, Part I: Methods of Establishing Grade Differences for Future Contracts*, May 4, 1908 [May 18, 1908, referred to the Committee on Interstate and Foreign Commerce] (Washington, DC: US Government Printing Office, 1908), 141.

25. Ibid., 193.

26. W. Whittam, "England's Cotton Industry," *Report on Cotton Exchanges*, 1908, 7.

27. "International Lint Merchant, Arthur H. Cleaver, Dies at 75," *Dallas Morning News*, May 12, 1948, sec. 1, 11.

28. "Cotton Exchange a Dallas Pioneer," *Dallas Morning News*, January 16, 1957, sec. 16, 4.

29. *Dallas Morning News*, November 21, 1913, 10.

30. *Dallas Morning News*, July 8, 1933, sec. 1, 4.

31. *Dallas Morning News*, March 13, 1965, sec. 4, 3.

32. "Hannay Heads Dallas Group," *Dallas Morning News*, February 7, 1957, sec. 3, 5.

33. *Dallas Morning News*, October 24, 1963, sec. 4, 5.

34. *Dallas Morning News*, February 17, 1969, sec. D, 3.

35. *Dallas Morning News*, July 11, 1960, sec. 4, 4.

36. *Dallas Morning News*, November 15, 1933, sec. 1, 2.

37. Roger L. Dixon, *The Cotton Bonanza, by a Participant, 1908–1960* (Dallas: University of Texas at Arlington Special Collections, 1978), 7.

38. *Dallas Morning News*, July 19, 1974, sec. E, 8.

39. Dixon, *Cotton Bonanza*, 4.

40. Ibid., 6.

41. Ibid., 21.

42. Ibid., 23.

43. Ibid, 27.

44. Ibid. 28.

45. Ibid. 22.

46. "International Lecturer Speaks for Alumni Here," *Dallas Morning News*, January 28, 1920, sec. 1, 4.

47. "As England Sees: Texas Theatricals Discussed Abroad," *Manchester Guardian*, August 11, 1929.

48. Ibid.

49. Dorothy Chansky, *Composing Ourselves: The Little Theatre Movement and the American Audience* (Carbondale: Southern Illinois University Press, 2004), 187.

50. "Former British Army Officer Has Role of General Burgoyne in Dallas Little Theater Play," *Dallas Morning News*, March 22, 1930, sec. 1, 12.

51. "Visit of London Writer Promised This Section," *Dallas Morning News*, January 6, 1925, sec. 1, 4.

52. "London Newspaper Man Visits in Fort Worth," *Dallas Morning News*, February 13, 1925, sec. 1, 4,

53. "English Union Officer Named," *Dallas Morning News*, January 15, 1928, Sports News, 5,

54. "Anglo-US Amity Urged," *Dallas Morning News*, November 21, 1926, sec. 1, 2,

55. Ibid.

56. "Exemplars of Round Table Ideas to Meet: Knights Hold International Convention in Dallas," *Dallas Morning News*, September 11, 1927, sec. 1, 6.

57. "Globe Trotter Lectures Here," *Dallas Morning News*, January 19, 1928, sec. 1, 6.

58. Ibid.

59. "Leading Lady Gives Program," *Dallas Morning News*, January 27, 1928, sec. 2, 20.

60. Ibid.

61. *Dallas Morning News*, December 21, 1930, sec. 1, 8.

62. Ibid.

63. *Dallas Morning News*, September 13, 1939, sec. 1, 12.

64. "British Lead List of New U. S. Citizens," *Dallas Morning News*, March 20, 1941, sec. 1, 6.

65. C. A. Wiley, *Agriculture and the Business Cycle since 1920: A Study in the Post-War Disparity of Prices* (Madison: University of Wisconsin Press, 1930), 22.

66. *Manchester Guardian Commercial*, December 16, 1933, 483.

67. Leslie A. Wheeler, *International Trade in Cotton*, Trade Promotion Series No. 13, Department of Commerce, p. VII (Washington DC: Government Printing Office, 1925), 45.

68. B. Bowker, *Lancashire under the Hammer* (London: Leonard and Virginia Woolf, 1928), 56.

69. *Handbook of Cotton Trade Statistics, 1924–1931* (Manchester: Cotton Trade Statistical Bureau, 1931), 5.

70. *Texas Business Review* 14, no. 8 (1940): 1–2 Bureau of Business Research, The University of Texas.

71. Natural Fibers Information Center, *The History of Cotton in Texas* (Austin: University of Texas Press, 1987), 6.

72. Ibid.

73. Committee on Agriculture, Report on Exchange of Cotton-Seed with Egypt, 43d Cong., 1st sess., H.R. Rep. No. 195–43 (February 27, 1874).

74. International Bureau of American Republics, John Barrett, Director, *Cotton: The Most Widely Used Staple in the World* (Washington, DC: US Government Printing Office, April, 1909), 2.

75. Lancashire Cotton Commission, *Cotton Fluctuation and Movement, 1902–1907, 34th Annual Edition* (New York: Latham, Alexander & Co. 1907), 1.

76. Chris Wrigley, ed., *The First World War in the International Economy* (Cheltenham, UK: Edward Elgar, 2000), 77.

77. Ibid., 33.

III

• • •

Identities

6

Working for Leisure

British Hunter-Writers in the American West, 1865–1914

Gregory Kosc

A *DOWNTON* INTRODUCTION

When the Granthams arrived at Duneagle Castle in the season 3 finale of the highbrow soap *Downton Abbey*, the camera panned across the entrance hall, taking in a majestic statue of a buck and walls covered with an assortment of hunting rifles, pikes, and armor. Nestled in a deerstalker's paradise in the Scottish Highlands, much of the action of the episode revolved around hunting. Most amusingly, one evening when Matthew Crawley, the presumed heir of Downton, tried to recall to his wife Mary his failed ten-hour foray "crawling through heather," she rolled her eyes, shooting back, "Really darling, it's boring enough to hear about when you succeed." Clearly, this was not the first time that Lady Mary had to endure such a tale, and when one considers the prodigious amount of British hunting literature that was produced in the nineteenth and early twentieth centuries, one might be able to sympathize. Lady Mary's exasperation notwithstanding, the episode did a nice job of dealing with some of the broader issues involved in turn-of-the-twentieth-century hunting and its attendant literary spawn. Throughout the episode, hunting and fishing were not only arenas for demonstrating one's manhood and enjoying a bit of leisure time, but these ventures and interludes also provided a safe space where men could broach personal and delicate topics of discussion with one another—seeking to cement homosocial bonds.[1] Although *Downton Abbey* is indeed a soap, the show nevertheless broaches the very real anxieties and issues revolving around class, gender, and national identity that the aristocracy faced during the late nineteenth century, all of which contemporaneous hunting literature sought to reconcile.

THE AMERICAN QUESTION

The United States played a critical role in forging various British identities in the second half of the nineteenth century.[2] In this chapter, I assert that upper-class British hunters constructed their identities in accounts of the American West from 1865 to 1914. In my dissertation, I analyze twenty-six different hunter-writers' accounts of the American West, but in this chapter, owing to space restrictions, I will discuss the accounts of only one author: Windham Thomas Wyndham-Quin Dunraven, the fourth Earl of Dunraven (1841–1926). Dunraven's accounts are long, sinuous, complex, and sometimes seemingly contradictory affairs that belie his attitudes toward a rapidly changing British society. Nineteenth-century travel accounts are akin to modern blogs because both have few space restrictions and their authors were/are trying to craft their public persona and identity. Although every author and his or her respective account(s) are singular, Dunraven's accounts are broadly representative of the trends that emerge in this genre and in British discourse about the United States.

DUNRAVEN'S ANXIETIES

Dunraven spent his childhood years in Wales and Ireland, and as a young man he led a rather peripatetic existence spending time in Rome, Paris, and Dublin, acquiring his schooling in a raft of Catholic institutions.[3] His father, the third Earl of Dunraven, was an ardent convert to Catholicism and chose these schools in an attempt to imbue his son with an appreciation for Roman Catholicism. These efforts backfired. Dunraven felt isolated on the Continent, and he failed to make any friends because he had little interaction with boys his age. In addition, due to the influence of his mother, the younger Dunraven never converted to Catholicism, and tension over his failure to convert persisted for the rest of his father's life. In fact, when he was ready to enter university, he and his father clashed over the school. His father wished that he would attend a Catholic college in Oscott, near Birmingham. Eventually, Dunraven won out and went on to log a few less-than-rigorous years at Christ Church, Oxford.[4] After spending most of his time hunting, sailing, and playing cricket at Oxford, he moved on to serve a stint in the First Life Guards in London, where he never saw any real combat. After leaving the army, Dunraven, who was not granted an extravagant allowance, became a war correspondent for a few different London papers during the Abyssinia expedition and the Franco-Prussian War. While we do not know his father's motivations, perhaps a lingering resentment over the younger Dunraven's unwillingness to convert had something to do with his stinginess. Even after his father's death in 1871, the issue of religion continued to vex their relationship, as Dunraven disputed his father's bequest to the local Roman Catholic church in Adare.[5]

Upon his father's death, Dunraven succeeded his father as the Earl of Dunraven and Mount-Earl, inheriting more than thirty-nine thousand acres. The landholdings were split between Dunraven Castle in Glamorganshire, Wales, and Adare Manor in County Limerick, Ireland. Although Dunraven always identified as an Irishman,[6] it was coal on the Glamorganshire property that was the key to his family's wealth.[7] Dunraven enjoyed his twenties immensely, though he clearly harbored doubts about his intellectual readiness for public life as he entered his thirties—even expressing his reservations to the sitting prime minister Lord Beaconsfield (Benjamin Disraeli).[8] Instead of taking a leadership role in the House of Lords or joining the fray of Irish politics where the issues of land reform and Irish Home Rule were coming to dominate the political landscape, Dunraven struck out to the American West and spent large portions of his thirties hunting and attempting to make Estes Park, Colorado, a private game reserve to the consternation of locals.[9] Dunraven visited the area nearly every year between 1869 and 1896—publishing a few books and articles about the place along the way.[10] And he was not alone. British hunters, and later huntresses, were crisscrossing the globe and publishing accounts of their exploits. All of this begs the following questions: Why would members of the upper class (like Dunraven) feel the need to write and publish their hunting narratives? What role does the American West play in all of this?

By the late nineteenth century, hunting had evolved into a ritualized test of manliness, virility, and social station. A hunting "code" evolved with an emphasis on "fair play" in order to even the playing field between hunter and quarry. These rules placed the onus on hunters to intimately understand their prey's anatomy and habits if they were to be successful. Rigidly abiding by this code and bringing home trophies allowed upper-class hunters to demonstrate their masculinity and justify their social superiority, especially vis-à-vis market and subsistence hunters. Thus, the physical act of hunting, with its bodily and mental tests, offered an opportunity to prove one's superiority in an activity more akin to a chess match than slaughter. Dunraven presented as articulate a summation of what hunting had become than anyone. He said, "I have not included hunting among the sciences, but in reality I might have done so. It is a very exact science, and one in which excellence is rarely obtained. Many men never become, never can become, good hunters. They are not endowed with the necessary faculties; and those who are gifted with them require years of study and hard work before they can be entitled to call themselves masters of the art. I hope no one labors under the delusion that hunting is a mere barbarous, bloodthirsty sport."

He went on to say that killing, in and of itself, did not give pleasure. Instead, "The charm lies in overcoming difficulties—in matching your natural intelligence and acquired knowledge and skill against the instinct, cunning, intellect, and reason of the animal you are endeavoring to outwit. The reward of the hunter is the same as that of the student of languages, of the archeologist, of the geologist. . . . His triumph is the triumph of unraveling a mystery, tracing and discovering a hidden fact, grappling with and overcoming a difficulty.[11] These rituals of scientific stalking and fair play would become cornerstones in hunters' literary efforts.

In the process of writing and constructing narratives, hunter-writers seized an opportunity to craft an upper-class and unassailable identity.[12] At a very basic level, these narratives allowed men such as Dunraven to claim masculinity and social superiority so that they reaffirmed their right to rule over others, but they also allowed men to assert that they could succeed regardless of the endeavor they chose—be it in Parliament or local politics or estate management or even business. Dunraven and his ilk did not view hunting as primarily a leisure activity or mere adventure. Rather, to the men who hunted in the American West, hunting was more fundamentally about work. In fact, it was about hard work that was dangerous. The use of the word and concept of "work" by Dunraven and others is key to understanding how they thought about their hunting. Those in the upper class were not immune to the criticisms of the aristocracy, nor were they blind to the tremendous social and political changes that were transforming their society. Thus, the hunter-writers deployed the concepts of fair play, hard work, and a "scientific" approach to hunting in order to preempt criticism that modern hunting was slaughter and that they were engaged in a meaningless activity. Performing work in a potentially lethal environment provided meaning and demonstrated one's composure and self-reliance. Self-reliance was the very foundation of these unassailable identities, which proved them to be the elite of an evolutionarily fit British nation.[13]

Of course, one might argue that in the late nineteenth century, Britain was reaching its apogee of power, thus obviating the need to prove anything to anyone. It is misleading, however, to take such a top-down view, or to use aristocrats' supercilious and paternalistic attitudes as our guide to the era. In fact, scholars of gender have noted that the late nineteenth century was a period of acute frustration for men and male ambitions in industrialized countries and should be characterized as a crisis of masculinity.[14] Additionally, the specific context of late nineteenth-century Britain seems to be a period that is also set apart by special pressures for the aristocracy. This particular period of 1865 to 1914 witnessed the erosion of patriarchy, deference, and privilege of the traditional upper class. In short, there were very pressing—and real—reasons for British aristocrats to feel as though their way of life were under assault. Concerns about the increasing geopolitical power of rivals and American influence on British politics and society were rife during this era. The diminution in elites' power had been occurring throughout the nineteenth century, but I would argue that the process intensified after 1865 and was happening in official and unofficial ways.[15] Legally speaking, reforms concerning hunting, voting, the civil service, the purchase system in the army, and—most important—landowning were carried out. These reforms were construed as a direct assault on the privileges of the aristocracy.[16]

For our purposes, the landowning situation in Ireland merits the most attention because Dunraven chose to live in Adare, Ireland. There had long been calls for reform and agitation on the island, and the 1870s witnessed continued activism—even after the Irish Land Act of 1870, which was designed to provide Irish tenants more security, compensation for improvements, and help purchasing land. In fact, the entire period was punctuated by a series of land reform measures that were intended to aid tenants in various ways and tamp down tensions. Although some of the act's effects were negligible for tenants, the long-term erosion of landed privilege was a reality. Furthermore, between the ongoing rural activism of the era and the activities of the Irish Republican Brotherhood, there was certainly the potential for unrest. In *The Great Divide*, Dunraven even mentioned the rancorous passage of the Peace Preservation

Acts of 1873, which sought to greatly curb gun ownership in an effort to preempt violence. Not only were British authorities concerned with the continuing potential for rural unrest, but they were also responding to the Irish Republican Brotherhood's terrorist activities.[17] Rural frustration eventually boiled over in the late 1870s as the Land League prosecuted its Land War (1879–82) in order to secure the "three F's"—fair rents, fixity of tenure, and free sale. Even after land sales commenced in the wake of the Land Act of 1881, there continued to be friction over prices and the speed with which these sales took place. Rural tensions continued throughout the era until the passage of the Wyndham Land Purchase Act of 1903, which brought considerable gains for Irish tenants. Dunraven personally participated in writing this legislation, which made the government fund the difference between the bid and ask prices for land and extend credit to tenants on favorable terms.[18]

The rise of women's rights activists and animal rights activists also posed questions that often put elite men in a defensive or uncomfortable posture.[19] Complicating all of this was an array of economic changes. The rise of an international plutocracy based on American and British industrial fortunes, the agricultural depression of the 1880s, and increasing American, German, Russian, and French international competitiveness in a spate of industries threatened not only the basis and exclusivity of aristocratic life but also Britain's position in the world.[20] From a cultural perspective, there was tension between noble ideals and *mentalités* such as libertinism, paternalism, status, honor, etiquette, and politeness and middle-class values such as hard work, domesticity, globetrotting, merit, brazenness, and manly independence and simplicity.

Many from the elite class began to see the United States and its influence as a common denominator in these changes and tensions.[21] This threat grew throughout the nineteenth century as Britain continued to incrementally democratize and American economic strength swelled.[22] Political radicals held up American democracy as an example to emulate, and in the debate over the Second Reform Act, which expanded the electorate and passed in 1867, Disraeli gave voice to the underlying fears about democratization by saying, "I think that this House should remain a House of Commons, and not become a House of the People, the House of a mere indiscriminate multitude, devoid of any definite character, and not responsible to society, and having no duties and no privileges under the constitution. Are we to consider this subject in the spirit of the English constitution, or are we to meet it in the spirit of the American constitution?"[23]

This fear of American democracy continued throughout the late nineteenth century and the early twentieth century as a Third Reform Act (1884–85) further expanded the vote and the Parliament Act (1911) ended the House of Lords' ability to veto legislation. As if a growing electorate was not enough to roil the landowning class, the incredibly popular radical philosopher/economist Henry George, who advocated a site tax on all land in order to redistribute land and alleviate tax burdens on the poor, was an American. As historian Antony Taylor notes, "His major work *Progress and Poverty* was selling 400,000 copies annually by the end of 1884 and has been continuously in print since its publication in 1880. . . . Moreover George's tours of Great Britain in 1881, 1882, 1884, and 1889 were sell-out affairs that galvanised a new generation of political radicals."[24]

If there was a region that radiated the American-ness that conservative elites in Britain abhorred, it was the West. The American frontier had always held an important place in the minds not just of Americans but also of British travel writers, immigrants, and novelists.[25] As a consequence, by 1865 the British public already had a vague idea of the American frontier, its landscape, and its people who were typified by their "roughness," "independence," and "egalitarianism."[26] And, although it is notoriously difficult to truly ascertain readership and even reception of certain books/genres, it should be noted that British investment and travel in the American West exploded after the Civil War. As cultural historian Monica Rico explains, "Roughly fifteen hundred British companies organized to do business in the trans-Mississippi West between 1865 and 1890. . . . In addition, the growth of Western tourism drew British investors and British tourists, who established themselves as a distinct community in many western resorts toward the end of the nineteenth century."[27] Some reviewers even bemoaned the sheer number of written accounts that emerged out of this veritable tourist stampede.[28] Because the American West seemed to be a place where American values were exemplified, indeed, amplified, it turned out to be a perfect setting for proving one could still lead in this rapidly evolving (and increasingly Americanized) world. One could confront presumptuous and assertive Westerners and put them in their proper place.[29]

As Dunraven was on the cusp of becoming an earl and being forced to shoulder the responsibilities of his rank, the world around him was slowly changing. He followed the example of so many before him (and probably his doctor's orders) and went west.[30] Although Dunraven never mentioned being diagnosed as neurasthenic, it was common for men to embark upon such trips "for their prophylactic effects."[31] He sought an escape to revitalize his body and mind in order to bolster himself upon his return to civilization, and, in the process, he sought psychological affirmation of his manhood, competency, and social station. The way that he pursued this reinvigoration and validation was not through a variety of leisure activities, but by performing hard work in a dangerous and egalitarian environment. Although the ideal trip for "overtaxed" men advocated a homosocial environment where men could reconnect with their "boyish selves" performing "demanding exercise," the average hunting trip to the West was no vacation.[32] In fact, Dunraven and other hunter-writers depicted these trips—and understood them—as deadly serious business and more about mental and physical "hard work" rather than "demanding exercise."[33] In Dunraven's *The Great Divide*, there are passages in which he luxuriated in languorous lassitude; on the whole, however, his account was not about relaxation, rest, and recovery. In fact, his trip to Yellowstone was at a point when the destination was still off the beaten path and, therefore, the entire enterprise was quite tedious and dangerous. Furthermore, when hunting, Dunraven narrated how he pushed his body and mind to the limit—sometimes by design and other times by accident.[34] By using the concepts of mental and physical hard work and danger over and over again, Dunraven and other elite hunters were trying to ward off accusations from radicals back home that they were superfluous relics incapable of work and engaged only in slaughter. By co-opting the middle-class virtue of hard work, elite hunters could preempt radicals' arguments, appeal to a large readership, and make it seem that they were not simply out on some lavish vacation, but, instead, they were out in the wilderness working for their leisure and, therefore, earning it. Additionally, by conceiving of hunting as work they were also able to convince themselves that they were capable of anything. In short, all of this made their resulting image and identity bulletproof.

DUNRAVEN'S *THE GREAT DIVIDE* (1876)

The first few pages of Dunraven's *The Great Divide* are crucial. Dunraven began with a picturesque comparison of the Rockies in relation to the Alps. After complaining of the Rockies' comparative aesthetic shortcomings, he countered, "But the one attribute peculiar to the continent is that of vastness. Everything is huge and stupendous. Nature is formed in a larger mould than in other lands." He went on to detail the savagery of nature in the West in a lyrical way: "Storms are fearful and violent, floods rise and sweep the country like seas. Mighty rivers, with fierce ungovernable tide, in a night scoop out fresh beds for themselves and laugh at man's shackles and restraints, or, in their struggles to break the chains that winter has bound around them, burst free and carry off, like cobwebs, the toilsome results of engineering skill. Lakes are seas. There are great deserts almost unknown and unmarked on any map."

He concluded by noting that one can only truly appreciate America's vastness "in the western wilds or far away territories; where Nature is strong and man is very weak, and where the powers of science have not yet been called into play, to supplement and make up for his feebleness."[35] In addition to pointing out the powerful forces of nature in the West and how truly isolated his hunting party was on this trek, Dunraven was keen to remind his readers throughout that some of their forays were into hitherto unknown and unexplored areas.[36] Just a few pages later, Dunraven set down another important principle that was reiterated in this book and every subsequent book that he published about hunting, that is, real hunting was not in a controlled environment and was hard work. "I have enjoyed pretty good sport occasionally myself, it is true," he explained, "but it is difficult to get; besides, it requires patience and perseverance, and entails *hard work*, and even then success is very uncertain."[37] These opening pages set the tone for Dunraven's account. Although the self-deprecating Dunraven stated that he was a mere "tourist" who had no "adventures" to relate, the book is filled with close calls, near-death experiences, and harrowing stalks—all of which pitted his hunting party against the harsh and lethal Western environment. Danger hung over this account from the first pages and only through Dunraven's and his comrades' grit and hard work was it overcome.

On his outfit's journey across the Great Plains, the threatening Rockies were ever present and forebodingly looming on the horizon. Once the party entered the mountains, descriptions of the environment filled page after page, and he quickly changed to threatening language to convey the increasing seriousness of the situation. He emphasized the "cruel look" or "cruel jaggedness" and "savage grandeur" of the mountain chain.[38] When a hunting expedition was eventually launched into the mountains, the difficulty of the terrain was constantly alluded to in recounting successful and unsuccessful stalks and chases after wounded game.

The weather and climate continually proved to be a formidable barrier to be overcome with hard work.[39] In stalking some bighorn sheep, Dunraven narrated, "Patiently we followed their trail all day over the most infernal ground. The mountain was very steep, and naturally quite bad enough; but on this occasion it was rendered unusually dangerous by the loose wet snow which covered the smooth surfaces of rock, and filled up all the interstices between the broken fragments of cliff, hiding the untrustworthy places, deceiving the foot and eye, glossing over little chasms, giving a false appearance of stability to tottering stones, and converting a difficult but feasible hill-side into a most dangerous and well-nigh impracticable slope."[40]

This particular stalk up a hillside ended in a failed attempt to locate game (similar to Matthew Crawley's frustrated pursuit of a buck in *Downton Abbey*), but Dunraven kept this story and several very similar anecdotes in the book. No doubt, similar to Crawley, Dunraven regaled dinner guests with such tales. Why, then, narrate something so seemingly inconsequential? For starters, by owning up to the failed stalks, Dunraven curried trust from his readers that he was not prone to inventing stories. It should be pointed out that Dunraven had already succeeded in bagging some wapiti (i.e., elk) in even harsher conditions; therefore, a failed stalk would not completely delegitimize his image. Second, and more important, Dunraven used these episodes to demonstrate his fearlessness in a deadly situation, as well as his persistence and physical endurance. In fact, after this particular failed stalk of bighorns, Dunraven gloated that he awoke the next day "tolerably refreshed," and, to add an exclamation point to the entire episode, he went out hunting in the mountains alone. Clambering up the side of a snowy and ice-riven mountain is hard work, and Dunraven was proving not only that he was up to the task, but that such arduous work energized him.

As terrible weather conditions continued in the mountains, Dunraven's physician, Dr. Kingsley, faced a life-threatening situation. Dr. Kingsley had wandered out of camp before dusk in search of dinner, but as the temperature dropped, fog descended and rain started falling so the doctor lost his way back to camp. Two guides set out to find Dr. Kingsley, and Dunraven was charged with staying in camp, tending the fire, and having to "occasionally emit a dismal yell to keep them [the guides] with the whereabouts of camp." The uncertainty of the situation was terrifying, and to Dunraven "the minutes were as hours. . . ."[41] Much like other portions of the account, this section allowed Dunraven to be self-deprecating and feign modesty while garnering esteem and validation. Even though Dunraven was terrified, he never gave in to his fear and never broke down mentally, nor did any of his companions. The party returned safely and without incident, testifying to their composure and self-control. As one hunter ruminated, "It takes moments of danger to discover a man's true grit—the 'bottom sand,' as a plainsman would say."[42] Each member of the group demonstrated his grit and composure in a difficult situation.

Dunraven had more occasions to prove his mettle, as later on in the account he related his own scare with being turned around near Fort Bridger. He explained, "It is a very mean feeling to be all alone and to fancy one's self lost; nothing so quickly upsets a man's mental equilibrium. I have been most fortunate. . . . and have never yet got out of my reckoning without getting in again pretty soon."[43] During this episode near Fort Bridger, Dunraven temporarily lost his bearings. He described it in detail,

> My head turned; my brain became quite bewildered; and an impulse to run straight ahead seized me. I was, to use the vernacular, for the moment completely "turned round." It seems to me most absurd, as I sit here writing, to suppose that one could be so easily thrown, even for an instant, off one's balance; but all men, except those who by long custom have acquired habits of complete self-dependence and self-control, are liable to such temporary aberrations—for it almost amounts to that;—and I have even seen very old and experienced prairie men become quite "turned round" after running elk, and so obstinate in their conviction that they were going right, when in reality the fact that they were moving in a totally wrong direction was clearly demonstrated by compass, that it required a strong effort on their part to force themselves to act according to the needle and not upon their own mistaken judgment.

> However, I was not so stupid long; I had sense enough to know that I must on no account leave the water.[44]

There are several key elements to this story that allow Dunraven to tell it without it compromising his equipoise and masculinity. By making it clear that his disorientation was only temporary, Dunraven demonstrated that his self-control was powerful for someone who was a relative novice in woodcraft. If true plainsmen could struggle with this, certainly a relative newcomer would have to be granted some leeway for a "temporary" loss of composure. To further drive home his competency, Dunraven used the next five pages to recount the story of a US assessor for Montana who got lost in the Yellowstone country and nearly died after he began hallucinating.[45] Again, the unstated message was that Dunraven—for a newcomer—was able to demonstrate considerable mental resolve and composure in the midst of several trying and potentially deadly situations. Because Dunraven's outfit was accompanied by two guides, Dunraven relished pointing out that he was now able to hunt alone and remain calm and composed in frightening conditions; Dunraven was crafting a narrative and image of independence and self-reliance.

Beyond detailing their own independence, hunters such as Dunraven also sought to reckon with their guides' presence by keeping up with them in every way: on stalks, in shooting, and in camp. Nonmilitary hunters such as Dunraven were also more apt to use personal gestures, such as guides' compliments, group banter, and friendships, to affirm their image and masculinity.[46] Dunraven's guides, Texas Jack and Fred Boteler, were portrayed as prototypical Westerners: independent and handsome.[47] Boteler was "[a]ctive, strong, willing, and obliging, a keen hunter, always in good humor, capable of great hardship, and a capital hand at making you comfortable in camp. . . ."[48] During one grueling joint stalk of a herd of wapiti, Dunraven recounted their efforts in detail: "Walking, or trying to run fast up an extremely steep hill-side, when the ground is rendered wet and slippery by melting snow, may be a very fine exercise, but, at an altitude of 8000 feet or so, certainly it is awfully trying upon the muscles and lungs. Boteler no doubt, if alone, would soon have overtaken the game [wapiti], he being very strong, hardy, and in first-rate condition; but I, soft as I was, and unaccustomed as yet to mountain walking, made rather a poor hand of it. However, I did my best, and ran till I was sea-sick. The work—to my great joy—was telling heavily upon Boteler also, for his nose began to bleed violently; and we would both willingly have given up the chase had not the sight of an unusually fine herd encouraged us to proceed."[49]

Dunraven's recitation of this stalk continued for several pages, describing how the two of them continued to doggedly pursue this herd. Eventually, "after about an hour's *very hard work*, for the snow was getting deeper and deeper as we ascended, and our progress was proportionately slow and *laborious*, we came upon them in some timber."[50] Both fired, killing the stag they were after. This quote brings together so many different facets of Dunraven's image making. Again, this stalk was not "exercise," but "work," and although Dunraven excuses his own efforts at mountain climbing, it is clear he was able to keep pushing his body to new limits even as Boteler, a seasoned guide, struggled. Stories such as this one served to show how much mental resolve, persistence, and physical fitness one needed to hunt in the West, and they balanced out the stories of frustrating misses and failed stalks.

The experience of camping and camaraderie was also crucial to Dunraven's account. By contributing to the smooth operation of the group, one could demonstrate one was capable of menial and hard work. The process of going into camp was recounted in painstaking detail in order to note everyone's role.[51] "Men soon get used to it," Dunraven commented, "and learn instinctively to undertake each a separate job, and not to interfere with one another." For instance, Dunraven was normally in charge of cutting young saplings for tent poles and cutting firewood. He clearly reveled in the interdependency of the camp experience and an illustration was even included depicting the men setting up camp. He did not feel the need to constantly assert his leadership within the group; instead, he was content to be a cog in the group's operation. Dunraven made it very clear that before going off to cut wood he would always ask Jack where the tents would be placed and how they would ultimately be oriented so he knew where to place the saplings.[52] Thus, he was happy to be accepted as one of the men's equals, take orders, and labor beside them. By deigning to participate in the democratic operation of the campsite and by succeeding in pulling his own weight, he was able to confirm his manhood and ingratiate himself to the group.

If hunters were successful in keeping up with their guides in hunting and in tending to camp, they would be recognized as one of the group by being included in group banter and by being acknowledged as a friend. Overall, Dunraven devoted five pages of text to routine camp life and he spent quite a bit of time detailing the group's camaraderie. He took an immense amount of delight in touching on subjects like Maxwell the cook's constant bickering over the distance to fresh water (it sometimes being too far or too near) and Texas Jack regaling the group with thrilling tales of cattle raids, conflicts with the Comanche, or just some "absurd" story told with that "quaint dry humour" particular to Americans. Although there were disagreements between members of the group, they were portrayed as being over frivolous matters, which were humorous in their predictability, such as Maxwell's carping about water or Campbell (Dunraven's Scottish gillie) and Maxwell's nightly fights over sleeping arrangements.[53] These incidents amounted to entertaining banter for the rest of the hunting party, all of whom were indirectly participating by serving as an audience and sniggering about them. Dunraven's recounting of bedding down each night was also representative of the group's camaraderie. During and after supper the men swapped stories and recalled their hunting feats, and therefore Dunraven was always "reluctant to leave the pleasant warmth of the fire." Eventually he lay down on the ground in his tent, which felt more comfortable than "the most luxurious bed." After falling asleep to the murmurs of a stream and the rustling of aspens, a chilly Dunraven would awake at about one or two in the morning to put more fuel on the fire and have a chat with the insomniac Jack. After a quiet smoke and talk, Dunraven would go back down until the morning.[54] Overall, the portrait painted of camp life is idyllic, and Dunraven would not have been able to participate in this dynamic nor would such a convivial atmosphere have been possible if he were not fully integrated and accepted into the group. Thus, being able to create and participate in the group dynamic was central to Dunraven's construction of his masculinity because these lighthearted interactions were proof of a general mutual respect between everyone in camp. If someone was not pulling his own weight in camp, or no one respected each other, there probably would have been much less bonhomie and storytelling around the campfire.

While group camaraderie was clearly important to Dunraven and made camp life rewarding. Dunraven's friendship with Texas Jack was also important to crafting his masculinity. The dependent economic relationship between guide and hunter did not compel guides to become friendly or friends with their employers. Many accounts bear this out and provide evidence of less-than-accommodating guides.[55] Thus, a friendship (or a perceived genuine friendship) with a Westerner, who only respected equally independent men, was a particularly symbolic recognition of masculinity and mutual respect.[56] It did not matter whether the realities of the companionship were complex and conflicting; what is significant, for understanding these writers' identities, was the way in which the hunters perceived their relationships and portrayed them in print.[57] In the case of Dunraven and Jack, there was clearly an already established bond because Jack had served as Dunraven's guide on his first trip to the West several years earlier.[58] When Dunraven requested Jack's services again, he was not optimistic about the prospects because Jack had recently been married. Dunraven, therefore, was pleasantly surprised when he received a letter from Jack "saying that he was ready for anything, that he would be delighted to come, and was prepared to accompany me anywhere." Since Jack had just recently started a new married life, this acceptance was intended to be interpreted as a sign of friendship. When the two finally met in Denver, Dunraven described their reunion as exceptionally warm and recalled how their reminiscing of the "old times" lasted well into the night.[59] Furthermore, as already mentioned, Dunraven and Jack enjoyed late-night chats around the campfire. These were signs of their mutual friendship and it meant a lot to Dunraven.

Another testament to their friendship came in *The Great Divide* when Dunraven recorded the fact that Jack cursed at him. The group caravan—with Dunraven and several others at the front guiding it—was moving on a trail when several deer jumped out in front of the procession. Not being ready for such a contingency, which they should have been, the deer made off easily and Texas Jack fumed:

> "G—d Al—ty d—m," says Jack, "there goes our supper! Why the h—11 don't you fellows in front look out?" Well, we fellows in front did look out after that, and before long I jerked my horse on to his haunches and slid quietly off. The others followed my example without a word, for they too had caught a glimpse of the dark-brown forms of some wapiti feeding quietly in the wood. Boteler, in his enthusiasm, seized me violently by the arm and hurried into the timber, ejaculating at every glimpse of the forms moving through the trees, "There they go! There they go! Shoot! Now then! There's a chance." All the time he was dragging me along, and I could not more shoot than fly. At last I shook myself clear of him, and, getting a fair easy shot at a large fat doe, fired and killed her.

This fit by Jack was proof that these men were not just acquaintances—they were friends. Only friends could speak to each other in this forthright way. Dunraven did not mind taking orders from Jack, upon whom he regularly heaped praise, nor did he object to being dragged through the forest like a child by Boteler—as long as there was a wapiti at the end of their jaunt. Dunraven's stalking ability and obvious hunting skill allowed him to dabble in self-deprecation such as this throughout the account.

In Dunraven's case, perhaps, there was an added bit of motivation for seeking out confirmations of friendship and respect. His relationship with his recently deceased father was unfulfilling because they had continually clashed over religion, and his father did not share his love of field sports. Furthermore, later in life Dunraven recalled that by not attending an elite public school he had "lost . . . the education, the discipline and the wholesome training of Eton, or any other great public school, and the intimate friendships that spring from public school life."[60] Dunraven seemed to be trying perpetually to make up for lost time. Thus, not only were these relations important to the masculine image that Dunraven crafted, but they were most likely important at a very basic psychological level.

Although "keeping up" with guides and earning their respect certainly demonstrated Dunraven's mental and physical abilities, he also sought to create an air of intelligence. For example, in his preface, Dunraven stated that he "did not undertake the expedition in the cause of Science," and added that he did not have anything more than a "slight acquaintance with natural history, geology, and minerology."[61] This false modesty did not stop him from offering several lengthy descriptions of the geological makeup of the mountain ranges he encountered, as well as his speculations about their formation.[62] Showing off his keen eye for observation, Dunraven described the Yellowstone and Gallatin mountain ranges, detailing their formations and the different deposits: "Peaks of very hard limestone tower from 1,000 to 1,500 feet above the silurian deposits, which rest upon quartz, mica-schists, and gneiss. The variety in texture, form, and colour of the metamorphosed rocks is infinite. The West Gallatin Mountains, and those on the west bank of the Yellowstone, are largely composed of conglomerates and breccia, and the peaks are of volcanic origin. . . . No doubt all these valleys have been scooped by the action of the water and weather out of originally homogeneous masses, for the signs of erosion and the effects of ice are universal; and there is abundant evidence that the entire country must have been under water, and subjected to the action of icebergs and glaciers for a very long period of time. Cretaceous and calcareous strata of considerable thickness are overlaid by vast deposits of clays, and every variety of tertiary formation; and the ranges are everywhere begirt with a fringe of foot-hills formed of drift, varying in size from large boulders to fine gravel."[63]

This passage with its specialized terminology clearly showed Dunraven's interest in geology and his ability to analyze the landscape before him. He also inserted several tables of various figures throughout *The Great Divide.* All of the tables that were included were pulled from the latest scientific publications about Yellowstone. The most important tables came from the well-regarded government survey report by Ferdinand Vandeveer Hayden detailing relevant information about springs and geysers.[64] Although Dunraven showed deference to these men's data collection, he was also keen to demonstrate his knowledge of the latest theories regarding the operation of geysers put forth by other geologists. After explaining two of the latest theories, he affirmed their ability to explain a short violent "explosion," but questioned their ability to adequately explain the sustained "eruption" of one of the larger geysers (Castle Geyser) that he observed in Yellowstone.[65] Clearly, Dunraven was demonstrating his diverse intellectual abilities and drawing attention to the fact that he was capable of truly comprehending complex geological theories.

Understanding game and their habits (i.e., field craft) as well as a hunter's commitment to humane hunting practices (i.e., small bags, one-shot kills) were other crucial indicators of intelligence and humanity among many of the hunters, but especially Dunraven. In the first chapter, he noted that knowledge about game is hard won and may take years to acquire. "And without this knowledge," Dunraven stated, "success is impossible." Furthermore, he was skeptical that useful information could ever be gleaned by relying on "local authorities, or indeed upon any authority at all." Thus, one could not be reliant on Westerners and therefore had to observe and learn for oneself. At this point, Dunraven went through a litany of observations that he had made about deer and wapiti in the Rockies, demonstrating his powers of observation. He also critiqued the hunting of buffalo, which he did not find sporting because of its ease.[66] By weighing in on scientific controversies and detailing his personal observations of Western game, Dunraven was showing the versatility of his knowledge and his ability to intellectually master any task he took on.

The role Native Americans played in hunting narratives about the West was less important than that of the environment and white guides, yet they were still important to the accounts in the 1870s and 1880s. Native Americans represented a direct racial, gender, and economic threat because of their well-known strength, endurance, and rejection of capitalism. Dunraven's account featured a large section devoted to the Crow tribe, whom he visited on their reservation. His account of the Crow was alternately empathetic and coldly Darwinist, and it belied a deep anxiousness about bodies and modernity.

The very first issue Dunraven chose to address when he visited the Crow reservation was men's bodies. "[A] fine race," he began, "tall, straight, clean-limbed, well-proportioned, and light in colour. Men of six feet two, three, and even four inches in height are not uncommon. . . . like all other savages, they lack the robust proportions and strong muscular development of the white man, and in consequence their limbs look long, rounded, and woman-like."[67] Although Dunraven later pointed out how strong and capable of amazing endurance Natives were, in this opening section, Dunraven sought to dispel any notions of Native physical superiority. Dunraven's descriptions of the Crow are a bit humorous considering his nickname in the British Army was "the Fly."[68]

Dunraven followed this up with a long section devoted to the ways that the US government had defrauded the Crow, and he detailed the risible terms of a new treaty. He then added that such a treaty was largely inconsequential because "[t]he Crow tribe will not, in all probability, cumber the earth for many generations." Interestingly, Dunraven then spent twelve pages covering the treaty negotiations and enclosed long sections of speeches made by different Crow. He heaped encomium upon Blackfoot (a Crow representative), and asserted, "To call such a man a mere savage and to assert that his race are irreclaimable barbarians who should no longer cumber the ground, is as untruthful as it is absurd."[69] After recounting the rest of his visit, Dunraven moved into a philosophical section in which he explored the reasons he believed Natives thought their civilization was superior to that of whites, and he owned up to the fact that Western civilization was struggling with poverty, squalor, overcrowding in cities, and the destruction of the environment. To reconcile this, Dunraven prophesized a brighter future in which white civilization, "growing out of present miseries, may, when the machine is in better working order and runs smoother, gladden the days of generations yet to come." He added that Natives were simply incapable of seeing this long-term picture. After acknowledging the chasm between notions of civilization that separated the two cultures, Dunraven spoke of the "inevitable" "extermination" of Native peoples because of this inability to see the long-term. At this point, Dunraven broached the question of whether Natives accurately understood white civilization's costs and benefits. Tellingly, Dunraven's list of costs was finely detailed and extensive, although he referred to the benefits only as "numerous and great." He concluded that no Native would choose to adopt such a system and that they would rather be "savage, uneducated and untutored, but with air to breathe, and water to drink; ignorant but independent, a wild but a free man."[70] It seems Dunraven believed Natives were not the racial equals of whites, but they were capable of learning and assimilating to Western culture. That said, he also surmised that the Natives' lifeways were so different from those of whites that they would refuse to assimilate; their refusal, in turn, doomed them to eventual extinction. Ultimately, although this section was not as outright racist as some other hunter-writers, and even though it was riven with anxieties about the present state of Western capitalism, it was a defense of the superiority of capitalism and Western civilization, which he believed would annihilate the Crow.

CONCLUSIONS

Hunter-writers' accounts and identities were singular; yet, they were all manifestations of writers' anxieties and the mental structures of empire. Economic competition, domestically and internationally, was coupled with a wave of reform, including land and voting reform, which seemed to eat away at the economic and political dominance of the elite class. Britain and the world were changing. Although Dunraven's economic future seemed secure enough, his lack of confidence in his own intellectual capabilities, the need for gun control in Ireland, and agitation for more Irish tenant ownership of land all combined to cause him concern. Hunting and writing became Dunraven's outlets to escape the messy realities of colonialism in Ireland, but these activities were also undertaken to prove and articulate his masculinity, social/national superiority, and competence in a world where specialized knowledge indicated legitimacy.[71] To do so, Dunraven wrote a truly sprawling travel account that showed him earning his leisure through hard work (mental and physical) in overcoming a dangerous Western environment and understanding every aspect of said environment. All of this was done in order to convince himself (and his readers) of his worthiness to assume a leadership position back home.

The elements the hunters encountered in the American West made it a space that forced British hunters to confront more challenges than any other place in the world, which also meant, therefore, that the vindication of British manliness coming from the accounts was powerful. Thus, a trip to the American West was, potentially, a high-risk and high-reward endeavor for the hunters. These risks paid off, psychologically speaking. The act of consciously constructing their various interactions with the natural environment, Westerners, and Natives gave the hunter-writers complete control over their identity. Even if the hunters' actual performances did not match up to those they wrote about and depicted, there must have been a great sense of security in knowing that they were able to control the reading public's perceptions of themselves. Although the act of constructing their stories (i.e., the mental/physical act of writing) was important for the hunter-writers, the accounts certainly had a long-term effect on their self-image. Surely, not every kill came to be ingrained in the minds of the writers, but certain concepts and encounters would have become definitional to their sense of self. Particular stories and phrases stand out and perfectly encapsulate everything the hunters were striving to prove about themselves. This phenomenon is clear in Dunraven's case. In his seventies, Dunraven wrote another hunting book, and in it he recalled a two-day stalk of a deer in Estes Park with his trusty Scottish gillie, Sandie, in amazing detail, all the while interspersing in the text lessons regarding the proper methods one must exercise in hunting deer.[72] The level of detail and the manner in which the story was told show that Dunraven thought the story itself was important. Even though Dunraven grumbled in old age that he wished he had not spent so much time hunting and engaged in field sports, those feelings did not stop him from continuing to write about hunting. In fact, in his autobiography, which he wrote in his eighties, he devoted an entire chapter to hunting.[73] Clearly, he wished to tell these stories because he felt they were important and they said something about his character and competence.

NOTES

1. Julian Fellowes, *Downton Abbey*, season 3, variously directed by Brian Percival, Andy Goddard, Jeremy Webb, and David Evans (United Kingdom: Carnival/Masterpiece, 2012), DVD.

2. As Catherine Hall and Sonya O. Rose have noted, there is more to British identity than its relationship with the empire. Yet, it seems British historians have been unable to free themselves from the analytical cage they have erected, especially when it comes to understanding the role of the United States, Russia, and Germany to British culture and identity. Perhaps it is the nature of university curriculum with its emphasis on the empire or the incredibly successful Manchester University Press series, Studies in Imperialism, that is to blame for the relative paucity of research devoted to the role of the United States in British identity, but newer organizations such as the British Scholar Society and its journal *Britain and the World* seem to be headed in the right direction. See Catherine Hall and Sonya O. Rose, "Introduction: Being at Home with the Empire," in *At Home with the Empire: Metropolitan Culture and the Imperial World*, ed. Catherine Hall and Sonya O. Rose (Cambridge: Cambridge University Press, 2006), 21. Regarding the United States, "the frontier," in particular, remained crucial to British identity throughout the long nineteenth century. The trans-Appalachian West was a critical space for British writers, thinkers, tourists, and politicians in the early nineteenth century. For a sense of the various meaning that the West had embodied during this prior era, see James Epstein, "'America' in the Victorian Cultural Imagination," in *Anglo-American Attitudes: From Revolution to Partnership*, ed. Fred M. Leventhal and Roland Quinault (Aldershot: Ashgate, 2000), 107–123. See also M. H. Dunlop, *Sixty Miles from Contentment: Traveling the Nineteenth-Century American Interior* (New York: Basic Books, 1995). On the flip side, for an understanding of how American identity rested on Anglophobia in the early nineteenth century, see Sam W. Haynes, *Unfinished Revolution: The Early American Republic in a British World* (Charlottesville: University of Virginia Press, 2010).

3. Most members of the Irish peerage sought to send their sons to top English public schools such as Eton or Harrow. Terence A. M. Dooley, *The Decline of the Big House in Ireland: A Study of Irish Landed Families, 1860–1960* (Dublin: Wolfhound Press, 2001), 71.

4. Windham Thomas Wyndham-Quin Dunraven, *Past Times and Pastimes* (London: Hodder & Stoughton, 1922), 1:7–10.

5. Ibid., 1:9, 210–11.

6. Monica Rico, *Nature's Noblemen: Transatlantic Masculinities and the Nineteenth-Century American West* (New Haven: Yale University Press, 2013), 88.

7. Muriel E. Chamberlain, "Wyndham-Quin, Windham Thomas," in *Dictionary of Welsh Biography* (Aberystwyth: National Library of Wales, 2001), http://yba.llgc.org.uk/en/s3-WYND-THO-1841.html

8. After noting that he informed Lord Beaconsfield of his doubts, Beaconsfield

tried to allay his anxieties by saying, "'Scholastic education is not so important as you think,' . . . 'You have seen men and cities, and that is the best of all education'" (quoted in Dunraven, *Past Times and Pastimes*, 2:98).

9. Dunraven was an important figure in the passage of the Land Purchase Act (1903), which made it easier for tenants to purchase land from their landlords. See John Kendle, *Ireland and the Federal Solution: The Debate over the United Kingdom Constitution, 1870–1921* (Kingston: McGill-Queen's University Press, 1989), 91. For the latest treatment of Dunraven's political life, see Michael V. Spillane, "The 4th Earl of Dunraven, 1841–1926: A Study of His Contribution to the Emerging Ireland at the Beginning of the 20th Century" (Ph.D. diss., University of Limerick, 2003).

10. John I. Merritt, *Baronets and Buffalo: The British Sportsman in the American West, 1833–1881* (Missoula: Mountain Press, 1985), 176–77; see also, Dave Hicks, Lord Dunraven, the Earl of Estes (Estes Park: Unknown, 1968); Dunraven, *Past Times and Pastimes*, 1:65–145.

11. Wyndham Thomas Wyndham-Quin Dunraven, *Canadian Nights: Being Sketches and Reminiscences of Life and Sport in the Rockies, the Prairies, and the Canadian Woods* (London: Smith, Elder, 1914), 26–27.

12. Others who have studied hunting often defer to the term "hegemonic masculinity." I prefer the term "unassailable identity" because—in my opinion—it offers a slightly more holistic understanding of what I believe British hunter-writers are looking to establish in their accounts (i.e., gender, racial, social/economic, intellectual, and national superiority).

13. Two recent relevant works differ slightly from my interpretation. First, J. A. Mangan and Callum McKenzie theorize that upper-class hunters sought "the transcendence of modern degeneracy and the survival of sound order." In short, what Mangan and McKenzie are saying is that elites would never condescend even to think about their ability to succeed in the marketplace. Aristocrats' haughtiness and superciliousness was no act, and they truly sought to simply perpetuate "sound order." I disagree. I believe that the hunters sought to prove they could do anything (including participate within the market economy) because they were experiencing so much change and criticism. See J. A. Mangan and Callum McKenzie, *Militarism, Hunting, Imperialism: "Blooding" the Martial Male* (London: Routledge, 2010), 184–85. Second, Monica Rico theorizes that Dunraven's accounts of the West are largely about leisure, adventure, and escapism, which proved Dunraven's masculinity and in reality provided revitalization for an increasingly embattled Dunraven, who was dealing with pressing land issues in Ireland. In the main I agree with Rico's conclusions, but I believe the concepts of work (mental and physical) and danger were far more important to the construction of Dunraven's narratives/identity than Rico. Rico believes that adventure necessitated "demanding exercise," but attention to the actual words Dunraven employs and some of the anecdotes that he tells shows that he believes he is performing "work" in very difficult and dangerous conditions. See Rico, *Nature's Noblemen*, 10–11, 109, 126–27.

14. Overall, I agree with John Tosh that this period witnessed a crisis of masculinity as well as a crisis of empire from 1880 to 1900. However, I believe that anxiousness about the empire actually dates back to 1865 because of worries associated with the potential rise of the United States. Tosh downplays the American and eventually the Russian threats to the empire in the second half of the nineteenth century, citing the locus of anxiety as Germany and its economic and territorial expansion after 1880. See John Tosh, *Manliness and Masculinities in Nineteenth-Century Britain* (Harlow: Pearson Education, 1005), 20–22, 193–95. Sofia Eriksson's work on British travel writing on Australia is crucial because it demonstrates that fears about "degeneration" were not a fin de siècle phenomenon, but rather they extended back into the early 1870s at the very least, and perhaps earlier. See Sofia Eriksson, "Meeting the 'The Coming Man'—Masculinity in British Travel Writing on Australia" (paper presented at the British Scholar Annual Conference, Austin, March 25–27, 2010).

15. For the most detailed examination of the structural transformations that the upper-class elites were dealing with during this period, see David Cannadine, *The Decline and Fall of the British Aristocracy* (New Haven: Yale University Press, 1990). Of course, it must be noted that even though the aristocracy found its position eroding, it was not completely swept away. Antony Taylor rightly notes, "In the nineteenth century, despite their depleted position, the aristocracy still held enormous sway and influence, and persisted as enormously powerful opinion-formers into the post-1945 period" (Antony Taylor, *Lords of Misrule: Hostility to Aristocracy in Late Nineteenth- and Early Twentieth-Century Britain* [London: Palgrave Macmillan, 2004], 8).

16. For a thorough account of the rural class antagonism that prevailed before Gladstone's Ground Game Act and the rise of the Humanitarian League, see Emma Griffin, *Blood Sport: Hunting in Britain since 1066* (New Haven: Yale University Press, 2007), esp. 159, 163–82.

17. Windham Thomas Wyndham-Quin Dunraven, *The Great Divide: Travels in the Upper Yellowstone in the Summer of 1874* (London: Chatto and Windus, 1876), 80; J. A. Fox, *Why Ireland Wants Home Rule: A Complete Handbook of the Views of Eminent Englishmen, Past and Present, as Expressed in Their Speeches and Writings* (London: The National Press Agency, 1887), 4:80. This period of legislative gains for Irish tenants and moderate activism was also punctuated by the creation of two terrorist organizations bent on establishing Irish independence: the Irish Republican Brotherhood and the US-based Clan na Gael. These organizations attempted or carried out a series of plots, assassinations, and bombings in the metropole and the colonies between 1867–68 and 1883–85. See Michael Burleigh, *Blood & Rage: A Cultural History of Terrorism* (New York: Harper Perennial, 2010), 1–18.

18. Cannadine, *Decline and Fall of the British Aristocracy*, 54–71.

19. Not only did the Humanitarian League bristle over the continuation of foxhunting, but also many hunters became disconcerted regarding the increasing artificiality of hunting and shooting within Britain itself. Callum McKenzie, "The

British Big-Game Hunting Tradition, Masculinity and Fraternalism with Particular Reference to the 'The Shikar Club,'" *The Sports Historian* 20 (2000): 74.

20. For a contemporaneous view of how one particularly important British railroad magnate saw America's economic potential in the wake of the US Civil War, see Samuel Morton Peto, *Resources and Prospects of America* (New York: Alexander Strahan & Co., 1866), esp. viii and 388–389. For economic threats in a hunting narrative, see Parker Gillmore, *Prairie Farms and Prairie Folk* (London: Hurst & Blackett, 1872), 1:14–15. To underscore the ubiquity of the threat that the United States posed as a competitor, in a book about German competition the economic threat that the United States presented was also mentioned—albeit it was considered less "insidious" than the German menace. See Ernest Edwin Williams, *Made in Germany* (London: William Heinemann, 1896), 60. For a view of American potential and power, see W. T. Stead, *The Americanization of the World: or, The Trend of the Twentieth Century* (New York: Horace Markley, 1901), or Frederick Arthur MacKenzie, *The American Invaders* (London: Grant Richards, 1902).

21. As Robert Saunders has pointed out, "For radical democrats, America was an inspiration, and their enthusiasm for the United States had attracted a significant commentary." Saunders also points out that nonradicals, generally, had a negative view of American-style democracy. Overall, contemporaries agreed that perceptions of the United States were colored by the voting reform question in Britain. Robert Saunders, *Democracy and the Vote in British Politics, 1848–1867: The Making of the Second Reform Act* (Surrey: Ashgate , 2011), 132, 144. Although the issue of land reform did not have its intellectual roots in the United States, the mid-nineteenth century witnessed land reform movements in both countries. Jamie L. Bronstein, *Land Reform and Working Class Experience in Britain and the United States, 1800–1862* (Stanford: Stanford University Press, 1999), 2. The word "Americanization" was actually coined in the 1830s. Paul Giles, *Atlantic Republic: The American Tradition in English Literature* (Oxford: Oxford University Press, 2006), 135–38.

22. I concur with Paul Giles's assertions that during the late nineteenth century the United States represented a political, social, cultural, and gender threat to Britain, and that the American threat surpassed the threat of French decadence and degeneration. This important position in the British imagination meant that the United States played a major role in forging British identity (Giles, *Atlantic Republic*, 135–38).

23. The well-known radical socialist Joseph Barker (1806–75) said, "As a rule, I held up America as an example in matters of government, but objected to a senate and a four years' president, preferring to place all power in the hands of one body, the direct representatives of the people." Joseph Barker, *The Life of Joseph Barker* (London: Hodder & Stoughton, 1880) 286–87. Benjamin Disraeli, quoted in Alexander Charles Ewald, *The Right Hon. Benjamin Disraeli, Earl of Beaconsfield, K.G., and His Times* (London: William MacKenzie, 1882), 2:12.

24. Taylor, *Lords of Misrule*, 46.

25. In fact, frontiers of all kinds have been crucial to British literature in general. John Tosh notes that other historians have traced this fascination with imperial adventure fiction and the romanticization of the frontier back to Defoe's *Robinson Crusoe* (1719) all the way through its explosion and dominance in the 1880s. He also points out that big-game hunting literature exploded in popularity in the late nineteenth century and built an audience based on this fascination. *Manliness and Masculinities in Nineteenth-Century Britain*, 199.

26. Literary historian M. H. Dunlop summed up the general mid-Victorian discourse relating to the trans-Appalachian West by saying, "The American assumption of equality that caused so much cross-cultural discomfort rose in the interior to an intensity that was unmatched anywhere on the East Coast" (M. H. Dunlop, *Sixty Miles from Contentment: Traveling the Nineteenth-Century American Interior* [New York: Basic Books, 1995], 50). For an evaluation of Western men, see Christopher Mulvey, *Transatlantic Manners: Social Patterns in Nineteenth-Century Anglo-American Travel Literature* (Cambridge: Cambridge University Press, 1990), 52.

27. Rico, *Nature's Noblemen*, 7.

28. Robert Brown, review of *Sporting Adventures in the Far West*, by John M. Murphy, in *The Academy* (London: Robert Scott Walker, November 8, 1879), 334.

29. Frederick Trench Townshend took this task seriously and he actually kicked a young, impudent newspaper hawker on a railroad platform in Omaha, Nebraska. Frederick Trench Townshend, *Ten Thousand Miles of Travel, Sport and Adventure* (London: Hurst & Blackett, 1869), 125.

30. Dunraven's personal physician, George Kingsley, actually accompanied Dunraven on his expedition in 1874, and this phenomenon of doctors embarking on trips with patients to various destinations was not unheard of. Such trips were often prescribed as an antidote to neurasthenia. For a synopsis of how such hunting trips were supposed to revitalize and harden men for their roles back in civilization, see Rico, *Nature's Noblemen*, 102–4.

31. Ibid., 104.

32. See note 13 for Monica Rico's argument regarding leisure and demanding exercise. Ibid., 102–4, 109.

33. It also bears pointing out that reviewers of the book noted the difficulty of Dunraven's treks through the West. One reviewer stated that Dunraven's trip was an "arduous, but enjoyable, expedition" (*The Morning Post*, May 26, 1876, 6). Another reviewer, after remarking on the scenery Dunraven described, said, "But the day's work must have been often tame and hard; and some of the flat deserts, sparsely sprinkled with sage bush and strewed with alkaline deposits, were the very pictures of dreary desolation" (*Pall Mall Gazette*, February 9, 1876, 12). I would like to thank my student at Tarrant County College, Juan Valentin, for researching these reviews.

34. Depending on the area or region that British hunters visited, any number of lethal threats could have conspired to kill them, and the hunter-writers were keen to point out the dangerousness and roughness of the environment. On the

Great Plains, Indians and grass fires were the most feared. Many hunters, such as Henry Astbury Leveson, Charles Alston Messiter, John Mortimer Murphy, and Paul Fountain, engaged in actual combat with different Native Americans. In fact, several of Leveson's hunting guides died while fighting with a band of Sioux. William Adolph Baillie-Grohman just barely survived a prairie fire, as he and his hunting party failed in trying to contain it three times before a fourth and successful counter-burn. William Adolph Baillie-Grohman, *Camps in the Rockies: Being a Narrative of Life on the Frontier, and Sport in the Rocky Mountains, with an Account of the Cattle Ranches of the West* (London: Sampson Low, Marston, Searle & Rivington, 1882), 35–38. See my dissertation for more on negotiating the environment and each of the aforementioned hostile encounters with Native Americans: Gregory Kosc, "Performing Masculinity and Reconciling Class in the American West: British Gentleman Hunters and Their Travel Accounts, 1865–1914 (Ph.D. diss., University of Texas at Arlington, 2010), chaps. 4 through 6. One hunter's friend died because of a fall on a mountain (John Turner-Turner, *Three Years' Hunting and Trapping in America and the Great North-West* [New York: Arno Press, 1967], 33–40). It also bears pointing out that nearly every hunter mentioned the debilitating effects and potential lethality of being "turned around" in a dangerous environment. For just one example, see John Mortimer Murphy, *Sporting Adventures in the Far West* (London: Sampson Low, Marston, Searle & Rivington, 1879), 34–6.

35. Dunraven, *Great Divide*, 2–3.

36. Ibid., xiii–xiv, 2–3, 60, 168, 294.

37. Ibid., 6. Emphasis mine.

38. Ibid., 132, 135.

39. For another excellent example of a protracted failed and excruciatingly frustrating chase of a wounded bear, see ibid., 158–61.

40. Ibid., 166.

41. Ibid., 175–76.

42. Baillie-Grohman, *Camps in the Rockies*, 16–17.

43. Dunraven, *Great Divide*, 238.

44. Ibid., 241.

45. Ibid., 242–47.

46. For more on the neediest hunter regarding compliments, see my coverage of William Adolph Baillie-Grohman's account in Kosc, "Performing Masculinity and Reconciling Class," 237–38.

47. Texas Jack's real name was John Baker Omohundro (1846–80). See Texas Jack Association, "Texas Jack History," http://www.texasjack.org/TJ/Texas_Jack_History.html

48. Dunraven, *Great Divide*, 136. Dunraven misspelled Bottler as "Boteler" throughout The *Great Divide*. Merritt, *Baronets and Buffalo*, 205.

49. Dunraven, *Great Divide*, 162.

50. Ibid., 163. Emphasis mine.

51. Dunraven also explained the process of packing up in the morning and moving camp in detail. Ibid., 138–44.

52. Ibid., 144–49. For another example of Dunraven ceding his leadership of a telescoping expedition while in wait for his friend, see 168.

53. He recalled, "By the time all this is done [cleanup from dinner] it is getting late. Campbell and Maxwell have finished their supper and washed up the things, and are now quarrelling about who shall have the best side of their tent" (ibid., 146).

54. Ibid., 147–48.

55. The economic relationship between hunter and guide did not mean that guides were always subservient to their bosses. The accounts are littered with stories of various struggles between the hunters and guides. See, for example, Murphy, *Sporting Adventures in the Far West*, 20–21; Turner-Turner, *Three Years' Hunting and Trapping*, 17–42, 101–3; Samuel Nugent Townshend, *Colorado: Its Agriculture, Stockfeeding, Scenery, and Shooting* (London: "The Field" Office, 1879), 35.

56. It is my view that male friendships and respect, which are solidified by shared sporting performances in a homosocial environment, offer important psychological affirmations of manhood and belonging. These confirmations of manliness also serve to convince men of their superiority to women. This process of justifying male power is still prevalent in modern athletics. Even though the "gap" in talent is closing—female athletes are still considered less talented by their male athletes and this belief justifies female inferiority. Paul Willis articulated a very similar theory in his work "Women in Sport in Ideology," in *Sport, Culture and Ideology*, ed. Jennifer Hargreaves (Boston: Routledge & Kegan Paul, 1982), 117–35. For insight into the pervasiveness of hetero-normative masculine bodily performances in arenas that were once considered alternative sites for sport, see Ian Wellard, *Sport, Masculinities and the Body* (New York: Routledge, 2009).

57. Monica Rico's examination of Sir William Drummond Stewart's relationship with his guide Antoine Clement is a good example of how complex realities of the relationships between hunter and guide could be. Although some attested to the two men's companionship in the field and Clement accompanied Drummond Stewart back to Scotland after his first expedition, Clement refused to return to Scotland after the second expedition and—for all intents and purposes—financially defrauded Drummond Stewart. See Monica Rico, "Sir William Drummond Stewart: Aristocratic Masculinity in the American West," *Pacific Historical Review* 76 (2007): 170–76. Establishing the true mutuality of these relationships would be impossible, but I think it is fair to say that respect between hunters and guides was not something completely unattainable.

58. Dunraven did not publish an account of his first visit to the West until after The Great Divide was published. Windham Thomas Wyndham-Quin Dunraven, "Wapiti Running on the Plains," *Nineteenth Century 8* (October 1880): 596.

59. Dunraven, *Great Divide*, 32–34.

60. Dunraven, *Past Times and Pastimes*, 1:9.

61. Dunraven, *Great Divide*, xxiv.

62. To see his theory of the process of formation, see ibid., 131–33, 185–86.

63. Ibid., 192.

64. A. C. Peale, a contributor to Hayden's report, was the author of several passages and a few of the tables that Dunraven included in his account. Ibid., 249–51.

65. Ibid., 289–91.

66. Ibid., 7–8.

67. Ibid., 62.

68. When Dunraven was living in London and serving with the First Life Guards, a man he rode horses for said that he "had the heart of a lion but the body of a fly" (*Past Times and Pastimes*, 1:208). It is also interesting to note that a few years after the initial printing of *The Great Divide*, Dunraven gave an interview to the *Newcastle Courant* and said, "As a rule I never have more than one white companion, and my Indians with me, and we live, bating bread on what we kill" (*Newcastle Courant*, July 4, 1879, 2). This comment is particularly interesting because there were no Indian guides on his trek, nor did he cede any physical superiority to the Crow in his account. Therefore, although the remark probably has no grounding in veracity, it does demonstrate Dunraven's continued preoccupation with the physical capabilities of Indians.

69. Dunraven, *Great Divide*, 69–82.

70. Ibid., 111.

71. Most hunters' articulation of national superiority was quite subtle. They relied on oblique criticisms of American government, game laws, or overall obsession with greediness to substantiate their national superiority. Dunraven criticized congressional Reconstruction because he believed Republicans divested plantation owners of their land through ruinous taxation (Dunraven, *Great Divide*, 309). In a later work, he critiqued American-style democracy for its "mob oratory," and the erosion of "statesmanship" (Dunraven, *Canadian Nights*, 10).

72. Dunraven, *Canadian Nights*, 40–47.

73. Dunraven, *Past Times and Pastimes*, 1:167.

7

"No Whiskey: A Liter of Vodka, and a Pickle Instead"

The American West in Polish Cinema and Literature during the Cold War

Pawel Goral

"For Harry Truman Presidential Library, we have brought from Poland some records of history of our road to freedom, among them—the poster of 1989 elections with a picture of Gary Cooper from the film '*High Noon*.' It helped us to win. For the people of Poland, high noon comes today."[1] With those words, Bronislaw Geremek, Poland's Minister of Foreign Affairs, finished his speech on March 12, 1999, in Independence, Missouri, at the ceremony of deposition of Protocols of Accession.[2] On that day, the North Atlantic Treaty Organization welcomed its three new members: Poland, Czech Republic, and Hungary. The former members of the Soviet-led Warsaw Pact raised their own flags and the flag of NATO side by side, accompanied by small public celebrations.[3] The poster could be seen all over Poland on the eve of the first democratic elections that took place June 4, 1989.[4] That political strategists used popular images of the American West in order to sway Poles toward voting for the Solidarity movement should not come as a surprise. Indeed, Western novels and films had been popular for a long time on both sides of the Iron Curtain in Europe, which led to the development of a well-established Western literary tradition.[5]

Polish filmmakers, novelists, and travelers influenced millions of Western enthusiasts' understanding of the myth of the American frontier, although their portrayal of the American West was shaped more by the works of a non-American author, rather than America's most famous Western authors such as James Fenimore Cooper or Zane Grey. Although Karl May is still virtually unknown in the English-speaking world, he has unquestionably been the most influential German novelist of all time. May created a distinctly German version of the myth of the American West and sold more than one hundred million copies of his books, in which the two main heroes were Winnetou, the Apache chief, and his German-American blood brother, Old Shatterhand. May's films, a series of West German Westerns produced in the 1960s, became the most popular series of films in the history of German cinema. Moreover, they precipitated the production of Westerns in other European countries. The East German DEFA film studio produced a successful series of *Indianerfilme* that spanned two decades and proved equally successful.[6] Sergio Leone admitted that the success of May Westerns enabled him to begin filming Italian "Spaghetti" Westerns.[7] In 1964, Filmove Studio Barrandov of Czechoslovakia released *Lemonade Joe*, a spoof of American Westerns; it was released in the United States two years later. In Poland, Zespol Filmowy "Rytm" produced a Polish Western in 1967 titled *Wolves' Echoes* (Wilcze Echa). Moreover, Polish writers eagerly adopted the American West as the setting for their novels, thus creating Polish heroes and a distinctly Polish conception of the American West. Among those, the most popular were Alfred Szklarski and Sat-Okh. Popular authors also used well-known Western characters, such as Winnetou, to become more appealing to readers and expand the circulation of their books. The author of one of the most popular series of adventure books, Zbigniew Nienacki, created a Polish equivalent of the fictitious popular Apache chief. Nienacki's Winnetou, however, unlike his portrayal in May's novels, was not an Indian chief fighting to preserve his nation at Llano Estacado, but a pioneer of conservation, struggling to preserve the purity of Mazury, the Masurian lake district.

May films proved to be tremendously popular in Poland. *Winnetou*, for example, was released in 1968, and even though it was seven years after the premiere of the first May Western, it nonetheless attracted 4.7 million Polish movie enthusiasts.[8] The 1960s proved to be the most successful decade during the Cold War for the Polish cinema industry; there were 3,935 movie theaters with a combined seating capacity of 732,000. Polish cinema grew during that decade; the number of films produced increased, as did the amount of money spent to make them. Consequently, Polish filmmakers could produce more costly, spectacular historical films, such as *Krzyzacy*, based on the book written by Henryk Sienkiewicz, a winner of the Nobel Prize in Literature.[9] Although Polish viewers could watch major European productions in the movie theaters, some suggested that the popularity of *Wolves' Echoes* could be explained by the fact that Poles did not have access to major American productions at the time and desired to watch more films that had "the motif of a lone defender of the law who clashes with gangster types."[10]

As much is evident from a 1990 summary of *Wolves' Echoes* plot: "It is 1948. Warrant Officer Slotwina, discharged from the military for insubordination, arrives at a small abandoned town in Bieszczady mountains. There he fights dangerous criminals who have taken over the police station and tries to find the treasure hidden in one of the many bunkers. After defeating the criminals, Slotwina and Tekla, a loyal and loving girl, move to another town in search of further adventures."[11]

This short description of *Wolves' Echoes* comes from a book concerning the history of Polish cinema between 1902 and 1988, written by one of Poland's most esteemed experts of film, Stanislaw Janicki. However, this description, with changed names of the characters and the region, might as well describe one of the many German Westerns and the German-American character created by May, Old Shatterhand, with one exception perhaps: many women were impressed with Old Shatterhand both in May books and films, but he never reciprocated their feelings and interest in him. Unlike the character Slotwina, Old Shatterhand was destined to remain a bachelor.

Here is another short description of *Wolves' Echoes* from a more recent issue of Poland's most prestigious film journal: "It makes one shed a tear! Here is a Polish Western set in the gaudy Bieszczady mountains, the Polish Wild East. In 1948, the defiant Warrant Officer Slotwina arrives at the emptied and ruined town of Derenica. He quickly discovers that the local militia (Police) are in fact a band of criminals led by Moron. And that they are all looking for the treasure of Tryzub, the money left over by the Ukrainian military unit, hidden somewhere in the area. There will be a bloody conflict to follow."[12] This review appeared in 2005 and accompanied the release of the film on DVD.[13]

Anyone familiar with May's novels could clearly see how the German Westerns released earlier in the same decade influenced the Polish filmmakers. The narration that opens *Wolves' Echoes* could almost serve as the opening scene of a May Western if the geographic names were changed. The narration is almost identical (see the accompanying comparison), with the crucial differences being Poland and the Bieszczady mountains instead of the American West, and the Ukrainian nationalists, responsible for the Wolyn Massacre during World War II, which resulted in at least forty thousand Polish civilian deaths, instead of Indians:

Winnetou	Wolves' Echoes
"What sounds incredible today was, a century ago, a bitter, cruel reality. This was the era of the last desperate attempt of the Indian to hold his own against the white man. Pushing farther and farther west came the hardy pioneers, and following them were the adventurers, bandits, desperadoes. The Mescalero Apaches were friendly to other white men, but their doom was inevitable."	"Bieszczady, the most remote corner of southeastern Poland. The war lasted here three years longer than in other parts of Europe. During those three years, Ukrainian nationalist bands burned towns and villages, slaughtering civilians. . . . When shots were finally no longer heard, the land looked like a desert. It took many more years for justice and law to triumph in the area."[13]

Following this brief introduction, the viewer sees a group of riders, Polish heroes who struggled to secure the frontier and helped to end World War II in that part of Europe. The riders then arrive at a fort where, sometime later, Warrant Officer Pietrek Slotwina must quickly put on his uniform, because his boss, the major, arrives unexpectedly and confronts Pietrek about his previous night's excursion. The major is angry. He points to soldiers waiting outside who testified against Pietrek and explains that Pietrek had advanced 14 kilometers into Czechoslovakia's territory while chasing after smugglers. Pietrek's adventure apparently ended after the Czechoslovaks finally apprehended him, though he resisted and even hit one of them. Pietrek explains that he is simply bored, but as it turns out, it was not his first insubordination. Indeed, he was denied a promotion earlier because he had sixteen warnings and penal reports combined. Pietrek reminds the major how they used to capture criminals together, and they seem to be friends. This time, however, Pietrek seems to have gone too far. "We have an international conflict," the major says, "you should be court martialed but you can request that you be honorably discharged." Pietrek is stunned, but complies. The viewer then sees him riding alone to an unknown destination. A few moments later, Pietrek will not notice that he is being watched by a man who stands in a typical Western fashion ready to pull out his gun and pull the trigger.

Pietrek finds what appears to have been a settlement; there are old cannons scattered there and he sees signs of destruction. He gets off the horse and decides to spend the night because he seems devoid of any purpose in his life, having been discharged from the Border Patrol unit.

At night he hears some noise that wakes him as he sleeps with his gun in his hand. Three of the Moron band arrive at the abandoned post to kill Pietrek; however, he decides to strike first and slips out of the hut while making it appear as though he were still in bed. The first bandit falls off a cliff and into the river below. Then Pietrek sneaks back into the hut and watches the other two bandits, who are about to hit the dummy he had left behind. "Do we wake him up?" one asks. "No need to, hit him in the head and that's it," says the other. Pietrek emerges behind them and tells them to drop their weapons, and when they refuse to comply, he fires a shot, which disarms them. The Polish Old Shatterhand will resort to violence only as his last resort. He did not even aim at either of them. The bullet strikes the wooden club that Pietrek was to be killed with. "I don't hide my gun when I hear militia," he says to them. "We're new here," they explain, trying to appear trustworthy. "But I am old here and I don't like such jokes," he responds. They finally drop their weapons and begin negotiating. Pietrek wants to know why they wanted to kill him, whether he resembled someone they were looking for. They tell him that they were simply being careful in the war-torn region of Bieszczady and did not trust newcomers. But they are newcomers to him.

Pietrek is surprised and suspicious to hear that they do not know anyone in the area whom he used to know. He thinks that a legitimate militia would at least know the people with whom he had served. He tells them that if he had not been tired, he would not have let them off the hook so easily. Nonetheless, he tells them to get undressed. They will be punished: they will have to walk back to their headquarters only in their underwear, but he assures them that they could pick up their belongings at their militia's headquarters the following day.

As one film critic pointed out shortly after the film was released, Warrant Officer Slotwina can be compared to May's Old Shatterhand because the film reminds the viewers of the books that most of them either read or with which they were familiar. Slotwina, like Old Shatterhand, does not promote violence and is more likely to use his fists rather than resort to his gun. In this regard, he, too, can ridicule his enemies and leave them unclothed, and his punch lines are as "shattering" as those of Old Shatterhand. His enemies are not the smartest either; they never shoot accurately, and chase after him in places he cannot be. Thus the audience quickly realizes the distinction between them and the main character.[14]

The following morning, Pietrek rides to the city, leading the bandits' three horses. His arrival causes a commotion and everyone stares at him. He enters the community and talks to the commandant. "I am bringing you your losses," says Slotwina, pointing to the horses. Commandant Moron notices the shoes and guns and wants to know where Pietrek got them. After a brief conversation, Pietrek finds out that the militia is looking for a man with a scar, who must be a criminal, which might explain why they attacked him. The commandant begins to like Pietrek and seems to trust him; he even tells Pietrek that he needs more deputies. He calls Tekla, the woman who works as the militia's maid and cook and who will eventually become Pietrek's girlfriend. Moron invites Pietrek to come through and drink vodka with him. They continue talking and ask each other questions but both remain cautious, though Pietrek's sarcasm makes him appear too self-confident and thus suspicious. "And what do you want to do?" asks the commandant. "I want to make money. I have been chasing smugglers for three years, and before that, five years in the forests. [Presumably, he was a member of a Communist resistance movement during the war.] I know every stone here," Pietrek adds. Hearing the word "stone," the commandant raises his head and, pointing to Tekla, says she is like a stone. Pietrek confidently states that if he were to join them, he would soon capture the girl's attention. Pietrek ultimately offers to help catch the mysterious man with a scar. They agree to meet again later,

Pietrek (Bruno O'Ya) surprises the two bandits who tried to kill him. (Fototeka Filmoteki Narodowej. Sygnatura: 1-F-318–42.)

Pietrek (Bruno O'Ya) enters the town the following morning, leading the bandits' horses carrying their belonging. (Fototeka Filmoteki Narodowej. Sygnatura: 1-F-318–52.)

as Pietrek refuses to drink with the man, telling him, "I don't like to drink to a pickle." "Hurry," says the commandant, "or I'll drink it all myself."

Pietrek then arrives at the home of the bootlegger's who happens to be his old friend. The bootlegger discourages him from becoming involved. He tells Pietrek that the city has become isolated from the rest of the world and has only one phone. He warns, "Don't ask questions, nobody will answer them and you can get hurt." Pietrek is at a loss. He asks his friend, "But we have known each other all those years and you won't tell me anything else?" It is obvious that the residents are afraid of the new commandant and his band. The next time Pietrek visits his old friend, he will be framed as a murderer and become an outlaw, which will justify Moron's band's actions against him. But that will not discourage Pietrek from fighting for justice. During the course of the film, Pietrek engages in fistfights, including those involving the athletic actor Marek Perepeczko, who later became one of Poland's most beloved actors thanks to his role in the tremendously popular television series *Janosik*, a Polish version of the escapades of Robin Hood, albeit in a mountainous setting. Pietrek is involved in gunfights before also being captured and tortured; eventually he is rescued by Tekla, who helps him escape from jail and with whom he later falls in love. That Pietrek is a noble and selfless character is best evidenced in one of the last scenes in the film in which he even risks his life to save the chief of the band, Moron, in order to have him face justice rather than leave him to die in a burning underground pit.

Ultimately, justice is served and the entire band is captured. In the final scene, Tekla is shown waiting anxiously, doubtful that she will see Pietrek again. She thinks he must have died in the final confrontation because the odds were certainly against him. How could he defeat a well-armed band of militia who are also the area's law enforcement unit? But anyone who read May knows that is exactly the manner in which European Western novels and films end. Pietrek returns and brings the prisoners along. The story does not end there, though. There is another similarity between Pietrek and Old Shatterhand. Old Shatterhand was entrusted with the knowledge of the hiding place of Native American treasures, but he would always keep it to himself and would never, even for a moment, have considered claiming his share. Neither does Pietrek. Moreover, Pietrek's companion, the wanted man with a scar, after finding the treasure hopes either to get rid of Pietrek or to convince him to share the riches. It is an emotional moment for Pietrek when he finds a letter from his former comrade in the treasure box: "I, sergeant Jan Wladeczek, am writing these words in order for everyone to know the truth as I am afraid that this might be the only way others can find out. The items found in this box belong to those murdered residents of this town and should be returned to their widows and orphans. I am now besieged by the enemies and cannot free myself or trick them and so I have to put these items in the old hiding place we created while fighting the Germans." The letter makes it clear that the enemies besieging him are Ukrainians. "I hope that this way the gold will be returned to the community."

In the last scene, viewers see soldiers riding again through the mountains and valleys just they did at the beginning. This is quite typical of May films, too, wherein Old Shatterhand and Winnetou are shown embark-

Pietrek (Bruno O'Ya) and Tekla (Irena Karel). (Fototeka Filmoteki Narodowej. Sygnatura: 1-F-318–16.)

ing on an unknown direction toward yet another adventure. The same major arrives, and again asks Pietrek where he was last night. "I was chasing horse thieves," says Pietrek. "Well," the major responds, "yesterday you crossed into another brotherly nation's territory, twelve kilometers deep. And returning . . ." Pietrek interrupts: "I know. What will happen now?" "Oh Pietrek, you are bored again," Pietrek hears in response.

Pietrek is last seen riding with Tekla, no longer wearing his uniform. He was discharged again but now, as they are crossing the river, new adventures await them, a new beginning. It is time to settle down, establish a family, and move on with their lives in the newly rebuilt country. The message the film conveys is straightforward and one should not expect to find any explicit anti-Communist overtones. One principal factor explains the dramatic transformation of the Polish film industry after World War II: the desire to align films with the propaganda of the Socialist government. As Dorota Ostrowska points out, making films in postwar Poland "was seen as paramount to the state propaganda machine, and thus a focus of much internal debate and bureaucratic effort [was] aimed at establishing a state-run national film industry which could contribute to the development of the Socialist culture in Poland."[15]

Marek Haltof and Norman Davies explain why Polish cinematic productions did not contain any antigovernment rhetoric. Polish filmmakers did not have the opportunity to posit questions regarding Poland's history, politics, or social issues because of the effective state censorship machine. Hence, some found a safe option in popular culture, whereas others stuck to the adaptations of national literary classics.[16] And, as Davies points out,

Marek Perepeczko. (Fototeka Filmoteki Narodowej. Sygnatura: 1-F-318–100.)

although "twenty years of National Communism in Poland provided an era of a relative stability . . . cultural life was closely controlled." Although some progress had been made, "yet political conformity remained the touchstone of success," and even some of the most popular authors and directors, such as Slawomir Mrozek, Roman Polanski, and Andrzej Wajda, were more likely to work abroad.[17]

There is another explanation for Westerns' popularity in Poland. Just because Poland was in the Soviet bloc does not automatically mean that Poles considered anything coming from the United States to be corrupt or evil. Despite the state's censorship machine and propaganda, which even blamed poor potato harvests on American-dropped Colorado potato beetles, the idea of America had always seemed appealing to Poles. In fact, streets were named after two American presidents, George Washington and Woodrow Wilson, and the Communist authorities did not choose to rename them. Significantly, millions of southeastern immigrants found stability and hope in the United States and that connection could not be disregarded or forgotten, because "movement to America was an affirmation of hope as well as a flight from poverty, and an optimism which could take collective expression imbued Polish American society with a future orientation," even though "migration of Poles was complex."[18]

Poles had also been present on the American frontier as the Indian Wars continued, and even there they did not become isolated from other communities. T. Lindsay Baker best summarized the importance of early Polish immigrants to Texas: "The Silesians who came to Texas were the precursors of the masses of Polish immigrants who followed them to America in the next half century. . . . They have constituted an important segment of the Texas population, adding to its economic prosperity and giving it a more varied culture; they have produced many individuals who have contributed significantly to the larger society in which they live; and they have preserved some aspects of their ethnic culture that have disappeared in Europe or have become modified there. But, above all, the Silesian Texans will be remembered as the pioneers who led the way for the thousands of Polish peasants who came after them to what they hoped would be the land of opportunity."[19]

Those Silesians, in fact, established the first permanent Polish settlements in the United States.[20] Moreover, although it is well known that there had been Poles fighting in the American Revolutionary War who became national heroes in both Poland and the United States (Tadeusz

Kosciuszko, in particular), Poles joined to serve in the US armed forces during the two world wars and even joined Texans during their rebellion against Mexico. At least one Pole, Frederick Lemsky, fought in the Battle of San Jacinto, which decided the war in favor of US Texans and led to a humiliating defeat of Santa Anna's forces.[21]

Another important dimension of the perceived relations among Communist countries and the importance of the frontier among Poles is worth mentioning. As Ewa Mazierska pointed out, "In the 1970s, when the restrictions of travelling were eased, thousands of entrepreneurial Poles travelled to the Soviet Union, nominally as tourists but in reality as black marketers, exchanging such homemade products as plastic sunglasses or plastic jewelry, for gold and diamonds. Needless to say, the character of this exchange smelled of the colonial trade, in which the Soviets were rendered as the new, easily duped 'Indians,' while the Poles saw themselves as superior, clever 'whites.' This has made a number of scholars regard Russo-Soviet colonization as 'reverse-cultural colonization.'"[22]

This is especially interesting when considering the attitude of Polish nobles centuries earlier who compared their activities along the Polish-Russian border and the drive to conquer and catholicize Russia with the Spanish conquistadors doing the same following the discovery of

Pietrek (Bruno O'Ya, in the middle), tortured by Moron (right) and a member of his gang. (Fototeka Filmoteki Narodowej. Sygnatura: 1-F-318–1.)

America. In fact, the myth of the "good savage," embraced by Bartolomé de Las Casas and Spanish conquistadors, was invoked by Polish nobles willing to either defend freedom or fight Poland's eastern neighbors.[23]

That the story of *Wolves' Echoes* was situated in the Bieszczady mountains should not come as a surprise. Topography mattered not only because the mountains are a beautiful tourist attraction, but also because of how politicized they were at the time, given the scope of fighting that occurred there during and after World War II. As Jakub Zajdel demonstrates, whereas northern and central parts of Poland were almost completely ignored, southern, southeastern, and southwestern areas, in particular, became the geographic centers of Polish postwar films. *Wilcze Echa* is just one of the many examples, next to *Sami Swoi* (All Friends Here), one of the most popular Polish comedies of all time. This choice awakened nationalistic feelings among the spectators. Although the ferocity of World War II does not need elaboration, the Polish army's struggle with Ukrainian nationalists was bloodstained and is still a controversial issue in both Poland and Ukraine. Even now, serious differences exist in the perception of Ukrainian nationalists and their leader Stepan Bandera. Although the Polish army also fought factions of the Home Army whose members did not all give up after 1945, it is logical to assume that images of the Polish army fighting fellow Poles would not find many enthusiastic supporters. On the contrary, focusing on Ukraine allowed Polish propagandists almost to equate the remaining "rebellious" Home Army members in hiding with the Ukrainian nationalists, as both fought against the legitimate authorities of Poland. Thus, anyone who was against the Polish army in Bieszczady was automatically considered a fascist and a nationalist, an ally of those who followed the anti-Polish movement of Bandera, which was associated with the massacres of Polish citizens. This also allowed the filmmakers to equate the Polish army fighting in Bieszczady with the Polish army fighting the Germans during World War II and protecting the Poles in the "Recovered Territories" (Ziemie Odzyskane) in Poland's West. Polish soldiers thus must be viewed unconditionally as "Polish patriots defending the borders." Last, one should not forget the natural advantages that Bieszczady offered; its pristine and wild landscape allowed filmmakers to create adventure films that were capable even of imitating a Western.[24]

The Bieszczady region thus seems ideal for a defiant and lone rider to appear in this isolated, roughneck world. At the same time, Polish films included Western elements, such as a lone sheriff, gunfights, horse riding and stunts, bandits, and the ultimate victory of good over evil, which is never in doubt. The choice of the Bieszczady mountains also emphasized a distinctly Polish interpretation of the Western genre, with the Polish eagle proudly displayed on the military uniforms of people dressed up just as they would have in the 1940s, and, instead of ordering whiskey, they ordered "a liter (of vodka) and a pickle."[25]

World War II was also one of the major themes in Polish cinema for decades after it had ended. In fact, the central theme of *Wolves' Echoes* is postwar reality in the "Recovered Territories."[26] In this regard, the film stands out as a clear endorsement of the Polish People's Republic's army, whose task did not end with the end of World War II, as the film implies. On the contrary, some of the bloodiest battles continued after the war as the army engaged the Ukrainian nationalists (and Polish anti-Communists) in the Bieszczady mountains. The film also shows the degeneration of the former partisans (the Home Army, supposedly). In this case, Moron's band is focused entirely on finding treasure, and they will torture, beat, and kill prisoners, clearly showing the methods applied by the enemies of Poland's People's Republic. And even if Slotwina makes a mistake, such as crossing the borders while pursuing smugglers, he does it for the right cause, that is, defending the homeland and capturing its enemies.

Unlike their Western counterparts, Agnieszka Cwikiel observed, "Polish popular genres had to perform several political duties outlined in the state's propagandist cultural policy. . . . [and] they had to be ambitious, show the achievements of the militia and thereby serve as a form of crime prevention. Finally, they had to entertain. . . . For filmmakers it was an almost impossible task to meet the demand of making an entertaining film that would also be apologetic toward the state and its representatives in blue uniforms." She then added that "the educational tasks of the 'militia genre' were achieved by including several stereotyped elements: the emphasis on the futility of crime ('crime does not pay'), the emphasis on the infallibility of the system, and the presentation of militia officers as dignified yet sympathetic characters with proper (usually working-class) backgrounds and beliefs."[27] *Wilcze Echa* certainly belongs to this category because it shows the courage and importance of the People's Republic's army during the early stage of formation of the nation after World War II, which encouraged the people to renew their trust in the authorities.

Because Poland considered itself a martyr nation, filmmakers and audiences would try to find characters that would reflect that attitude, characters who, although individualistic and defiant, would always differentiate between good and evil, and would not hesitate to fight for the right cause, even if outnumbered.[28] The idea of a martyr nation goes back to the final partitioning of Poland among Prussia, Russia, and Austria in 1795, which caused Poland's disappearance from maps for 123 years. The short revival after the end of World War I was brutally ended with Hitler's invasion of Poland on September 1, 1939.[29] Moreover, it is likely that Polish filmmakers and audiences could easily accept the Western convention of a lone hero clashing with "gangster types" because of the still-recent war memories; in addition, interest in American Westerns and American products stemmed from their limited availability in Poland.[30] This is best evidenced by the fact that Polish filmmakers even considered proposing that Kirk Douglas (born Issur Danielovitch) star in Polish Westerns.

Douglas's arrival in Lodz, Poland, in 1966, attracted crowds of fans. His popularity behind the Iron Curtain shocked even Douglas himself. The Polish filmmakers seriously considered the possibility of Kirk Douglas playing Slotwina, and Douglas, upon arrival, enjoyed "roughhousing" with the students of the Film Academy in Lodz. They dressed up as cowboys and gunslingers and tried to provoke him by challenging his image as a tough cowboy; he had to defend himself by using his fists and, on at least one occasion, his elbow.[31] As Douglas wrote, "There was no script, no choreography—just mob hysteria. They're thinking, 'The Great Kirk Douglas. Invincible.' I had to be very cool. One of the Polish cowboys came at me, blood in his eye. I reached out and kicked him right in the face, and knocked him down. Another guy came over, and—pretending to be very playful—I had to give him an elbow in the throat. And knock a few of these guys off. Or they would have knocked me off the horse, and probably trampled me. And my reputation. I don't know what they would have done if John Wayne had been there."[32] Ultimately, following the Six Days' War in the Middle East and the expulsion of thousands of Jews from Poland, Douglas, himself of Jewish origin, supposedly expressed his disinclination to participate in a Polish film. For that reason, the filmmakers had little time to find someone to replace him and asked a former water polo and basketball player who was more than 2 meters tall, Bruno O'Ya from Estonia, to play the character. He had settled in Wroclaw and later was cast in one of the biggest film productions in Poland, *Deluge*, as Jozwa Butrym.[33]

What makes Slotwina an appealing character? He is somewhat independent but he is loyal and knows what he fights for. Most important, like Old Shatterhand, he fights for the right cause and does it honorably. Therefore, the viewer is able to identify with him, even though Slotwina can be insubordinate at times. The prevailing theme is the lone hero's struggle to bring criminals to justice, which certainly seems to be a plot of a typical American Western, and the viewer is certainly aware of it. In fact, from the very beginning the viewer probably thinks he is viewing a Polish version of a Western. Opening titles in red showed galloping horses across the Bieszczady mountains, followed by the introduction, reminding the viewers of how brutal and prolonged the war in the region was because of the presence of the Ukrainian nationalists. *Wilcze Echa*'s opening certainly resembles May's German Westerns, and American Westerns to a certain extent as well.[34] As the film progresses, it looks perhaps less like a Western because the plot revolves around Slotwina's investigation of a murder case. Toward the end of the film, however, this film again becomes a typical Western in which good defeats evil, with a shootout on the frontier in one of the last scenes, and the finding of treasure that will be selflessly given away to the community to which it belongs.[35]

Although it is Poland's most important Western, *Wolves' Echoes* never received any awards at domestic films festivals. (Interestingly, it received an award at a film festival in Phnom Penh in 1968.)[36] What Polish film critics did praise, however, was the high quality of the cinematography. Accordingly, Stanislaw Loth could have easily found a job in Hollywood because his depiction of the Bieszczady mountains was not inferior to those of Monument Valley in American Westerns. Likewise, film critics underscored the fact that the sound track was written by Wojciech Kilar, a well-known Polish composer, whom they even compared to Ennio Morricone.[37] Another appealing element in the movie was an effective depiction of action scenes, including horse chases, fistfights, shootouts, and pyrotechnic effects. In fact, some of the crew members were injured in accidents, including a stuntman who broke his collar bone when he fell off a horse.[38]

However, as enticing as the images of the Bieszczady mountains were and as appealing as the soundtrack was, nothing attracted viewers' attention more than the motif of a classic Western-like clash between good and evil and law and lawlessness. Danuta and Aleksander Scibor-Rylski wrote the script. The latter was also the film's director, who later established himself as one of Poland's most important directors.[39] In fact, Scibor-Rylski never hid the fact that he wanted to attract a mass number of viewers. He believed that the postwar years in Poland served the same mythological role that Western films had in America.[40]

Although the hero is a man, as was always the case in Westerns, Slotwina would not have defeated the bandits without the help of the woman who later became his partner. Irena Karel, a popular actress, looked like a contemporary woman, with her revealing dress showing her knees, rather than a less-revealing dress from the 1940s. Her blond hair certainly made an impression on male viewers as well.[41] As one article stated, the "lethally handsome" actor infatuated many women in the Bieszczady mountains. It was even rumored that the men who lived in the village where the film was produced got together and beat up the actor, jealous of his popularity with their women. But, as the article states, we do not know whether it really happened, which means that it was probably a rumor.[42] The greatest attribute of the film was indeed its cast, which, aside from those already mentioned, included one of the idols of postwar Polish film, Marek Perepeczko, known especially for his role in the revered television series *Janosik*, depicting the Polish Robin Hood, stealing from the rich and giving to the poor. The cast included other well-known Polish actors, including an icon of Polish cinema, Bronislaw Pawlik, and Janusz Klosinski.[43]

What contemporary historians pointed out, however, is that a significant portion of viewers today would consider the hero, Warrant Officer Slotwina, as a representative of the oppressive apparatus of the Communist regime instead of a lone hero fighting for justice. Jerzy Eisler points out that *Wilcze Echa* has as much to do with the truth of postwar reality as American Westerns do with the truth of the conquest of the American West.[44]

The filming process itself attracted a great deal of attention in Poland. A crowd of people watched galloping horses, armed police officers chasing suspects, and some of the major stars of the Polish cinema, including the Estonian actor Bruno O'Ya and Marek Perepeczko, who played Piwko, a bandit who ultimately switched sides and helped Pietrek defeat the criminals. Witnesses saw O'Ya fall off his horse, which led to minor head and spine injuries, and an argument with the doctor, who ordered that O'Ya not leave the hospital and tried to stop him from doing so. According to the nurse present at the scene, it appeared comical, as the doctor was quite short compared to the tall and athletic Estonian actor.

As the film director Aleksander Scibor-Rylski said, the filmmakers wanted to create a Polish version of the American Western film, with dynamic scenes, shootouts, adventures, horse chases all situated in the raw landscape of the Bieszczady mountains. What seemed difficult at first, because of the remote location and the altitude, became a mission accomplished, according to film reviewers.[45] Rafal Marszalek pointed out that many Polish filmmakers at the time had to face technological challenges, the most significant of which being outdated equipment. Although Scibor-Rylski and the crew had to face a similar challenge, one of the biggest problems that the filmmakers of *Wolves' Echoes* faced was the inadequate training of the horses used in the film.[46]

Interestingly, although film critics approved of the didactic value of the film, they did point out that the scene in which Slotwina is tortured might have been the reason only teenagers above the age of fourteen should be allowed to watch the film. At the same time, setting the age at fourteen excluded a great number of viewers who would actually love to see the film: the youngest movie enthusiasts.[47]

Although the Polish Western literary tradition cannot compare with that of Germany, some of the most popular Polish writers were influenced by May and his Winnetou novels. The most popular of them all was probably Alfred Szklarski. Born in 1912 in Chicago, he came to Poland in 1926 and, as a member of the Home Army, fought in the Warsaw Uprising in 1944 during World War II. He was sent to prison after the war because of his membership in the Home Army. Although he wrote novels for both adults and adolescents, his most popular hero became a young Polish boy, Tomek Wilmowski, who, along with his father and their two friends, trav-

The cameraman, Stanislaw Loth (left), and the director, Aleksander Scibor-Rylski (right). (Fototeka Filmoteki Narodowej. Sygnatura: 1-F-318–74.)

eled all over the world as a hunter and an explorer. The third in the series of the adventures of Tomek Wilmowski, *Tomek on a War Path* (Tomek na wojennej sciezce), was published in 1959 and described Tomek's adventures in the American Wild West.

In the novel, Tomek befriends a Native American boy, Red Eagle, an Apache, who later helps Tomek free his best friend, Sally, an Australian girl whom Tomek met a couple of years earlier on his first visit to Australia and whom he will later marry. As one reviewer wrote, Szklarski's narration sometimes resembles an encyclopedia with a significant number of footnotes explaining different geographic, historical, or anthropological aspects of subjects under discussion. Szklarski researched extensively before writing his books, using many academic sources as well as copies of *National Geographic* sent to him from the United States.[48] This method resembles that of May, who undertook meticulous research to authenticate his own stories.

Szklarski often cites factual entries to validate his novels; for example, he refers to the research conducted by Professor Emil Dunikowski of Lwow, who had published a few books about the American West; the reader still notices echoes of May. Specifically, the author focuses on the same geographic area that May had before him, the American Southwest, and the same Native American tribe that May had, the Apache. Moreover, one of the main Polish characters, Bosman Nowicki, like Old Shatterhand, was always reluctant to reach for his pistols; instead, he could knock down an opponent with one blow to the jaw. Another, Jan Smuga, seems to have inherited all of the best qualities of Winnetou and Old Shatterhand: he was the best at shooting, tracking enemies, and knowing the languages and habits of a variety of people and tribes. Moreover, in the story titled *Tomek na czarnym ladzie* the reader finds out that he was one of the few white explorers who had acquired the language of tam-tams, African hand drums. Also, as in May's books, the noblest characters are Europeans (in this case, the Poles), there are good and bad Indians, good and bad Americans and Mexicans; but the courageous Poles, valued by their foreign employers, do not hesitate to risk their life to fight for the right cause, just like their German counterparts in May's novels. Even when facing death, Tomek will not reach for his revolver when fighting a Native American armed only with a knife. Instead, he will risk his life to fight a fair fight and thus prove to the Native American that Polish explorers are noble human beings who, just like the Natives, are fighting for their freedom, having been occupied by Tsarist Russia and the monarchies of Prussia and Austria.[49] This book series sold more than ten million copies in Poland before the collapse of Communism and an additional million after 1989.[50]

Several generations of young Polish readers have been influenced by Zbigniew Nienacki, the creator of the Mr. Automobile (Pan Samochodzik) book series. Nienacki admitted in the 1980s that he had actively fought against the enemies of the Communist Polish state in the 1940s, later castigated the Solidarity movement, and did not object to the implementation of martial law.[51] Although his novels are rarely set outside Poland and certainly not in the American West, one of the most interesting characters he developed in *Mr. Automobile and Winnetou* (Pan Samochodzik i Winnetou) was Mr. Automobile's partner. According to the writer, "My hero is such as he is; because he reflects my own attitude toward life. He is what I would like to be and will strive to become."[52] Indeed, he wrote the book after he had bought land at a village in Mazury, where he lived without electricity. This led to the development of the character of Winnetou, a pioneer of conservation in Communist Poland.[53] There are some elements of Nienacki's life that can be found in the character of Mr. Automobile; for example, both Nienacki and Mr. Automobile had a passion for art history and the environment.

Ultimately, the character he created was Tomasz N.N., a detective for the Ministry of Culture who had a car that changed into an amphibian when in water and that had the engine of a Ferrari that allowed him to win any car chase and conquer the heart of even the most resistant woman. Nienacki became tremendously popular and millions of copies of his books were sold, some of which were also made into movies.[54] A connection can be made between *Wolves' Echoes* and Nienacki. He wrote novels for adults in which he portrayed anti-Communists as criminals, including those who belonged to the Home Army.[55]

Nienacki is still read and remembered by many, and some of his enthusiasts meet annually at the site of one of his stories.[56] In his books, Winnetou is a defender of the environment, but, unlike May's Winnetou, he has no rifle and neither does Mr. Automobile, who despises violence. In Winneotu, an ecologist fighting for the protection of Mazury, Poland's lake district, he finds an ally and a friend. *Mr. Automobile and Winnetou,* published in 1976, demonstrates a struggle to resist what seem to be American/Western influences, such as commercialism. Only with the help of the selfless character of Winnetou can Mr. Automobile eradicate the corruption endemic within the local government and protect the lake district against those who had violated the sacred rules of how one should interact with nature.

By implication, in order to become righteous, one must become like Nienacki's Winnetou, which does not mean that one should become less Polish. The book does not criticize the political system in Poland; on the contrary, it shows how to improve it by rejecting commercialization and Western pop culture.[57] Many examples demonstrate how Nienacki's Winnetou was influenced by May. For example, like May's character, Nienacki's Winnetou can also sneak up within reach of a person without being noticed. As one reviewer stated, Tomasz becomes a defender of the environment, and he can achieve his goal only with the help of Winnetou, with whom he will smoke the pipe and whose friend he will become forever, just as Old Shatterhand did in May's novels.[58]

Another author of popular Polish Indian stories was Stanislaw Suplatowicz, nicknamed Sat-Okh, who was born in 1920 in Canada and described himself as Native American. He claimed to have been raised in Canada by his Polish mother, to be an escapee from a Siberian gulag, and to have a Shawnee father, Leoo-Karko-Ono-Ma. He traveled to Poland in 1937, was arrested by the Gestapo, and sent to Auschwitz, but managed to escape from the transport. He was arrested by the Communist authorities after World War II because of his involvement with the Home Army. In the late 1950s, he began to write his Indian stories in which he alluded to his Indian past.[59] His novels were translated into many languages. He often appeared on TV shows for children and met children at cultural centers and schools throughout Poland in order to talk about Native Americans and his Native American heritage.[60]

May's novels, including his most popular Winnetou series, also became popular in southeastern Europe shortly after they were published in Germany in the last decade of the nineteenth century. Poland's most popular authors were heavily influenced by May's novels, and their most popular adventure novels clearly exhibit his impact on them. Polish Indian literature is certainly not as profuse as German Indian literature, however. Polish authors and movie producers were inspired by May's books and films, and they created their own versions of the American West that, in many ways, resembled the German American West. Although *Wolves' Echoes* did not become a blockbuster, it is still remembered as the most important of the Polish Western films, a Polish attempt to combine Polish history and culture with the appealing myth of the American West. It also created a Polish Old Shatterhand, a role model in the difficult times of postwar reconstruction and transformation who was capable of inspiring and entertaining millions of Poles.

NOTES

1. Frank Fox, "Poland and the American West," in *Western Amerykanski: Polish Poster Art & the Western*, ed. Kevin Mulroy.(Los Angeles: Autry Museum of Western Heritage; Seattle: University of Washington Press, 1999), 69, http://www.nato.int/docu/speech/1999/s990312d.htm

2. Fox, "Poland and the American West," 69.

3. Jane Perlez, "Expanding Alliance: The Overview; Poland, Hungary, and the Czechs Join NATO," *New York Times*, March 13, 1999, http://www.nytimes.com/1999/03/13/world/expanding-alliance-the-overview-poland-hungary-and-the-czechs-join-nato.html

4. Fox, "Poland and the American West," 69.

5. Richard Cracroft, "World Westerns: The European Writer and the American West," in *A Literary History of the American West* (Forth Worth: Texas Christian University Press, 1987), 159.

6. Pawel Goral, *Cold War Rivalry and the Perception of the American West* (New York: Palgrave Macmillan, 2014), 2–3.

7. Christopher Frayling, *Spaghetti Westerns: Cowboys and Europeans from Karl May to Sergio Leone* (New York: I. B. Tauris, 2006), 115.

8. Marek Haltof, *Polish National Cinema* (New York: Berghahn Books, 2002), 111–12; Marek Haltof, *Kino Polskie* (Gdansk: Slowo, Obraz/Obraz Terytoria, 2002), 136.

9. Jacek Fuksiewicz, *Film w Polsce* (Warszawa: Wydawnictwo Interpress, 1972), 38.

10. Haltof, *Polish National Cinema*, 123.

11. Stanislaw Janicki, *Polskie Filmy Fabularne 1902–1988* (Warszawa: Wydawnictwo Artystyczne I Filmowe, 1990), 224–25.

12. Film review of *Wolves' Echoes* (kino domowe), *Kino* 2 (2005): 84.

13. Goral, *Cold War Rivalry*, 69; Karl May and H. G. Petersson, *Winnetou I*, directed by Harald Reinl (Germany: Rialtofilm, Preben, Philipsen/Jadran-Film, 1963); Danuta Scibor-Rylska and Aleksander Scibor-Rylski, *Wolves' Echoes* [Wilcze Echa], directed by Aleksander Scibor-Rylski (Poland: Zespol Filmowy "Rytm,," 1967).

14. Rafal Marszalek, "Konie," *Film* 16 (1968): 4.

15. Dorota Ostrowska, "An Alternative Model of Film Production: Film Units in Poland after World War Two," in *A Companion to Eastern European Cinema*, ed. Aniko Imre (Malden, MA: Wiley-Blackwell, 2012), 453.

16. Haltof, *Polish National Cinema*, 110.

17. Norman Davies, *God's Playground: A History of Poland*, vol. 2, *1975 to the Present* (New York: Columbia University Press, 2005), 440–53.

18. William J. Galush, *For More Than Bread: Community and Identity in American Polonia, 1880–1940* (Boulder: East European Monographs, 2006), 21, 43.

19. T. Lindsay Baker, *First Polish Americans: Silesian Settlements in Texas* (College Station: Texas A&M University Press, 1979), 170–71.

20. T. Lindsay Baker, *The Polish Texans* (San Antonio: University of Texas Institute of Texan Cultures, 1982), 9.

21. Ibid., 5.

22. Ewa Mazierska, Lars Kristensen, and Eva Naripea, "Introduction: Postcolonial Theory and the Postcommunist World," in *Postcolonial Approaches to Eastern European Cinema: Portraying Neighbors on Screen*, ed. Ewa Mazierska, Lars Kristensen, and Eva Naripea (London: I. B. Tauris, 2013), 9–10.

23. Janusz Tazbir, *Polskie przedmurze chrzescijanskiej Europy: Mity a rzeczywistosc historyczna* (Warszawa: Wydawnictwo Interpress, 1987), 6.

24. Jakub Zajdel,"Filmowy Obraz polski powojennej," in *Syndrom Konformizmu? Kino Polskie Lat Szescdziesiatych*, ed. Tadeusz Miczka and Alina Madej (Katowice: Wydawnictwo Uniwersytetu Slaskiego, 1994), 102–5.

25. Bozena Janicka, "Western bez Kowbojow," *Film* 35 (1967): 10–11.

26. Haltof, *Polish National Cinema*, 123.

27. As quoted in Haltof, *Polish National Cinema*, 110.

28. Zajdel,"Filmowy Obraz polski powojennej," 109–10.

29. Marek Haltof, *Polish Film and the Holocaust: Politics and Memory* (New York: Berghahn Books, 2012), 1–2.

30. Ibid., 123.

31. Jerzy Eisler,"Prawda Czasu Prawda Ekranu: *Wilcze Echa*," *Biuletyn IPN* 2, no. 11 (2013): 56–58.

32. Kirk Douglas, *The Ragman's Son: An Autobiography* (New York: Simon & Schuster, 1988), 390–91.

33. Eisler, "Prawda Czasu Prawda Ekranu," 56–58.

34. Ibid.

35. Zajdel,"Filmowy Obraz polski powojennej," 109–117.

36. Fuksiewicz, *Film w Polsce*, 130. The Phnom Penh International Film Festival took place twice, in 1968 and 1969, when the king of Cambodia, who had made approximately thirty films during his acting career, proposed the ambitious idea that "Cambodia should challenge Cannes." Nick Ray, *Cambodia* (Oakland: Lonely Planet, 2010), 56.

37. Eisler, "Prawda Czasu Prawda Ekranu," 56–58.

38. Ibid.

39. Ibid.

40. Ibid.

41. Ibid.

42. "Aktorski Najazd." Obszerne fragmenty reportażu, który ukazał się w

zbiorze Krzysztofa Potaczały 'Bieszczady w PRL-u' opublikowanym nakładem Wydawnictwa Bosz, Olszanica 2012." *Przeglad*, nr. 34/2012, August 20, 2012, 58.

43. Eisler, "Prawda Czasu Prawda Ekranu," 56–58.

44. Ibid.

45. "*Wilcze Echa*," in *Bieszczady od A do Z*, September 20, 2013. http://www.biesyiczady.eu//?s=wilcze+echa&x=8&y=4

46. Marszalek, "Konie," 4.

47. Ibid.

48. Błażej Popławski, "Afryka widziana z peerelu (1): Tomek," February 3, 2011, http://www.afryka.org. http://afryka.org/afryka/afryka-widziana-z-peerelu—1—-tomek,news/

49. Alfred Szklarski, *Tomek na wojennej sciezce* (Warszawa: Muza SA, 2012).

50. Popławski, "Afryka widziana z peerelu (1)."

51. Piotrek Szymczak, "Zbigniew Nienacki." December 10, 2009, http://www.nienacki.art.pl/r_winnetou.html

52. Ibid.

53. Ibid.

54. Bozydar Brakoniecki, "Co ukrywal pan samochodzik?" *Polska Times*, July 27, 2013.

55. Marcin Wyrwal, "Zbigniew Nienacki: Pan Samochodzik i człowiek o wielu twarzach," July 8, 2013, http://ksiazki.onet.pl/pan-samochodzik-i-czlowiek-o-wielu-twarzach/7z71tf

56. Ibid.

57. Zbigniew Nienacki, *Mr. Automobile and Winnetou* [Pan Samochodzik i Winnetou] (Wroclaw: Wydawnictwo Siedmiorog, 2010).

58. Piotr Szymczak, "'Mr. Automobile and Winnetou' [Pan Samochodzik i Winneotu]: A Review," *internetowy klub nienackofanow* [the Internet fan club of Nienacki], October 20, 1998, Nienacki.art.pl.

59. Dariusz Lipecki, Muzeum Indiańskie im. SAT-OKHA [The Indian Museum of Sat-Okh] Sat-Okh - Długie Pióro - Stanisław Supłatowicz. Stanisław Supłatowicz SAT-OKH (Długie Pióro), http://www.huuskaluta.com.pl/sat_okh/

60. Ibid.

About the Contributors

Marcus Rediker is distinguished professor of Atlantic history at the University of Pittsburgh. He is the author of numerous acclaimed books, including *The Many-Headed Hydra: Sailors, Slaves, Commoners, and the Hidden History of the Revolutionary Atlantic* (with Peter Linebaugh) (2000); *The Slave Ship: A History* (2007); and, most recently, *The* Amistad *Rebellion: An Atlantic Odyssey of Slavery and Freedom* (2012).

Benjamin Mark Allen, associate professor of history at South Texas College, is the author of *Naked and Alone in a Strange New World: Early Modern Captivity and Its Mythos* (Cambridge Scholars Group, 2009). He is also editor/author of *Captivity, Past and Present: A Compendium of Interpretations and Observations* (2011), and (with Dahia Messara) the editor/author of *The Captivity Narrative: Enduring Shackles and Emancipatory Language of Subjectivity* (2012).

Emmanuel M. Mbah is associate professor of history and director of African and African Diaspora Studies at the City University of New York, College of Staten Island. He has edited and coedited numerous books and authored several chapters in anthologies/edited volumes. His most recent book is *Environment and Identity Politics in Colonial Africa: Fulani Migrations and Land Conflict* (Routledge, 2016).

Julie L. Holcomb is associate professor in the Department of Museum Studies at Baylor University. Her new book, *Moral Commerce: Quakers and the Transatlantic Boycott of the Slave Labor Economy*, was recently published by Cornell University Press. She is also working on a biography of nineteenth-century Philadelphia reformer George W. Taylor, who was active in the free produce, antislavery, peace, and temperance movements.

Tom Aiello is professor of history and head of the Department of History and Political Science at Gordon State College. His most recent publication is the article "Jacob de Cordoba: Immigrant, Messenger, Prophet," which appears in *FHC Annals: Journal of the Florida Conference of Historians*, Vol. 23, 2016.

GREGORY KOSC is professor of history at Tarrant County College-Southeast in Arlington, Texas. He is a 2010 graduate of the Transatlantic History doctoral program at the University of Texas at Arlington. His current research is focused on the experiences of female travel writers in the British publishing industry in the early twentieth century.

PAWEL GORAL is professor of government at Grayson College (Denison, Texas) and lecturer at the University of Texas at Arlington. He is the author of *Cold War Rivalry and the Perception of the American West* (Palgrave Macmillan, 2014).

Index

Other Titles in the Walter Prescott Webb Memorial Lectures Series:

African Diaspora
Alusine Jalloh and Stephen E. Maizlish

Creolization in the Americas
David Buisseret and Steven G. Reinhardt

Sacrifice and National Belonging in Twentieth-Century Germany
Greg Eghigian and Matthew Paul Berg

Beyond Black and White: Race, Ethnicity, and Gender in the US South and Southwest
Stephanie Cole and Alison M. Parker

Transatlantic History
Steven G. Reinhardt and Dennis Reinhartz

Traveling between Worlds: German-American Encounters
Thomas Adam and Ruth Gross

Lights, Camera, History: Portraying the Past in Film
Richard V. Francaviglia and Jerry Rodnitzky

Catholicism in the American West: A Rosary of Hidden Voices
Roberto R. Trevino and Richard V. Francaviglia

Baseball in America and America in Baseball
Donald G. Kyle and Robert B. Fairbanks

Manifest Destiny and Empire: American Antebellum Expansionism
Sam Haynes and Christopher Morris

Assumed Identities: The Meanings of Race in the Atlantic World
John D. Garrigus and Christopher Morris

Crossing the Atlantic: Travel and Travel Writing in Modern Times
Thomas Adam and Nils H. Roemer

Folly of Jim Crow: Rethinking the Segregated South
Stephanie Cole and Natalie J. Ring

Mexican Revolution: Conflict and Consolidation, 1910-1940
Douglas W. Richmond and Sam W. Haynes

Cold War Crossings: International Travel and Exchange across the Soviet Bloc, 1940s-1960s
Patryk Babiracki and Kenyon Zimmer

Contested Empire: Rethinking the Texas Revolution
Sam W. Haynes and Gerald D. Saxon

CPSIA information can be obtained
at www.ICGtesting.com
Printed in the USA
LVOW04*0748090517
533759LV00006B/9/P

9 781623 495428